Resources for Teaching

Practical Argument

A TEXT AND ANTHOLOGY

Laurie G. Kirszner
Stephen R. Mandell

Prepared by

Courtney Novosat
Jeffrey Ousborne
Cara Snider

Bedford/St. Martin's
Boston ♦ New York

Manufactured in the United States of America.

5 4 3 2 1 0
f e d c b a

For information, write: Bedford/St. Martin's, 75 Arlington Street, Boston, MA 02116 (617-399-4000)

ISBN-10: 0-312-61310-5
ISBN-13: 978-0-312-61310-5

Preface

As the title suggests, *Practical Argument* strives to make the methodologies and nuances of argumentation *practical* by helping students to realize that arguments are, indeed, *everywhere.* Accordingly, the introductory chapter focuses on reframing students' understanding of arguments as fights or quarrels; in addition, by focusing on common examples that students encounter in everyday life, the introductory chapter allays the trepidation many feel when confronted with formal argument. More than most texts, *Practical Argument* focuses on demystifying argumentation by offering common and *practical* explanations and examples in each chapter. And, recognizing the demands of teaching, here in this manual, we distill the key ideas of each section and essay, suggest additional teaching ideas or resources, help to negotiate some of the common problems students encounter with the material, and provide responses for each *exercise.* In short, we've striven to make *Practical Argument* not only *practical* for students but *practical* for instructors.

The manual for *Practical Argument* mirrors the pattern of the text. For example, as the text's introduction is divided into seven sections, so is the manual's coverage of it. As we have done for the introduction, for each chapter of the text the instructor's manual offers a comprehensive guide to ensure that you will find assistance and support for each page of the text.

Contents

Model Syllabi

Here are two model syllabi. The first is for a standard semester course and the second for a school on the quarter system, planned for a fourteen-week term and ten-week term, respectively. They reflect a scaffolded approach to teaching the forms of argumentation presented in *Practical Argument.* Both syllabi follow a progressive pattern of teaching less-sophisticated to more-sophisticated concepts in argument. The page numbers on the syllabi refer to the student edition of *Practical Argument.* Suggestions for additional topics for writing assignments supplement those in the book.

FULL-SEMESTER SYLLABUS

fourteen-week term, three meetings per week

WEEK 1: INTRODUCTION

INTRODUCTION: Understanding Argument 3

Chapter 1: The Structure of Argument 11

- At Issue 11
- The Pillars of Argument 12

Chapter 2: Thinking and Reading Critically 33

- Reading Critically 34
- Becoming an Active Reader 34

Chapter 1 Readings:

- **PolandSpring.com,** Poland Spring Water [ADVERTISEMENT] 27
- **PureWater2GO.com,** Pure Water 2GO [ADVERTISEMENT] 28
- **Zak Moore,** Defying the Nalgene 22
- **Tom Standage**, Bad to the Last Drop 24

Writing Assignment: Construct a template for your own argument about bottled water.

WEEK 2: VISUAL ARGUMENTS

Chapter 3: Decoding Visual Arguments 53

- Thinking Critically about Visual Arguments 53
- Using Active Reading Strategies with Visual Arguments 54

Chapter 1 Readings: Look again at water visuals.

- **PolandSpring.com,** Poland Spring Water [ADVERTISEMENT] 27
- **PureWater2GO.com,** Pure Water 2GO [ADVERTISEMENT] 28

Chapter 3 Readings (visuals):

- Distribution of Language, Sex, and Violence Codes in PG-Rated Movies [CHART] 57
- Homicides per 100,000 Population [GRAPH] 58
- **EveryLifeCounts.info,** "I Saw 7,000 People Killed" [PHOTOGRAPH] 58
- **Act Against Violence,** Media Violence & Children [WEB SITE] 59

Writing Assignment: Analyze and decode the argument of a visual text.

WEEK 3: WRITING A RHETORICAL ANALYSIS

Writing Assignment: Write a rhetorical analysis that compares Stanton's use of rhetoric to Jefferson's, and explain the rhetorical value of using Jefferson's work as a model.

WEEK 4: EVALUATING SOURCES

Writing Assignment: Choose one of the At Issue debates covered this week, and use one article that you've evaluated as a source to write an evaluation argument of Facebook or the Harry Potter texts.

WEEK 5: ROGERIAN ARGUMENT, TOULMIN LOGIC, AND ORAL ARGUMENT

Writing Assignment: Write either a Toulmin or Rogerian argument that supports your position in the debate on distance learning; then highlight the key points, and reformulate the argument in brief for oral delivery.

WEEK 6: UNDERSTANDING LOGIC AND RECOGNIZING FALLACIES

Writing Assignment: Choose one of the debate topics our readings have addressed this term, and write either an inductive or a deductive argument supporting your position.

WEEK 7: UNDERSTANDING LOGIC AND RECOGNIZING FALLACIES

WEEK 8: ARGUMENT BY DEFINITION

Writing Assignment: Spend some time thinking about the debate on vegetarianism, about the words used to define it, perhaps about the word *vegetarianism* itself, and write an argument by definition.

WEEK 9: CHAPTER 17–ETHICAL ARGUMENTS 481

Writing Assignment: Find a visual image of an ethical question that you are passionate about; for oral delivery, write an ethical argument that also makes reference to your visual image.

WEEK 10: DO WE STILL NEED UNIONS?

Writing Assignment: Interview a union or nonunion worker. Use his or her responses as a source for an argument about whether or not we need unions; write an oral argument for use in your class debate.

WEEK 11: CHAPTER 12–ARGUMENT BY DEFINITION 315

Writing Assignment: Choose a position in the rights-of-homeless debate or in the debate over awarding driver's licenses to undocumented immigrants; remember to consider the ethics of the argument as you use a Rogerian or Toulmin model

WEEK 12: SHOULD FELONS PERMANENTLY FORFEIT THEIR RIGHT TO VOTE?

Writing Assignment: Write an evaluation argument summarizing and analyzing the four authors' opinions before presenting your own response to the debate.

WEEK 13: SHOULD EVERY AMERICAN GO TO COLLEGE?

Writing Assignment: Using a Toulmin structure, write an argument in which you take a position on the college-access debate.

WEEK 14: CLASSIC ARGUMENTS

Writing Assignment: Using the structures covered in the preceding weeks, write an argument that responds to one of the selections in this chapter.

QUARTER-SYSTEM SYLLABUS

ten-week term, three meetings per week

WEEK 1: INTRODUCTION TO ARGUMENT

Writing Assignment: Choose one of the At Issue debates covered this week, and use one article that you've evaluated as a source to write an evaluation argument of Facebook or the Harry Potter texts.

WEEK 5: ROGERIAN ARGUMENT, TOULMIN LOGIC, AND ORAL ARGUMENT

Writing Assignment: Write either a Toulmin or Rogerian argument that supports your position in the debate on distance learning; then highlight the key points, and reformulate the argument in brief for oral delivery.

WEEK 6: UNDERSTANDING LOGIC AND RECOGNIZING FALLACIES

Writing Assignment: Choose one of the debate topics our readings have addressed this term, and write either an inductive or deductive argument supporting your position.

WEEK 7: UNDERSTANDING LOGIC AND RECOGNIZING FALLACIES

WEEK 8: ETHICAL ARGUMENTS

Writing Assignment: Find a visual image of an ethical question that you are passionate about; for oral delivery, write an ethical argument that also makes reference to your visual image.

WEEK 9: ARGUMENT BY DEFINITION

John Derbyshire, Throw the Bums Out:
But Do So with Compassion—Coolidge-Style Compassion 543

America, The Meanest Cities 546

Writing Assignment: Choose a position in the rights-of-homeless debate or in the debate over awarding driver's licenses to undocumented immigrants; remember to consider the ethics of the argument as you use a Rogerian or Toulmin model.

WEEK 10: SHOULD EVERY AMERICAN GO TO COLLEGE?

Chapter 26 Readings and Class Debate:

Pharinet, Is College for Everyone? 635

Margaret A. Miller, The Privileges of the Parents 628

Charles Murray, What's Wrong with Vocational School? 631

Robert T. Perry, On "Real Education" 625

Writing Assignment: Using a Toulmin structure, write an argument by definition focusing on the term *education* as you weigh in on the college-access debate.

PART

1

Understanding Argument

Introduction: Understanding Argument

Encountering Arguments, p. 3

This part of the introduction offers examples of common arguments (lawyers defending clients, an employee who thinks she or he deserves a raise, a job-application letter) and concludes by offering a few reasons why they are assigned. By pointing to argumentation's real-world efficacy, the text makes a case for the importance of assigning arguments in school.

Since the text offers real-world examples and a list of debatable questions students might encounter in your course, you might consider asking students to list more real-world examples or to compose more questions you might debate in a college classroom. This could be a good time to talk about debatable claims, which segues to the next section, "Defining Argument."

Defining Argument, p. 4

Introducing terms such as *spin* and *propaganda*, this part of the introduction first defines an argument by what it is not: a quarrel, positive or biased slant, or denial of another's position. It then offers a brief differentiation between informal and formal arguments and resolves that "An argument takes a stand and presents evidence that helps to convince people to accept the writer's position" (p. 5).

Teaching tip: Many of your students are likely familiar with right-wing commentators Sean Hannity and Ann Coulter and left-leaning commentators Rachel Maddow and Keith Olbermann. To discuss bias and spin, consider bringing in a documentary news story about a recent event that two of these politically disparate commentators discuss. Read the news story first, and then view and discuss clips of each commentator. You may naturally begin discussing debatable claims here—it's likely one of the commentators will resort to a statement of taste or an expression of faith, both problematic, nondebatable statements that are also discussed in this section of the text.

As you discuss debatable claims, consider preparing a list of facts that students could turn into debatable claims. Since the text stresses the idea that arguments have multiple sides and the commentators we watch frequently show only two, this is a good place to encourage students to think from multiple viewpoints as they reformulate facts as claims and attempt to negotiate the **either/or fallacy** (p. 7); you might even rewatch the clips of the commentators and encourage students to think about perspectives left out of their coverage.

Logos, Pathos, and *Ethos,* p. 7

Drawing from argument's Aristotelian roots, here the introduction defines **persuasion** as "a general term that refers to how a speaker or writer influences an audience to adopt a particular belief or to follow a course of action" (p. 7) and focuses on the three major appeals Aristotle names in *The Art of Rhetoric*: logic (***logos***), emotion (***pathos***), and character (***ethos***). Generally, students easily grasp appeals to emotion, but appeals to logic and character are a bit more difficult.

Teaching tip: To explain these appeals, you might turn to television commercials for insurance or medication; encourage students to see the use of experts such as doctors or others we esteem, such as celebrities, as appeals to ethos (character) that attempt to establish credibility for a product. Further, these commercials also frequently compare price or effectiveness, making an appeal to a viewer's logic. For example, if a commercial proclaims, "Nine out of ten doctors recommend X," then the viewer who doesn't use X asks him or herself, "Why am I using Y?"

Teaching tip: Advertisements, the most common everyday arguments we encounter, are a great place to find visual appeals (like the images included in this text) and textual appeals. Clip a few ads, and distribute them to groups of two or three students. Have students discuss the ads in their groups and then present their ideas to the larger class. In lieu of presenting, have students write about the appeals they identified.

CHAPTER 1

The Structure of Argument

Centered on the benefits and costs of buying bottled water, this chapter focuses on identifying and learning to mirror effective argument structure. The chapter first introduces several key concepts and a useful metaphor for thinking about argument.

The Pillars of Argument, p. 12

Drawing on students' existing knowledge of the essay format (*introduction, body, conclusion*), the text suggests that argument is built from these basics: the introduction contains an argumentative *thesis statement*, the body includes *evidence* and *refutation*, and the conclusion resolves with a convincing *concluding statement*. The building metaphor continues as the text uses words and visuals of an Ancient Greek temple to conceptualize argument. The argument—the top of the temple—is supported by a thesis, evidence, refutation, and a concluding statement—the four pillars, which give shape to and buttress the argument. As the metaphor is presented, the text briefly defines each pillar.

Teaching tip: Remember that thesis statements are difficult for students no matter how many times they've been taught and that students frequently do not evaluate the sources from which they draw evidence. You might want to spend some time talking about both thesis statements and good and bad evidence. Consider giving students practice by assigning a topic and having small groups work out mock thesis statements for each topic. Further, it's likely that students have been taught that a conclusion summarizes the main points of an argument, while a concluding statement asks students to think about a logical next step or recommendation for future action. Help students transition from summary-focused conclusions to concluding statements by suggesting that they consistently ask of essays they read and write, "So, what do we do now?" Since refutation will likely be the newest concept for your students, you may want to have the class share their team-generated thesis statements on the board and together think of at least one possible counterargument and refutation for each thesis. This approach shows students the importance of a thesis statement in directing the content and shape of an argumentative essay.

Sample Student Essay: "Why Foreign-Language Study Should Be Required," p. 14

With each structural element clearly labeled in the text, this student essay argues in favor of college foreign-language requirements because the global economy necessitates that Americans speak more than one language. The student argues that speaking a second language makes students more employable, enriches students' understanding of culture and education, and even strengthens relations between nations. The author poses and refutes the counterargument about the time and work required to learn a second language by arguing in favor of cutting less-important requirements (such as physical education) to meet the demands of language study. The author poses a second counterargument and refutation: positing that some may argue that requirements limit students' control of their own studies (including their majors), the author reminds us that students may change majors and that studying another language exposes students to other possibilities. In a concluding statement, the author claims that students have become too narrowly focused and overlook the broader implications of language study for their future.

Exercise 1.1, p. 16

This exercise directs students to read Arnold Schwarzenegger's "An Immigrant Writes" and to answer four questions (p. 18) about the essay's argument structure. You will find a brief summary of the essay and sample responses to those questions below.

Summary of "An Immigrant Writes" by Arnold Schwarzenegger, p. 16

In this brief argument, Governor Schwarzenegger urges federal immigration reform predicated on a simple philosophy: control of the borders, compassion for the immigrant. He concedes that in a post-9/11 America, stronger borders are necessary but suggests that in addition we need a temporary worker program that sheds light on the 12 million undocumented—but contributing—workers in American society.

Identifying the Elements of Argument, p. 18

1. Schwarzenegger's thesis appears in the fourth paragraph of his argument when he writes: "control of the border . . . and compassion for the immigrant. These are the twin pillars around which we must construct a new immigration policy. They are both essential elements in our overall immigration strategy. Without both, our strategy is destined to collapse." Student rewrites of Schwarzenegger's thesis will vary but should stress that a new immigration policy, to succeed, must have a two-pronged approach—control and compassion.

2. Students are asked to list three arguments the author uses; here is a list of the author's arguments, paraphrased:
   - In a post-9/11 world, we must think about security (para. 5).
   - Citizens' groups at the border remind us that the federal government is failing to do its job (5).

- Brick walls and chains (a unilateral focus on security) will not stop "a father who is desperate to feed his family" (6).
- Twelve million undocumented workers support our economy because business depends on these workers to do jobs no one else will do (6).
- A free trade zone throughout the Americas will help to create economic growth elsewhere and, therefore, give us greater security (7).
- Immigrants are just like us (8).
- It's un-American to punish charities and individuals who help immigrants (8).

3. In the third paragraph of the essay, Schwarzenegger writes against several straw-man arguments he introduces early in the essay; he suggests that some people falsely and thoughtlessly argue that "in a free society it's not possible to have border security" and that "we must deport 12 million people." In paragraph 5, he refutes deportation by reminding readers of the need for security in a post-9/11 America, while in paragraph 6, he argues in favor of a temporary worker program by pointing out that the work of those 12 million undocumented workers supports the economy. He also refutes the latter by reminding readers of the ironic link between complaints about outsourcing and the use of immigrant workers in America; thus, he suggests that the use of immigrant workers actually keeps jobs in America, supporting the American economy.
4. Students should point to Schwarzenegger's final paragraph as his concluding statement, when he writes: "Yes, immigration reform is a difficult issue. But it must be guided by a simple goal: compassion for the immigrant, control of the borders. Congress should not rest until it achieves both."

Teaching tip: Because Schwarzenegger enlists several rhetorical strategies and appeals, consider using this essay to review the content covered in the text's introduction by asking students to identify his means of persuasion.

Reading and Writing about the Issue: Do the Benefits of Bottled Water Outweigh the Costs? p. 19

Returning to the questions raised about bottled water at the outset of this chapter, this section collects three argumentative essays and two visual arguments on this debate. Each essay and image is followed by an At Issue section with several questions about the structure of the argument; below, you will find a brief summary of each written argument and sample responses to the questions in each At Issue.

Teaching tip: Since students are likely consumers of bottled water and, as such, may take even more interest in this debate, this might be a good time to ask students to bring in their favorite bottle of water or for you to supply empty bottles for in-class analysis. Analyzing the packaging is a good way to reinforce the ideas covered in the introduction. *Hint*: Ethos brand water, frequently sold at Starbucks, always makes for an interesting analysis. Further, to help students think more broadly about consumption and refuse, consider asking students to collect and document (textually, photographically, or by other means) their plastic trash for a few days.

Summary of "In Praise of Tap Water," *New York Times*, p. 20

As the title suggests, this argument favors drinking tap water in the United States, which the author claims has "some of the best public water supplies in the world" (para. 1). He points to the extensive negative environmental impact the bottled water industry has on the environment as well as on consumers' pocketbooks.

At Issue: The Structure of Argument, p. 21

1. The author's actual thesis statement is at the end of the first paragraph. Student responses will vary but should clearly assert that we should stop consuming bottled water because of its environmental impact.
2. The arguments used in paragraphs 1–3 to support the thesis are as follows:
   - The United States offers the cleanest public water in the world (para. 1).
   - Spending up to $1,400 annually on bottled water; same amount of tap water is only $.49 (2).
   - Manufacturing water bottles, made from natural gas and petroleum, uses 1.5 million barrels of oil per year (3).
   - Water bottles are frequently excluded from local recycling (3).
   - Transporting water, because of its weight, consumes substantial fuel (3).
3. The essay's concluding statement is its final paragraph; students should mention that change will come only when consumers realize that they can save money and the environment by drinking tap water.
4. The author could raise additional arguments against his position. He does raise the idea that tap water may not always be the equal of bottle water but suggests that any decline in tap water will be politically motivated by consumers' preference for bottled water. He argues that, in part, because of consumers' desire for bottled water, eventually less money will be invested in supporting clean public water (4). Other arguments and refutations might include the following:
   - *Argument:* Because of its diffuse network and the sheer volume of its distribution, pipes for tap water are always at risk of contamination. *Refutation:* Because of the number of humans at bottling plants in contact with bottles and because of a single filling source, bottled water may also be contaminated.
   - *Argument:* Tap water in all communities is not equal, despite the fact that, on average, U.S. water is highly drinkable. *Refutation:* Interest in bottled water may divert funding from improving tap water in these regions, but the population of these regions is so low that they barely increase bottled-water consumption.

5. Paragraph 5 is both an example of a grass-roots movement against bottled water and a call to action aimed at the reader; it suggests the mass movement toward bottled water is stoppable and that even city governments are getting involved.

Summary of "Defying the Nalgene" by Zak Moore, p. 22

In favor of drinking bottled water, Moore suggests that beyond the better taste and more sanitary production of bottled water, arguments for the negative environmental impact of excess bottles and their transportation are unconvincing. He also suggests that the price argument fails in practice because the expense of water is low—comparable with or less than that of other staples—when purchased.

Teaching tip: Consider having students evaluate or try to substantiate Moore's evidence; unlike the other two articles in this set, "Defying the Nalgene" does not name any sources.

At Issue: The Structure of Argument, p. 23

1. While responses will vary, students should mention that the arguments against bottled water are unconvincing. For example, a student may write: Bottled water comes under a great deal of criticism for its negative environmental impact; however, closer examination of environmental and price-based arguments against drinking bottled water reveals that they are unconvincing, even specious.
2. In paragraph 2, Moore introduces related counterarguments he eventually refutes convincingly: (1) producing, disposing of, and transporting bottled water are bad for the environment; (2) consumers should drink tap water because bottled is expensive and has minimal health benefits.

   Other arguments students might raise against Moore's position include the following:
   - Most plastic is not biodegradable.
   - Plastic may be cheap, but as a finite resource, the oil to produce it is not.
   - One bad experience with Nalgene does not mean that all reusable bottles are problematic.
   - When tap water is drinkable and the expense of bottled water is tallied yearly, the expense becomes both visible and unnecessary.
   - Supply and demand in the United States does not necessarily affect pricing in other countries.
3. *Moore's arguments:*
   - Nalgenes are unsanitary because they are hard to clean.
   - Bottled water is more convenient.
   - The demand for low-priced bottled water in the United States keeps prices down elsewhere in the world where clean water is scarce; choosing to drink bottled water is humanitarian.

Other arguments Moore might present:

- The demand for bottled water employs countless Americans.
- The demand for bottled water ensures consistent and competitive quality.
- Some bottled water brands contribute to improving clean water supplies in developing nations (Ethos is one such brand).
- Manufacturers of bottled water are already striving to reduce waste by using postconsumer recycled materials in packaging, making the purchase an ethical choice.

4. Moore's actual concluding statement is the last paragraph of his argument; it states that few facts or convincing arguments support the case against drinking bottled water and that readers should choose to drink it freely.
5. Answers will vary, but since Nalgene was a first-generation refillable bottle, it has come to function generically—as a general term for all refillable bottles. In other words, Nalgene is very well-known, particularly among college students.

Summary of "Bad to the Last Drop" by Tom Standage, p. 24

Reporting on a taste test that reveals that only one of ten can discern tap water among bottled water, Standage argues against the consumption of bottled water. While he makes traditional arguments about the financial and the environmental impact of bottled water, his later focus on the lack of clean water in developing nations adds complexity to the bottled-water debate. He argues that a fraction of the money spent annually on bottled water would enable everyone on earth to have clean water and sanitation, so he concludes by advocating donation to water charities in lieu of buying bottled water.

Teaching tip: Consider asking students how Standage's essay responds to Moore's—particularly, to Moore's claim that consuming bottled water is a humanitarian gesture. Then ask students to evaluate which essay seems more credible and why.

At Issue: The Structure of Argument, p. 26

1. The introduction, an anecdote about a water tasting the author and a group of friends conduct, lends him credibility and appeals to a reader's logic. From the outset of the essay, readers question, If only one out of ten people can identify the tap water in the lot, could I? Beginning in this manner unsettles readers, forcing them to second-guess themselves and, in this manner, opens up the possibility they may change their opinions.
2. Student responses will vary, but most will suggest that Standage wants to relate to his audience by establishing a common understanding of the bottled-water industry and rate of consumption. After the facts and figures Standage cites, he anticipates objections and logically disarms readers prior to making his

case; this tactic may gain support as objections are raised and dismissed, forcing readers to rethink their own position.

3. The opposing arguments and refutations are as follows:
   - *Argument:* Both types of water are at risk of contamination. *Refutation:* Tap water is much more stringently regulated than bottled (para. 8).
   - *Argument:* Bottled water allows you to avoid chemical additives. *Refutation:* Some bottled water contains the same chemicals, and chemicals in water are unavoidable if you shower or use a dishwasher, as both appliances strip chemicals from water and put you in constant contact with them (9–10).
   - *Argument:* Bottled water is associated with purity and cleanliness. *Refutation:* Bottled water wastes fuel and money; bottles overload landfills (11).
   - *Argument:* Tap water is not abundant in the developing world. *Refutation:* Thus, the choice to drink bottled water in a country with safe tap water is an indulgent lifestyle choice that merely flaunts wealth in the face of those for whom "access to water remains a matter of life or death" (12).

   On the question of why Standage doesn't wait to refute opposing arguments until after he makes his case, answers may vary. Students may suggest that refuting the arguments early shows how easily Standage can wipe them out, how dismissive he can be.

4. The arguments in support of Standage's thesis follow:
   - More than 40% of the world's population lack basic sanitation; more than 1 billion people lack safe drinking water (13).
   - The World Health Organization estimates that, worldwide, 80% of illness is due to water-borne diseases (13).
   - Widespread illness (which he has linked to water) makes countries less self-sufficient, more reliant on aid, and less able to combat poverty (14).
   - The need to transport clean drinking water is one of the chief reasons girls in developing nations do not attend school (14).
   - For $1.7 billion dollars a year (above current spending), everyone could have clean water (15).
   - Improving sanitation would cost an additional $9.3 billion a year (15).
   - Combined, the money to improve sanitation and provide clean water worldwide amounts to less than one quarter of the money spent annually on bottled water (15).

5. Standage's thesis is a directive to stop spending money on bottled water and to donate that money to water charities. While opinions about the delayed thesis may be mixed, students will likely agree that the thesis is a radical suggestion that a skeptical audience would initially reject and dismiss; it might even stop this audience from continuing to read the essay. The essay's structure and thesis position are strategic—as is Standage's lengthy introduction.

6. Standage's concluding statement urges readers to try their own taste test, to see if they can actually distinguish tap water from bottled or if they are mindlessly

and needlessly buying water and consuming it. His use of the phrase "bitter taste" points to the taint bottled water acquires when consumers learn how their money could be much better spent.

At Issue: The Structure of Argument, p. 27

After reading all three essays, students are likely to name the following opposing arguments:

- Compared with the number purchased, very few water bottles are recycled, and most communities do not recycle the plastic (frequently different) used to make lids.
- Smaller labels may use less paper or plastic, but given the number of bottles produced each year, conservation through sparse labeling is nominal.
- While some water advertisements or labels brag about using less plastic, they still use a lot of plastic and with it large quantities of petroleum and natural gas.
- Reusable or filter bottles are as easy to carry as bottled water, sometimes more so as many clip onto bags or come with a strap.

At Issue: The Structure of Argument, p. 28

Student responses should focus on the enormous waste caused by consuming bottled water versus the conservation possible by using refillable, filter bottles.

Exercise 1.2, p. 29

For this exercise, students follow the template and fill in the blanks to create their own argument. A sample response against the use of bottled water is provided below; the given text is in boldface.

Template for Structuring an Argument

The use of bottled water is a controversial topic. Some people claim that bottled water is environmentally unfriendly and even hard to distinguish from clean tap water. **Others, however, believe that** bottled water tastes better and has little more impact on the environment than any other consumer product. **Although both sides of this issue have merit, I believe that** the impact bottled water has on the environment is substantial, so when we have access to clean tap water, we should limit or stop consumption of bottled water **because** bottles frequently go unrecycled, their manufacture depletes petroleum resources, the water offers little health benefit, and the money would be better donated to clean-water charities.

Exercise 1.3, p. 29

This exercise asks students to revise their response for the template exercise by taking into account two friends' opinions on the issue. Remind students that academic debate is useful and that every issue has multiple viewpoints—not just two sides. Emphasize respect for others' opinions. Perhaps, redirect students to the structure of Standage's essay, which seeks to build rapport and to refute counterarguments logically before proposing a thesis.

Exercise 1.4, p. 29

This exercise asks students to write an essay addressing the question "Do the Benefits of Bottled Water Outweigh the Costs?" and to cite the texts from pages 20–28. First, you may want to remind students that the facts and ideas they've encountered in the preceding essays and visuals can be used as supporting evidence in their own arguments. To that end, it may be useful before assigning this exercise to review direct quotation—including the introduction of quotations—and MLA or APA format for in-text citation. You might also consider allocating a class meeting or portion of a class meeting to a partnered or small-group writing assignment where students can work together (in a computer lab or in the classroom) to negotiate a position and compose a single essay. If you're concerned that some students may not be able to argue their own or multiple perspectives, consider assigning students to rewrite the joint essay from a different perspective as homework.

Exercise 1.5, p. 29

This exercise asks students to review the argument checklist on page 14 and to label each portion of the essay: thesis statement, evidence, refutation of opposing arguments, and concluding statement.

Teaching tip: to give students extra practice identifying these elements, consider having students label classmates' essays rather than their own.

PART 2

Reading and Responding to Arguments

CHAPTER

2

Thinking and Reading Critically

This chapter focuses on what has become a passionate debate in our time — the relationship between violence in the media and violent behavior of young people. While most students will likely be familiar with this discussion, the chapter's content seeks to draw out the complexities surrounding the issue (parental responsibility, gun regulations, the history of violence on television and in video games) and reminds students that this is not a simple two-sided debate.

Reading Critically: Becoming an Active Reader, p. 34

To make the chapter relevant beyond just this one issue, the text asks students to learn to become critical readers. You may need to underscore this point with students — specifically, because most students will assume that to be critical is to criticize. Instead, remind them that to read critically is to assess and examine rather than simply argue against or challenge. Secondly, this chapter encourages students to be active, rather than passive, readers, and it introduces them to various techniques that will help them with reading comprehension (highlighting, annotating, summarizing).

Teaching tip: Your students are likely to have very strong opinions about the subject matter of this chapter, so you'll want to make sure that their discussions about violence in video games or in movies stay centered on the essays provided. Consider having them brainstorm a list of who is affected by this discussion (children, parents, media companies, government leaders, victims of violence, gun manufacturers, and so on) so that they have in mind what kinds of arguments would work for what kinds of audiences. This list will help them build, as well, on the means of persuasion covered in the book's introductory chapter. In other words, by discussing what kinds of arguments would work for parents of young children versus what arguments a teen video gamer might believe, your students will quickly see the value of critically assessing arguments for strength or for bias (another concept that is introduced in the beginning pages of this chapter).

Exercise 2.1, p. 35

This exercise asks students to read "Violent Media Is Good for Kids" by Gerard Jones and then answer a series of questions, in preparation for class discussion. You will find a brief summary of the essay and possible responses to those questions below.

Summary of "Violent Media Is Good for Kids" by Gerard Jones, p. 35

In this magazine article, comic-book author and father Gerard Jones argues that in some cases "creative violence" can provide children with much needed outlets for their fears and anger and even bring a sense of empowerment and selfhood. Jones draws on his own experiences as a child, when he found courage through the dual-identity of the Incredible Hulk, and he describes how his son followed a similar path to empowerment through comic-book characters. Finally, Jones discusses recent psychological studies arguing for the usefulness of violent entertainment that allows children to explore feelings they're often told to suppress. Using real-life examples to support these studies, Jones details the ways that several children dealt with difficult family situations by writing violent stories or listening to rap. In the end, Jones does not argue that violent entertainment is harmless but rather that it helps more people than it hurts.

Identifying the Elements of Argument, p. 39

1. Because Jones's essay relies so heavily on personal experiences, his thesis is delayed until the end, when in the next-to-the-last paragraph he writes, "I'm not going to argue that violent entertainment is harmless. I think it has helped inspire some people to real-life violence. I am going to argue that it's helped hundreds of people for every one it's hurt, and that it can help far more if we learn to use it well." Students may paraphrase the quotation as saying that more good derives from violent entertainment than ill. Talk with your students about why a delayed thesis is useful in this essay and how the author builds his credibility and support in a way that leads to this statement as a conclusion.
2. Jones's main arguments rely on personal experience: the way he found courage as a child in the character of the Incredible Hulk (paras. 2–5), the way his son has used "creative violence" in comic books as an outlet (6), the experiences of several children Jones has known or worked with who found ways to express their anger and fear through violent stories and even "gangsta rap" (13–15). Jones also weaves in current psychological studies regarding violence and creative expression among children (9–12).
3. Jones acknowledges the current debate surrounding violence in the media and the effects of so-called junk culture (7), and he admits in his concluding statements that, in some cases, violent entertainment does cause children to act out violently (16).
4. Students should look at the second half of Jones's final paragraph, which broadens the discussion to a more historical view. He says parents condemn "Mortal Kombat" and play-fighting, alike, in ways that suppress their children's need to "feel what they feel," and he compares this suppression with the ways Victorians suppressed their children's sexuality. He advocates balance, instead,

in a way that allows for "natural aggression" without necessarily condoning extreme violent behavior.

Highlighting, p. 39

This section introduces the technique of highlighting important parts of an essay (such as the thesis, topic sentences, supporting points, and so on). Suggestions for markings to highlight text appear in a box. Then, a sample essay shows how a student, Katherine Choi, highlighted a magazine article titled "When Life Imitates Video" by John Leo.

Teaching tip: Remember that most of your students will feel a bit strange about writing in their actual books (in fact, many of them have been told *not* to write in books at all). To help ease their anxieties, think about showing them your own highlighted books or articles and explaining how and why you highlight your own reading material. This sharing will make active reading seem like less of an activity for inexperienced readers.

Exercise 2.2, p. 42

This exercise asks students to read through student Katherine Choi's highlighting of Leo's essay "When Life Imitates Video." When students are through reading, you might open things up for discussion and ask them to consider what markings they've seen in Katherine's highlighting and what they would do differently if they were to highlight Leo's essay. Remind them that they want to highlight the main points of the essay so that they can quickly reference them but that students' highlighting will vary, depending on their particular ways of reading.

Exercise 2.3, p. 42

This exercise directs students to reread the first essay in the chapter, "Violent Media Is Good for Kids," and to practice highlighting by underlining, starring, circling, and marking the essay's main points. It also reminds students that it can be useful to mark words or references they don't understand by putting a question mark above them, then coming back to them later. When they're finished, have students discuss this experience, either in small groups or in a large group, so that they can consider the benefits of such focused attention to an essay. Most students (especially, first-year students) say they have a hard time with reading comprehension, so you might remind them that highlighting will help them find ways to remember and engage with what they read.

Annotating, p. 42

This section introduces annotating as a supplement to highlighting. A box provides suggested questions that will lead students to make notes on an essay. Then the Leo essay appears again, this time with notes by Katherine, the student.

Exercise 2.4, p. 45

For practice with annotating — marking their responses to what they read — this exercise has students return, again, to "Violent Media Is Good for Kids" by Jones. Students should mark where they agree or disagree with Jones and why, summarize the most important points, look up unfamiliar words or references and write in the definitions, and note passages they'd like to return to when writing about Jones's essay.

Exercise 2.5, p. 45

To compare their new annotating methods, have students exchange their annotated essays with one another and consider the ways that their responses to the text were similar and different. Also, have them discuss how their classmate's responses help them to realize new things about Jones's essay.

Exercise 2.6, p. 45

This exercise allows students to consider how highlighting and annotating help them to compare and contrast arguments by two writers. Students are directed to examine readers' responses that appeared in *USA Today* after the 2007 massacre at Virginia Tech University. The opinion pieces provide counterpoints to Jones's arguments, and students should mark areas where these contributors agree or disagree with Jones. You may also ask them to mark places where the writers address concerns that Jones ignores.

Teaching tip: Most students say that they have difficulty organizing sources and information for papers that they write, so you may want to suggest ways of keeping their annotations clear. Offer them simple ideas, like putting an *A* next to parts of essays they agree with and a *D* next to parts they disagree with; or they may jot *NI* if they think the author "needs more information" to support a certain point. These practical suggestions can help students to organize their notes and papers better.

Summaries of Newspaper Opinion Pieces, p. 46

There are two letters from readers in this section. The first one, titled "Media Violence May Be Real Culprit Behind Virginia Tech Tragedy," argues that the way violence is portrayed in the media (television, movies, coverage of wars in Iraq and Afghanistan) makes students believe that violence can solve problems. The second piece, titled "Take Aim at Guns," argues that the availability and prevalence of guns in America lead to outbursts of violence like the Virginia Tech shooting. Further, this author references the National Rifle Association, the Constitution, and even the Bureau of Alcohol, Tobacco, Firearms and Explosives.

Exercise 2.7, p. 47

To help students interact with a fellow college student's opinion on the effects of violent media, this exercise asks them to read a letter to the editor of a college newspaper and then highlight and annotate the letter in response to several questions. Possible responses to these questions appear below.

- Students should identify the thesis at the end of the first paragraph where the writer states, "Some states have already passed laws which ban minors from the viewing or purchasing of these [violent] video games without an accompanying adult. I believe this law should not exist." As students restate the thesis, they should acknowledge that the writer's main argument is against laws that prohibit the sale of graphic, violent video games to minors; the author is not against laws that rate such games, as she indicates in paragraph 2.

- In paragraph 3, the writer cites studies reported by universities such as MIT and UCLA. The studies denounce laws that prohibit the sale of certain video games to minors because, according to the studies, such games are not found to have adverse effects on children. Then the writer takes this conclusion a step further by saying there are benefits to violent video games — that they provide a "safe outlet for aggression and frustration, increased attention performance, along with spatial and coordination skills" (para. 3). The idea that violent entertainment provides an outlet for emotions is Jones's primary argument, and he discusses several children he's known who, after needing an outlet for anger and fear as children, went on to success in school, college, and beyond.
- In paragraph 4, the writer of the letter to a college newspaper notes that there are people who disagree with her opinion, and she writes that they believe research shows that violent video games lead to antisocial behavior and even delinquency. For this reason, some people believe there should be laws restricting who can play graphic or violent video games. But the writer says that children know the difference between real life and video games and are also aware of the consequences of turning to violence and weapons. In some ways, Jones addresses similar concepts when, in the concluding paragraph of his essay, he argues that parents should allow their children to express natural feelings of aggression or anger, not keep feelings bottled up. Both writers, then, argue that some expressions of anger or frustration are *natural* for children and that these feelings shouldn't be repressed. Consider asking students their opinions, and ask them which writer seems more effective in making his or her argument.
- The writer to the college paper seeks to overturn laws restricting the sale of violent video games to minors. In her closing paragraph, she implores the major software companies that make violent video games to write to Congress and protest these laws. Jones, in his essay, argues more for the emotional and personal value of "creative violence," which he claims can help children develop a sense of selfhood and stability — a different approach from this letter's arguments about legality.

Writing a Critical Response, p. 48

The final section of this chapter asks students to go a step beyond simply understanding arguments and, instead, demonstrates how they may *respond* to arguments critically. To do so, this section reminds students that critical evaluation involves both examining the features of any given text to identify how the writer makes his or her argument and asking plenty of *why* and *how* questions: why did a writer include this particular means of persuasion, why did the author include this information as support, why is the writer taking this stance, how will the writer's strategies impact readers? After reading previous sections of this chapter, students should be able to identify the main parts of an argument essay and should have strategies for how to highlight these main parts and annotate their response to the text while reading. Specific questions for critical reading are also provided in this section, along with a paragraph that outlines, step by step, how to write a critical response (pp. 48–49). You might consider writing out these various steps on the board so that students can easily know whether they've included enough elements for a critical response.

Teaching tip: Students often have a difficult time transitioning from identifying the parts of an essay to being able to write about an essay critically. Keep reminding them that while they should identify the main parts of the writer's argument, they also should include their response — not just whether they liked the essay or not but whether the author's argument was successful or well supported or how the author attempted to connect with readers. And remind students that they can actually identify elements that are not successful; often students hesitate to criticize published work.

Summary of Sample Critical Response by Student Katherine Choi, p. 49

Providing a sample critical response for your students is crucial if they are to understand how to go about writing such a text. Keep in mind that most of them have never written this kind of essay before, so a focused discussion about Katherine's method and organization could be quite helpful to them. Katherine responds to the essay "When Life Imitates Video" by John Leo. She opens her response by stating the main point of Leo's essay — that violent video games can actually lead to violent behavior. Then Katherine goes on, in paragraph 2, to outline Leo's subsequent main points and to explain both their usefulness and their shortcomings. She acknowledges that Leo's argument is "convincing, up to a point" but says that the study he relies on most for evidence is never cited by name and that his rhetorical style is weak. In later paragraphs, Katherine criticizes Leo for speaking in generalizations, for misunderstanding why children play violent video games in the first place, and for making unsubstantiated connections between violent video games and the military. Ultimately, Katherine argues in her response that Leo does not establish a substantial cause-and-effect relationship between violent video games and violent behavior and that his argument is not convincing.

Teaching tip: After reading Katherine's critical response, students will likely feel that their responses have to *criticize* the authors they're writing about. Remind them that when an author is successful in his or her argument they will want to tell *why* the writer is able to make such an argument, and they might even discuss why it's a fresh or new argument as well.

Exercise 2.8, p. 51

In this one-paragraph exercise, students fill in the blanks to create their own argument about Jones's essay on creative violence. A sample response appears below with the given text in boldface.

Template for Writing a Critical Response

According to Gerard Jones, violent media can actually have positive effects on young people because those media can give children much-needed outlets for feelings of anger, frustration, sadness, and aggression. **Jones also believes that violent media are a positive influence on children because** they allow children to explore these feelings in a controlled environment. **Jones makes some good points. For example, he says that** "even in the most progressive households, where we make such a point of letting children feel what they feel, we rush to substitute an enlightened discussion for the raw material of rageful fantasy. In the process, we risk confusing them about their natural aggression in the same way Victorians confused their children about their sexuality" (para. 16). **However,** Jones does still acknowledge that a link between violent media and violent behavior likely exists, but he believes that for every one person hurt by violence in media, one hundred people are helped by using such media as an outlet. **All in all,** Jones's essay is a well-balanced and personal look at the issue of violence in the media, both addressing the need for children to express their feelings and cautioning us to remain aware of the possible risks of violent media.

Exercise 2.9, p. 51

Now it is time for students to try their own hands at writing a critical response. This exercise asks them to return to the paragraph they wrote in the template exercise and to develop it into a more substantial response to Jones's essay. Remind them to refer to the highlighting and annotating they did earlier and to think in terms of what was successful about Jones's essay and what was unsuccessful (or less convincing).

Teaching tip: One of the things students will struggle with the most in writing a critical response is organization. Before you ask them to write a fully developed response to Jones's essay, you might return to the paragraph that discusses the various parts of a critical response (pp. 48–49). Listing these components bullet-style might supply the students with a ready-made outline for their own critical responses.

CHAPTER

3 Decoding Visual Arguments

Continuing the debate about violent media images begun in Chapter 2, Chapter 3 asks students to broaden their discussion by considering the cultural effects of violent visual images. At the same time, this chapter encourages students to apply the critical-reading strategies learned in the previous chapter to visual arguments. Clarifying that not all images are visual arguments, the text differentiates an advertisement, chart, or Web page from an informational diagram, for example.

Teaching tip: Because we live in a society where we are inundated by images, students frequently receive those images passively—they consume them without thinking critically about them. As a continuation of the prior chapter, consider asking students to collect or document violent images they see around them. Ask them to watch TV with paper and pen or their camera phones in hand. Also, consider bringing in a variety of visual images (diagrams, ads, posters) for students to categorize, first, by whether or not they make an argument and, second, by the dominant appeal that the image uses. This activity reinforces the text's introductory chapter and introduces this chapter's attention to identifying appeals in visual arguments.

Thinking Critically about Visual Arguments, p. 53

Drawing on the previous chapter's focus on thinking critically, the text asks students to see similarities between written and visual arguments and to evaluate the logic and fairness of those arguments.

Teaching tip: Help students learn to read visual texts through in-class analysis. By and large, students do not know what to look for or how, so thoroughly cover and discuss the list of reading strategies in the next section of text (see p. 54).

Using Active Reading Strategies with Visual Arguments, p. 54

This section reminds students that *highlighting* and *annotating*, tools for actively reading a written text (covered in Chapter 2), can help with decoding visual arguments as well. As when approaching a written text, students should approach a visual text with pen in hand in search of main ideas, purpose, and intended audience. As the text points out, encourage students to look for words/body copy, the size and orientation of images, use of white space, use of color and shading, presence of people, activities, expressions, and gestures.

Teaching tip: The text box entitled "Comprehension Clues" (p. 54) offers a good list of things to consider when approaching visual images, but it is not exhaustive. Consider reading and discussing these clues as a class, applying them to a particular image. Then, try to add to the list other clues students should look for when approaching a visual text.

Reminding students that visual images also make appeals, a second text box (p. 55) describes how visual images deploy *logos*, *pathos*, and *ethos*. A cartoon and brief analysis of it follow; spend time talking about the cartoon's intended audience and purpose, how it makes an argument, and what appeals it makes.

Teaching tip: If you did not earlier have students identify and categorize visual arguments by dominant appeals, have students identify and classify them now; advertisements (drawn from a variety of magazines) or comic strips are great visuals to use for this assignment.

Crime Victims per 1,000 Citizens (graph and explanation), pp. 56–57

This graph refutes the popular assumption that crime rates rose with the advent and popularization of violent video games. To help students identify the purpose of visual arguments quickly and succinctly, the text illustrates naming the argument of the image in a single sentence.

Teaching tip: Provide or have students bring in other visual arguments to practice this valuable skill.

Exercise 3.1, pp. 57–59

Identifying the Elements of Visual Arguments, p. 59

1. The four images are a pie chart labeled "Distribution of Language, Sex, and Violence Codes in PG-Rated Movies" (informative); a bar graph labeled "Homicides per 100,000 Population" (informative/argumentative); a photo of a child with a sign saying "I saw 7,000 people killed before I was 14" (argumentative); and a screen shot of a Web page, "Media Violence & Children" (informative/argumentative). The images labeled "informative/argumentative" convey information, but they do so in an argumentative fashion. For example, the simple bar graph lists the United States first and shows a line three times longer than the lines of other major developed nations; the juxtaposition of the lines seems to convey a comparative argument in a way that a chart listing homicides as numbers would not.
2. A main idea of each may be stated as follows:
   - "Distribution of Language, Sex, and Violence Codes in PG-Rated Movies" *Main Idea:* Nearly half of all movies rated PG earn that rating because of

violence only or some violent content in addition to the prevalence of sex and language in the film.

- "Homicides per 100,000 Population" *Main Idea:* The United States has a homicide rate over three times higher than the rate of all the other major developed nations shown on the chart.
- "I saw 7,000 people killed before I was 14" *Main Idea:* Young children witness many murders on television, a fact that underscores the prevalence of violence in media.
- "Media Violence & Children" *Main Idea:* Media violence has a strong influence on children's behavior.

3. How each visual supports its main idea follows:
   - "Distribution of Language, Sex, and Violence Codes in PG-Rated Movies" shows the prevalence of violence in PG-rated films surpasses the prevalence of only sex or only language.
   - "Homicides per 100,000 Population" clearly shows the much higher U.S. homicide rate.
   - "I saw 7,000 people killed before I was 14" focuses on that single striking statistic.
   - "Media Violence & Children" links witnessing media violence to aggressive behavior.
4. Answers will vary, but students should generally suggest a link between media violence and actual violence or between media violence and aggressive behavior among children.
5. Answers will vary; most of the visuals could appeal to a variety of audiences. Suggestions follow:
   - "Distribution of Language, Sex, and Violence Codes in PG-Rated Movies": neutral audience
   - "Homicides per 100,000 Population": neutral, hostile, or friendly audience
   - "I saw 7,000 people killed before I was 14": friendly audience, possibly neutral audience as well
   - "Media Violence & Children": friendly or neutral audience

Highlighting and Annotating Visuals, p. 60

Highlighting and annotating visual arguments, just like highlighting and annotating textual arguments, help us to look more carefully at each element in an image. The text suggests that students star, box, and circle important parts of an image and write about each of the identified elements in the margins.

A sample student annotation of a video game called *Grand Theft Auto IV* follows.

Teaching tip: Ask students to critique and add to this sample annotation; it's a good annotation but intentionally not exhaustive.

Exercise 3.2, p. 61

This exercise asks students to (1) highlight and annotate a visual argument and (2) identify its central message. The image, entitled "Media Violence" shows a white hand holding a gun emerge from the screen of a laptop to shoot its white male user in the head; blood splatters the wall behind him.

In their highlighting and annotating, students should note that the hand and gun are central to the image and that a black glove makes the hand stand out. The black-gloved hand and the silver gun reinforce the color of the laptop, turned to an angle to make it appear more prominent. The victim's neutral-colored clothing and the image's general lack of color make the blood on the wall behind the victim appear even more vivid.

Some may read the central message of the ad as "Media violence contributes to claiming real lives"; despite the cautionary note accompanying the image, others may want to focus specifically on violent video games.

Exercise 3.3, p. 61

This exercise asks students to interview a classmate about an experience with video games and actual violence, to discuss any links that classmate sees between the two, and to write a paragraph summarizing the interview.

Teaching tip: Because the assignment does ask students to consider their experiences with actual violence, discussion may touch on uncomfortable areas of student disclosure (child abuse, domestic violence, assault, etc.). As you present the assignment to students, you may want them to focus on violence in their communities rather than on themselves, or you may want to preface the assignment by reminding students that they do not need to talk about more than one experience that they feel comfortable sharing.

Exercise 3.4, p. 61

This exercise asks students to recall Gerard Jones's argument in "Violent Media Is Good for Kids," which they read in Chapter 2 (pp. 36–39), and to assess the images included in that essay with a critical eye. Students should discuss whether or not the images support Jones's central argument.

While student responses will vary, each image reinforces Jones's central argument that comic-book images and fantasy violence help children to negotiate their own feelings of powerlessness. Each visual is empowering: a central figure gains control of a situation and indulges in over-the-top self-expression. The images combat what Jones sees as a society problematically encouraging only acceptable social behavior to the detriment of developing healthy aggression in children.

Responding Critically to Visual Arguments, p. 62

Encouraging students to recall what they learned in Chapter 2 about writing critical responses to written arguments, this section offers a useful series of questions to prompt students to write a critical response to visual arguments. The text suggests that students first identify audience and purpose before analyzing a visual text. A sample student analysis of the advertisement for *Grand Theft Auto IV* (p. 60) follows.

Teaching tip: If you spent time asking students to add to the annotation of the *Grand Theft* advertisement, continue this work by having students add to this sample response. Ask students to evaluate the sample essay, to provide more evidence, and to make and support additional assertions about the visual text.

Exercise 3.5, p. 65

For this exercise, students follow the template and fill the blanks to create their own argument. A sample critical response to a visual argument follows; the given text is in boldface.

Template for Responding to Visual Arguments

A visual posted on Flickr.com shows a white hand holding a gun emerge from the screen of a laptop to shoot its white male user in the head; blood splatters the wall behind the computer user. **This visual makes a powerful statement about** media violence. **Its images show** media as the perpetrator of real violence, as violence reaches past the screen into the real world. **At first glance, the photographer's goal seems to be to** critique violent screen media, perhaps even violent video games. **The photo's stark images support this position. For example,** the gun appears as the central and most prominent image in the photo, **and** the neutral colors in the photo make the victim's red blood even more vivid. **A note that accompanies the photo states that it is not a statement against video games. Still the impact on its audience is likely to be** upsetting since so many video games are played on computers.

Exercise 3.6, p. 65

This exercise asks students to reflect on their paragraph response to Exercise 3.5 and to write a more fully developed critical response to the "Media Violence" image. Have students return to the highlighting and annotating of the image they did in Exercise 3.2 as they construct a more in-depth response to the image.

Teaching tip: Since this is a difficult image to analyze (it's stark, has no text, and seems deceptively simple) and may be your students' first sustained attempt at analyzing a visual argument, consider having them work in small groups to develop their ideas together before they write on their own.

CHAPTER

4

Writing a Rhetorical Analysis

What Is a Rhetorical Analysis? p. 68

Focusing on Martin Luther King Jr.'s "Letter from Birmingham Jail" (p. 68), the text asks students to begin thinking about rhetorical analysis—that is, how a writer uses strategy to convince his or her audience. As the text warns, students may know or focus on the negative connotation of *rhetoric* as empty manipulation, so here the text explains *rhetoric* from the academic perspective. The text defines *rhetoric* and *rhetorical analysis* in terms of the situation within which the writer is writing: for whom she or he is writing, how she or he attempts to persuade, and what strategies she or he uses to form an argument.

Considering the Rhetorical Situation, p. 70

Considering the rhetorical situation of any piece of writing requires analyzing the writer, purpose, audience, topic, and context of the writing. The text explains each of those five concepts through examples from King's "Letter from Birmingham Jail" and offers lists of universal analytical questions for each. (As students perform their own rhetorical analysis in Exercise 4.2, p. 87, direct them to return to these questions.)

Context is perhaps the most difficult of these concepts for students to grasp, largely because it requires social, political, and historical knowledge students might not have; always remind students to read headnotes and to scan a text for historical or cultural references (p. 74). While you should encourage students to recall what they have learned about the time period during which a text was written, this is also a good time to make a plug for the importance of research.

Teaching tip: To encourage research, you might ask students to underline any of King's references that they do not understand and to look them up later; parlay this advice into a short writing assignment asking students to discuss how learning this new information affected their thoughts about the letter.

Considering the Means of Persuasion: *Logos, Pathos, Ethos,* p. 75

This section reviews the terms *logos, pathos,* and *ethos,* introduced on p. 7. Generally, students easily grasp appeals to emotion, but appeals to logic and character are a bit more difficult.

Teaching tip: While the text draws on King's letter to give examples of these appeals, the identification of them is certainly not exhaustive. Consider giving students an excerpt of King's letter and asking them to mark each kind of appeal in a different color highlighter/marker/pen. Also, advertisements, the most common everyday arguments we encounter, are a great place to find visual appeals (like the images included in this text) and textual appeals. Clip a few ads and distribute them to small groups (two or three works best); have students discuss the ads in their groups and then present their ideas to the larger class. In lieu of presenting, have students write about their ad's rhetorical situation and the appeals they identified.

Considering the Writer's Rhetorical Strategies, p. 76

As writers and readers, it's important to think about rhetorical strategy on the structural and stylistic level. As this portion of the chapter makes clear, the tenor and placement of the thesis statement as well as the organization—the arrangement of points or ideas—are important components of an essay's rhetorical effect. You might use this opportunity to discuss the type and caliber of evidence or sources that an author may include and why he or she might choose to include or exclude the refutation of opposing viewpoints.

The text reacquaints students with the stylistic techniques of metaphor, simile, and allusion and again offers examples from King's letter. Students will most likely be more familiar and adept at spotting metaphor and simile than they will be at recognizing allusion. Since the examples given of each strategy are not exhaustive, have students search for more examples in King's text; pay particular attention to what they identify as allusion. Additionally, expect students to be unfamiliar with the uses of the second set of stylistic rhetorical strategies the text names: parallelism, repetition, and rhetorical questions. Parallelism will likely be the most difficult concept of the set for students to identify because it is more difficult to define and identify (perhaps try diagramming a few sentences to teach the concept). Students usually quickly grasp the use of repetition and rhetorical questions for effect and reflection.

Assessing the Argument, p. 79

It is important for students to understand that the purpose of rhetorical analysis is to assess an argument's effectiveness. The text evaluates "Letter from Birmingham Jail" as a highly effective argument because of its expert use of appeals and rhetorical strategies. A checklist for performing a rhetorical analysis is available for students to refer to as they write their own analyses.

Sample Rhetorical Analysis, p. 80

Summary of "Terror's Purse Strings" by Dana Thomas, p. 81

In this *New York Times* op-ed, author Dana Thomas argues that the long-reaching arms of terrorism affect even the counterfeit handbag industry and that only consumers can stop this crime. She delays this thesis until the article's final paragraph. Appealing to *ethos* by citing reputable research from Interpol and the Global Anti-Counterfeiting Group, Thomas also appeals to *logos* as she argues that we must stop purchasing counterfeit bags because the "rackets are run by crime syndicates that also deal in narcotics, weapons, child prostitution, human trafficking and terrorism" (para. 6). Offering her own experience as evidence as well, she appeals to *pathos* in the story of a raid on a "decrepit tenement," where children aged eight to thirteen, who were likely "sent off" or "sold" by their families, were left "jobless" and "homeless" afterward (8–9). Here Thomas also makes a literary allusion to *Oliver Twist* and a bit later makes a historical allusion when she likens luxury manufacturers that will not authenticate goods to complicit Victorians, who wished to distance themselves from the taint of ill repute. She insists that consumers must stop buying fakes to end the supply chain; consequently, she claims, illicit activities, terrorism, and child labor will end.

While Thomas makes a compelling and persuasive argument, encourage students to question her conclusion. The conclusion is too far-reaching—she seems to think that counterfeit purses hold, as her title suggests, terrorism's purse strings. This is a provocative argument that largely capitalizes on our contemporary political context and the popular memory of former president George W. Bush's "war on terror." Finally, Thomas's conclusion that the children who labor in counterfeiting sweatshops would be returned home overlooks numerous other industries unrelated to handbag counterfeiting that rely on child labor.

Student Response: "A Powerful Call to Action," p. 82

Student author Deniz Bilgutay clearly identifies the means of persuasion and the rhetorical strategies that Thomas uses in "Terror's Purse Strings." As marginal notations throughout the essay point out, Bilgutay analyzes context, topic, purpose, audience, stylistic rhetoric, evidence, appeals, organization, and thesis. While she does recognize that Thomas's conclusion relies on "the simple logic of cause and effect," she could be a bit more critical of the author's overzealous conclusion.

Exercise 4.1, p. 85

For this exercise, students follow the template and fill the blanks to create their own one-paragraph rhetorical analysis of "Sweatshop Oppression" by Rajeev Ravisankar on pp. 86–87.

Exercise 4.2, p. 87

Student responses will vary. The following sample rhetorical analysis identifies in brackets the elements of the argument's rhetorical situation, the means of persuasion, and the rhetorical strategies that Rajeev Ravisankar uses in "Sweatshop Oppression."

> In the opinion section of the *Lantern*, Ohio State University's student newspaper [context], Rajeev Ravisankar, a college senior [writer] majoring in political science and international studies [*ethos*], argues that the blame for sweatshop oppression should be placed on the corporations leading "the race to the bottom"—that is, the race to pay their workers the lowest wages possible [topic]. As a member of the college community, Rajeev establishes a rapport with his audience by using *we* and *us,* thereby avoiding the finger-pointing that might ensue from discussing such a hot-button topic [audience]. His attempt to forge a community with his readers and his early focus on the facts of sweatshop labor [organization] build to a delayed thesis that places blame on corporations [thesis].
>
> Rajeev not only wants to gain support for grass-roots movements for fair labor, such as University Students against Sweatshops, but also wants to set the record straight about the nature of corporate and consumer rhetoric surrounding sweatshop labor [purpose]. Usefully, he critiques "free-market economic fundamentalist" rhetoric that supports the corporate use of sweatshop labor. While fundamentalists argue that labor activists actually harm laborers by "forcing" corporations to move elsewhere, Rajeev points out that corporations are "forced" only by their lust for profit as they choose to "shift to locations where they can find cheaper labor and weaker labor restrictions" [refutation].
>
> Rajeev advances his argument by using figurative language such as "pits of poverty" and "race to the bottom" [stylistic technique], which helps readers to understand workers' impoverishment and the pace of corporate greed. Emotional appeals such as "the plight of the poor" and "total disregard for human well-being" [*pathos*] and the use of other stylistic techniques such as asking the reader, "So what can we do about it?" [rhetorical question] persuade the reader to align with the author's perspective. Finally, Rajeev concludes with an appeal to *logos* when he cites research from *The Nation*, a reputable source [evidence, *ethos*], that testifies to the billions of dollars spent annually on clothing with university insignias; he suggests that pressure to sell sweatshop-free goods would encourage corporations to rethink their practices rather than lose such a large amount of revenue [*logos*].

CHAPTER 5

Understanding Logic and Recognizing Fallacies

To further students' understanding of what makes a solid argument, this chapter focuses on the difference between arguments built on logic and those propped up by logical fallacies. The chapter—divided into sections on deductive reasoning, syllogisms, enthymemes, inductive reasoning, and inferences—shows how to construct and write deductive and inductive essays. Next, the chapter covers logical fallacies so that students may recognize them in others' arguments and avoid such fallacies in their own work. The final part of the chapter brings together all these discussions about good and bad arguments in a debate over whether schools should provide merit-based aid to students. Because this debate is one that your students are close to, it's accessible and helps combine all that they've learned to this point.

Teaching tip: Sometimes the principles of logic, reasoning, and logical fallacies can seem academic and somewhat removed from students' day-to-day lives. To motivate students, you might have them practice recognizing these concepts in familiar pop-culture texts such as magazine ads. Ask each student to bring in a magazine ad or two; then have students examine the ads to see what kind of reasoning they use and even what kinds of fallacies they rely on (and there will be many). This activity will give students quick practice and will serve as good preparation for the more weighty and substantial set of readings that they will work with at the close of the chapter.

What Is Deductive Reasoning? p. 91

This section describes the kind of argument built on a series of premises, or assumptions, that leads to a certain conclusion. Traditionally, this process is illustrated with a **syllogism,** which the text tells us consists of a **major premise** (a general statement that relates two terms), a **minor premise** (an example of the foregoing statement), and a **conclusion**. That is, deductive reasoning moves from true statements to a logical conclusion. Examples from the Declaration of Independence show students a real-life example of deductive reasoning, but you may want to provide a few everyday examples of your own to help them understand the logical progression of this kind of argumentation.

Constructing Sound Syllogisms, p. 92

Building on the previous section on deductive reasoning, this section provides a closer look at syllogisms and how they are used to construct **sound arguments** (arguments that are both valid and true). It also stresses that a valid syllogism is not true if one of the premises is false. The text provides examples of true and untrue syllogisms, and these examples relate to the At Issue topic for the chapter—merit-based scholarships. This section goes on to examine syllogisms in more depth looking at syllogisms with illogical middle terms, syllogisms with key terms that shift meaning, and syllogisms with negative premises. Be sure to cover all these examples, and give your students plenty of time to practice with these terms.

Recognizing Enthymemes, p. 94

Here the text introduces **enthymeme** as a syllogism that leaves out part of its argument—usually, the major premise—because it is obvious or assumed. But sometimes the omitted underlying belief or assumption is questionable and undercuts the argument.

Bumper-Sticker Thinking, p. 96

Students can use this box to practice what they've learned about syllogisms and enthymemes. Or they can collect their own bumper-sticker sayings. The goal is to analyze the kind of logic used by each bumper sticker: what is being said, what is assumed, what logic is combined, and so on?

Exercise 5.1, p. 97

This exercise asks students to read a short paragraph about drunk driving and then present its main argument in the form of a syllogism. An example follows.

Major premise: Laws should deal only with actions that damage person or property.

Minor premise: Laws that make it a crime to drive with a blood-alcohol concentration of .08 or higher allow the government to criminalize the content of drivers' blood rather than drivers' actions.

Conclusion: Drunk-driving laws are a violation of civil liberties.

Students may discuss whether the major premise begs the question of what laws are. It makes an assumption that not all legal scholars would share.

Exercise 5.2, p. 97

This exercise asks students to read an excerpt from a passage about human rights and to answer a set of questions. Possible answers are provided.

1. By citing the United Nations and the Declaration of Independence, this writer assumes, first, that readers recognize the authority of both the international organization and a founding document of the United States. The writer also, without stating so directly, operates on current interpretations of the Declaration of Independence (that "basic rights apply to everyone"); while the writer mentions slavery, she does not acknowledge that slavery was a part of U.S. history even after the declaration was signed. The writer also uses phrases such as *basic rights* and *inherent value* without defining them, thereby assuming readers will know what the terms mean. Finally, the writer assumes that everyone *should* have basic human rights and that, ethically, governments are supposed to uphold those rights.
2. The writer supports her argument by referencing both the United Nations and the Declaration of Independence as evidence. The writer also uses a common-sense approach, saying that because everyone experiences life, all individuals have inherent value.
3. The major premise is that a person's inherent value means he or she should be afforded certain basic human rights.
4. A syllogism that expresses the essay's argument:

   Major premise: A person's inherent value means he or she should be afforded certain basic human rights.

   Minor premise: Each person's value comes from his or her capacity to experience life, not from intelligence or usefulness to others.

   Conclusion: Everyone is entitled to basic rights.
5. Ask students to consider their own syllogisms and evaluate them for truth, validity, and soundness.

Exercise 5.3, p. 98

This exercise asks students to evaluate the soundness of arguments. Suggested responses are provided in parentheses after each given argument.

1. Sound.
2. Not sound because there is no qualifier. The first premise does not state that Alison *always* orders eggs or oatmeal; it just states that she *should*.
3. Not sound because syllogisms in which both premises are negative cannot have a valid conclusion.
4. Sound.
5. Not sound, because the first premise is untrue. Only equilateral triangles have three equal sides.

Exercise 5.4, p. 98

This exercise asks students to read the enthymemes that appear on bumper stickers, to supply their missing premises, and to evaluate them as arguments. Possible responses follow each enthymeme.

1. Missing premise: if you love your pet, you love animals, so you shouldn't eat meat because to do so causes cruelty and death to animals. This is not necessarily a strong argument, because, in reality, the animals people eat are not usually the same animals they keep as pets.
2. Missing premise: that civilized nations do not engage in terrorism. Here the bumper sticker is arguing that there is no difference between terrorism and war, and it assumes that, in both cases, there are civilian casualties and planned destruction. This argument is a difficult one to identify as sound, because often the strategies of war and terrorism are quite different, however, depending on one's political leanings, certain comparisons can be made and argued.
3. Missing premise: that men don't need to ask for help and that doing so makes them less "manly." This argument is certainly not sound, because it relies on antiquated assumptions about masculinity.
4. Missing premise: that everyone in a given place belongs equally. Such rhetoric is often used when discussing immigration policies and who does and does not belong to a certain place. While powerful in its idea, this is not a strong argument because, certainly, according to government policies, people *are* designated as either citizens or foreigners.
5. Missing premise: what matters in life cannot be bought or measured according to monetary worth. Some students may be critical of this statement because they may subscribe to the idea that materialism equates with happiness or a certain level of success; however, "the best things in life aren't things" is pretty strong because it relies on a more universal meaning of *best*—that the best aspects of life—for example, life itself, family, a place—are not *things.*
6. Missing premise: both the driver of the car and the person reading the bumper sticker don't approve of the job being done by a current elected official. That major premise coupled with the stated minor premise "I didn't vote for him" leads to conclusion "Don't blame me."
7. Missing premise: people need a "cure" for all their years of work. This bumper sticker is difficult to assess as an argument, however, since retirement is not "medicine" at all, and for some people, retirement can be difficult because of lack of income, health problems, and so on.
8. Missing premise: love can and should solve all problems. This bumper sticker says that love is the only solution, presumably excluding other actions such as war or any other aggressive behavior. Of course, this can be a difficult argument to make, and likely your students will have strong opinions on this idea. While loving in all situations can be very difficult and even a powerful response, there are often situations that require more aggressive actions. And

the wording of this bumper sticker presents a problem because, in reality, love is not the "only" solution.

9. Missing premise: discussions surrounding abortion should focus on the fetus as a child rather than uphold the idea of a woman's choice. Clearly, this bumper sticker would be on the car of someone who is pro-life. This argument is hard to evaluate objectively because it is based on individual beliefs about ethics and when life (and the designation *child*) actually begins.

10. Missing premise: people who don't go to hear live music are missing out on a unique experience. Likely the driver of the car is advocating not only live music, but also local music, so there may be other concerns behind this statement. This argument is based purely on opinion.

Writing Deductive Arguments, p. 99

Here students learn how to make deductive arguments into strong deductive essays. Most important, students who write deductive arguments should remember to support them with pieces of evidence that, together, reach a specific conclusion. A student essay provides an example of a deductive argument.

Summary of Student Essay "Higher Education for All," p. 99

In this essay, student Crystal Sanchez lays out the reasons that every U.S. citizen should be encouraged to attend college and get a degree. Additionally, at the end, Sanchez moves her argument a step further when she states that the government has the *obligation* to offer all students access to a college education. Sanchez's essay relies on a deductive style of argumentation, and each topic sentence provides support for the argument. Her evidence for why everyone should go to college includes "a college education gives people an opportunity to discover what they are good at" (para. 2); "many current jobs will not exist in this country in ten years; many will be phased out or shipped overseas. Americans should go to college to develop the skills that they will need to get the jobs that will remain" (3); and "education is an essential component of a strong democracy" (4).

Identifying the Elements of Deductive Argument, p. 102

1. A paraphrase of Crystal's thesis: Given that education means advantages such as higher income for individuals and a more robust government, all U.S. citizens should go to college and earn a diploma.

2. Crystal's main points are her topic sentences: the first sentences of paragraphs 2, 3, and 4. In spite of Crystal's designation of her third argument as "the best reason," students may differ in identifying the strongest argument and the weakest.

3. Crystal refutes the opposing arguments of insufficient room for all students and underprepared students. She could have addressed the extreme cost of

providing higher education to every willing U.S. citizen, changes in government spending since the time of the G.I. Bill, and government's current role in making college more affordable to students (in the way of grant money, loans, scholarships, and so on).

4. In the conclusion, Crystal reiterates that every American should be able to go to college, and she restates her main points of support. Finally, Crystal looks to the future and argues that not only will Americans who go to college benefit personally but also the entire nation will benefit from having a more prepared workforce.
5. A syllogism that expresses the essay's argument:

Major premise:	People who have a college education enjoy increased wages, opportunities, and benefits.
Minor premise:	Only 28% of Americans had a bachelor's degree in 2004.
Conclusion:	The U.S. government should encourage every citizen to attend college and get a degree.

What Is Inductive Reasoning? p. 102

In contrast to deductive reasoning, **inductive reasoning** refers to arguments that come out of a list of observations and lead to a certain conclusion. The section opens with a series of observations about pollution and how, given these observations, we conclude that runoff pollution is a problem that must be addressed as soon as possible. Following that is a discussion about Francis Bacon's use of the scientific method, and the text gives real-life examples of the various ways that argumentation can reach inductive conclusions (particular to general, general to general, general to particular, and particular to particular).

Making Inferences, p. 104

One of the primary components of inductive reasoning is the **inductive leap,** or **inference.** This section discusses how an inference is what allows a person to make a conclusion based on observations. It reminds students, too, that because inductive conclusions are based on a person's ability to infer, they are never certain (as deductive arguments are), only probable. Students are also cautioned to be on the lookout for hasty generalizations, which are overly broad inferences—meaning the gap between the observations/data and the conclusion is too big.

Constructing Strong Inductive Arguments, p. 105

Finally, with this section, it's time to show students how all this information about inductive arguments can be used in their own work. Here, students see that the conclusions they reach through inductive reasoning are only as strong as the support they provide. In a sense, this section instructs students on what problems can occur when trying to make inductive arguments, including the dangers of broad generalizations, insufficient evidence, irrelevant evidence, and an overlooked exception to the rule.

Exercise 5.5, p. 106

This exercise asks students to read a series of arguments and label those that use deductive reasoning with a *D* and those that use inductive reasoning with an *I*. The answers appear in parentheses after each argument.

1. Deductive; you may ask students' input on whether this is a sound argument.
2. Inductive; the argument infers that "it makes more sense" to buy the Charger because it gets better gas mileage than the Crown Victoria.
3. Inductive; one has to infer, based on the evidence, what Montresor's plans were and how long he had these plans.
4. Deductive; since a patient is a person, the minor premise is a form of "Garrett is a person," and the syllogism is sound.
5. Inductive; this argument does not lead to a certain conclusion, but it does lead to a probable one. Reaching this conclusion, however, depends on assuming that the pollution found in the ocean is harmful to swimmers.

Exercise 5.6, p. 107

This exercise asks students to read a series of arguments and decide whether they are deductive or inductive. If the argument is inductive, students should tell how strong or weak it is; if the argument is deductive, students should evaluate its soundness. The answers appear in parentheses after each argument.

1. Inductive. This argument is strong, based on the evidence provided, though the conclusion is not certain. Instead, one needs to infer that *The Farmer's Almanac* and the National Weather Service know what they're talking about and can make reliable predictions.
2. Deductive. This argument starts with a larger premise about small towns in Europe, and the conclusion that follows is a logical one.
3. Inductive. This argument is based on a series of observations that lead to a probable conclusion—that the boys who were playing broke the window.
4. Inductive. Because the argument is overly simplistic and incomplete, it is weak.
5. Deductive. The major premise and minor premise—the first and second statements, respectively—lead to a logical and strong conclusion that George Martin has an advanced degree.
6. Inductive. The inference that all men are like the speaker's last two boyfriends is a hasty generalization.
7. Inductive. This argument infers that the pharmaceutical company knows best, and it leaves out a vital explanation of why the government pulled the drug.

8. Inductive. Because the two statements have no correlation, this is a weak argument.
9. Inductive. Inferring that Harry Potter is the *only* exception to the rule makes for a weak inductive argument.
10. Inductive. This is a strong argument, based on what the speaker has observed and his or her inference that the teacher will be consistent.

Exercise 5.7, p. 108

This exercise asks students to read an inductive paragraph and to answer questions that follow it. A short summary and answers are provided below, with given text in boldface.

Summary of "Football Fanatics" by Pooja Vaidya, p. 108

In this brief excerpt, Pooja Vaidya describes going to a football game between the Philadelphia Eagles and the Dallas Cowboys and experiencing what a professional football game is like in the United States. Pooja describes the aggressive, emotional behavior of the Eagles fans and explains various fan rituals and cheers. Pooja concludes that, for many Eagles fans, "a day at the stadium" is just an "opportunity to engage in behavior that in any other context would be unacceptable."

Questions for Essay by Pooja

1. The first statement cannot be concluded from the paragraph. Although some fans engage in violent behavior at Eagles games, there's no indication that *all* of them do so.
2. The writer's conclusion is that fans at a football game behave in ways that would be unacceptable in any other context. All the following observations lead him to his conclusion:
   - Fans at the stadium paint their faces or chests.
   - Fans at the stadium wear capes, jerseys, and colored wigs.
   - Fans at the stadium join in cheers and fight songs; they become outwardly emotional when their team is losing.
   - Fans at the stadium often drink a lot before and during the game, causing them to become unruly in public.
   - Some Eagles fans treat fans of the other team (the Cowboys) with disrespect and won't let them sit in their section.
3. The writer could have given more examples of what the fans do at the game (things they yell or say to one another, other rituals or superstitions about the game, and so on), or he could have provided some contrast to what he wrote about; for instance, how did the people he was with behave? Or how was the atmosphere at the football stadium different from the atmosphere at arenas where other sports are played? As it stands, his argument requires readers to infer what is normal and acceptable based on what he describes as abnormal and unacceptable behavior; his answers to these other questions might have helped readers.

4. Your students will probably disagree on this question.
5. Students will probably conclude that the paragraph makes a strong inductive argument: most people do not engage in these behaviors anywhere else, nor would such behavior elsewhere be acceptable. However, students may disagree with Pooja's apparent disappointment at the fans' behavior.

Writing Inductive Arguments, p. 109

As in the section on writing deductive essays, this section helps students to put what they know about inductive arguments into prose form. As with deductive essays, students learn to present evidence (facts, observations, or examples). In addition, they learn that because their readers will need to take an inductive leap to reach a conclusion, writers need to be sure their link between the data and conclusion is strong.

Summary of "Please Do Not Feed the Humans" by William Saletan, p. 110

In this essay, Saletan examines the current obesity epidemic and explains that it is a problem not just in the United States or Europe but has become a global issue. He cites data from both the World Health Organization and the United Nations that concludes "for every two people who are malnourished, three are now overweight or obese" (para. 3). Saletan explains the ways that socioeconomics and technology have led to an overweight population—how fast food, technological advancements, and everyday work requirements have changed. He also notes that the historical relationship between economic class and health has completely inverted itself. In the past, the rich were the ones who could afford luxury and excess, and they were the ones who became fat; now, the cheapest foods are often the least healthy, so those who are poor are the ones who are fat. As a result of all these observations, Saletan concludes that we must change our behaviors, from the foods we eat to the amount we exercise, and he says programs that help the poor must begin providing and subsidizing healthy food choices like fruits and vegetables.

Identifying the Elements of Inductive Argument, p. 112

1. Saletan's thesis comes in paragraph 13, when he states that we must burn more calories and eat fewer calories to begin with.
2. You might want to point out to students that Saletan's thesis is an example of the delayed thesis—a way of accumulating support for a thesis before making it. (Tom Standage in Chapter 1 also delays his thesis.) There are several reasons that authors choose this structure, and in Saletan's case, he likely puts the thesis later in his essay so that readers are more likely to accept his solution. If he had started the essay by saying that we need to exercise more and change the foods we eat, readers may have felt that they were being criticized and may have been less receptive to his argument. As it is, by the time readers

reach Saletan's thesis, his argument is so strong that readers can't help but agree with him.

3. Saletan amasses several lines of support for his conclusion, as follows:
   - Statistics from the World Health Organization and the United Nations prove that people around the world are overweight and suffering health problems as a result (para. 3).
   - Socioeconomic information reveals that "fat is no longer a rich man's disease" and that obesity has actually become more of a problem among the poor (4).
   - Technology has made life easier so that we work less and burn fewer calories (5, 6, 11, 12).
   - Our diets often include processed foods, more sweeteners, and high levels of animal fat and salt (7 and 8).
   - The abundance of fast food and larger portions make unhealthy foods more affordable and accessible, while healthy foods are more expensive and less affordable for lower-income families (8 and 9).
   - Our mentality about food, eating, and exercise has not changed to compensate for our easy lifestyles (14).
4. Saletan's conclusion comes right after his thesis, at the end. So when he states that we need to change how we eat and to exercise more, he quickly follows with advice about tackling the mentality that keeps us from doing so. See if your students follow this inductive leap and if it makes sense to them.
5. Have students explain *why* they think Saletan's reasoning is strong or weak. If they say it is weak, ask them what Saletan could have covered to make the argument more compelling.

Recognizing Logical Fallacies, p. 113

Now that students have covered ways to make deductive and inductive arguments, they also need to understand what lines of argumentation are weak and should be avoided. This substantial section on logical fallacies covers a variety of ways that some seemingly valid arguments rely on inaccurate or intentionally misleading uses of logic. Several examples are given for each. The logical fallacies covered include begging the question; circular reasoning; weak analogy; *ad hominem* (personal attack); hasty or sweeping generalization; either/or fallacy; equivocation; red herring; slippery slope; you also; appeal to doubtful authority; misuse of statistics; *post hoc, ergo propter hoc* (after this, therefore because of this); *non sequitur* (it does not follow); and bandwagon appeal.

Exercise 5.8, p. 123

This exercise helps students identify logical fallacies. It directs them to decide which of the given statements are logical and which rely on fallacies. If the statement is not logical, students are asked to identify the fallacy that best applies. Keep in mind that, in some cases, more than one logical fallacy can be identified. Answers follow.

1. Hasty generalization
2. Non sequitur
3. Non sequitur
4. Slippery slope fallacy
5. Begging the question
6. Hasty generalization
7. Weak analogy
8. Circular reasoning
9. Weak analogy
10. Bandwagon appeal
11. Non sequitur or hasty/sweeping generalization
12. Appeal to doubtful authority
13. Bandwagon appeal
14. Either/or
15. Logical argument using deductive reasoning
16. You also
17. Slippery slope
18. Circular reasoning
19. Because this argument says that the new software "must be" the cause of the problem, it relies on the *post hoc, ergo propter hoc* argument. There could be other reasons that the computer is not working.
20. Bandwagon appeal

Exercise 5.9, p. 125

This exercise asks students to read the essay "Immigration Time-Out" by Patrick Buchanan and identify logical fallacies that he uses as part of his argument. Here is a summary of the essay followed by a list of the fallacies your students may identify.

Summary of "Immigration Time-Out" by Patrick Buchanan, p. 125

In response to recent debates surrounding immigration policies in the United States, politician and conservative political commentator Patrick Buchanan argues in this essay that America needs to call a time-out on immigration. He opens his discussion with a reference to California's Proposition 187—legislation that proposed to cut off social welfare benefits to illegal aliens in the state—and states that this referendum reveals conflicting visions of what America can and should be in the future. Buchanan believes that continued or increased levels of immigration would cause unrest in the United States and would uproot traditional American culture.

Logical Fallacies in "Immigration Time-Out" by Patrick Buchanan, p. 125

- **Non sequitur:** Buchanan cites the chancellor of the University of California at Berkeley, who argues that, by 2050, the "majority of Americans will trace their roots to Latin America, Africa, Asia, the Middle East and Pacific Islands" (para. 4). Buchanan argues that this increase in immigrant populations will automatically lead to social and political unrest. He states that "consequences will ensue" and says these new immigrants will break the law, protest, and get into conflicts with one another. This is a non sequitur because he is arguing that one thing will inevitably result from another, when in reality, Buchanan's argument is based on panic and illogical assumptions. You may also ask your students what they think about his apparent fixation with Mexicans and other Hispanics, as he constantly cites them in negative ways.

- **Either/or fallacy:** Buchanan's whole argument involves an either/or fallacy because he states that either immigration must be stopped entirely (if even for a short time) or "if no cutoff is imposed . . . the message will go out to a desperate world: America is wide open" (8). He leaves no room for anything in between. Also, Buchanan uses the either/or fallacy when, in his conclusion he states that either "we" must decide what America will be like in 2050 or "others will make those decisions for us" (13).
- **Begging the question or circular reasoning:** Buchanan begs the question when he states, "If America is to survive as 'one nation, one people' we need to call a 'time-out' on immigration, to assimilate the tens of millions who have lately arrived" (12). He assumes that America is "one nation, one people," when one could argue that America has always been a diverse nation, made up of immigrants living side by side and constantly changing what it means to be American. This line of thinking can also be considered circular reasoning because one would have to subscribe to his first statement (that America once was "one nation, one people") to believe his subsequent statements.

Teaching tip: There are several other logical fallacies that your students may find, so make sure you open up discussion for their input. Also, the Buchanan essay will likely spark discussion in class, as many of his statements are built on controversial, even xenophobic, thinking about people from other nations.

Exercise 5.10, p. 126

This exercise asks students to choose three logical fallacies they identified in the Buchanan essay and then to rewrite the passages in a way that changes Buchanan's statements into logical arguments. Suggest that students remove words such as *must* and *will* and substitute language that allows for more discussion of the issue. For instance, Buchanan states, "Crowding together immigrant and minority populations in our major cities *must* bring greater conflict"; this statement could be tempered by replacing *must* with *may* or *could*. Part of the problem with Buchanan's essay is that he speaks as if chaos and crime are a *certain* result of more immigration, a relationship that cannot be proven ahead of time. Because most of Buchanan's arguments are based on logical fallacies, your students may find it difficult to rewrite excerpts in ways that don't change his thinking altogether. Take this as an opportunity to discuss how his whole essay might be reworked to be more logically sound.

Reading and Writing about the Issue: Do Merit-Based Scholarships Make Sense? p. 127

This section includes five texts from a variety of genres—essay, article, newspaper story, and even a Web page. The texts comment on the debate surrounding merit-based scholarships. You will find a summary of each argument and sample responses to the questions in each At Issue.

Summary of "At the Elite Colleges—Dim White Kids" by Peter Schmidt, p. 128

In his article, Peter Schmidt addresses what he perceives as unfair admissions policies by American colleges and universities. Specifically, Schmidt identifies a trend in higher education that privileges the well connected. In some cases, these students are the children of donors or alumni, and in other cases, they or their family just happen to know someone in a position of power at the school. Schmidt also argues that a disproportionate number of white students are admitted based on their connections, and he also identifies a link between the well-connected students and merit-based aid for students who are from wealthy families. In the end, Schmidt states that such policies stifle social mobility because talented but less connected or less wealthy applicants are kept out of prestigious schools, these policies sending the message that hard work will not be rewarded.

At Issue: Sources for Developing a Logical Argument, p. 130

1. Schmidt uses a delayed thesis in his article. It doesn't come until nearly the end, when he states, "rather than promoting social mobility, our nation's selective colleges appear to be thwarting it, by turning away applicants who have excelled given their circumstances and offering second chances to wealthy and connected young people who have squandered many of the advantages life has offered them" (para. 14). Usually, when authors decide to delay the thesis, it's because the topic is a controversial one, and they want to amass their support first, then explain what their observations and facts actually add up to. See if your students think that the delayed thesis here is an effective strategy or think that it may not work as well as a thesis stated in the opening of the essay.
2. Schmidt addresses an opposing argument in paragraph 9, when he says that leaders of universities often argue that they have to "reward" those who support them financially (by admitting students of donors and so on), because if they don't keep donors happy, they won't have money to help the underprivileged students who are also admitted. Schmidt attempts to refute this thought in paragraphs 10 and 11, when he says that most elite colleges are already "well-financed" and that "most served disproportionately few students from families with incomes low enough to qualify" for federal aid (11).

3. Schmidt focuses on those students who are "connected" in some way, so your students will likely refer to that aid as connection based. Some students may know the term *legacy admissions*.
4. *Schmidt's objections:*
   - Schmidt argues that students who are accepted based on their connections are disproportionately white; as a result, others who apply and are not privileged and/or white are not treated fairly (4, 5).
   - Schmidt states that athletes often have connections and are accepted regardless of academic ability or performance (6).
   - Schmidt laments that students who get into college based on their connections are no different from people who get into "trendy night clubs, by knowing the management or flashing cash" (8).
   - Schmidt says that while universities state that these "connected" students (and their donor-parents) are footing the bill for underprivileged students, statistics do not support that statement (11–12).
   - Schmidt says that privileging connections and pedigree over academic ability sends the wrong message to students. In other words, this "trend" leads to a breakdown in social mobility and does not allow talented students from lower-income families to move up the social ladder through hard work (14–16).
5. See what your students say in response to this. You may need to explain a bit more about the *Chronicle* and perhaps remind them of a writer's "ethos." Ask them how disclosing his position might lead to increased credibility and respect from readers. Also ask them what the downside of such a disclosure might mean.

Summary of "Paying for College" by Zoe Mendelson, p. 131

Compared with the previous selection, Zoe Mendelson's essay is a more personal look at the issue of scholarship money. She tells of two friends and their difficulties affording college, based on current qualifications for need- and merit-based financial aid. Mendelson places the blame on universities for raising their price tags but not using their large endowments to help the "impoverished and qualified" (para. 10). Ultimately, Mendelson argues that colleges and universities need to rethink their aid policies in a way that accounts for middle-class families—those who make too much to qualify for certain types of aid but who do not have enough resources or savings to keep up with the increasing cost of higher education.

At Issue: Sources for Developing a Logical Argument, p. 133

1. Mendelson states that such a suggestion "undermines the meritocracy that we claim as a nation. Those worthy of the best are not the richest or the poorest but the brightest" (para. 5). You might ask your students what they think

Mendelson is basing this argument on (perhaps on the idea that Americans are entitled to the "pursuit of happiness" or that fairness and equality should be upheld in the realm of education). This might also be a good time to ask what kind of "inductive leap" Mendelson is making here, regarding American ideals.

2. Mendelson's thesis is that schools need to rethink qualifications for student aid in ways that take into account not just each family's income but also other expenses such as family size, health-care expenses, cost of education for siblings, and so on. In paragraph 15, Mendelson praises Harvard for including these expenses in their "sweeping middle-income initiative," but Mendelson never states outright that she wants all colleges and universities to do the same. Mendelson comes close to stating this thesis in paragraph 16 but is not as clear as she could be. Encourage students to revise Mendelson's thesis to be more direct.
3. Because your students are just learning argumentative writing strategies, it is a good idea to encourage them to address opposing arguments in all their papers so that they think through their own opinions more thoroughly. Therefore, it is a good exercise to consider why Mendelson does not choose to speak to arguments against her position and how she could have done so. Remind your students of strategy used by Peter Schmidt in his essay.
4. This essay is primarily an inductive argument. Mendelson cites a number of specific examples—her own experience and that of other college students—before moving to a general conclusion about "the right direction" for college admissions criteria.

Summary of "A Broader Definition of Merit: The Trouble with College Entry Exams" by Brent Staples, p. 134

This *New York Times* editorial opens the question of what makes for a deserving student. Rather than focusing on the question of merit aid versus need-blind aid, Staples begins his essay with a compelling narrative that will have students engaged in a real question: which student should get the aid?

At Issue: Sources for Developing a Logical Argument, p. 135

1. Students may see that the hypothetical situation makes the issue concrete in a way that abstract questions of need-based or merit-based aid do not.
2. Staples's thesis appears in the second paragraph, when he writes "the pressures that are driving colleges—and the country as a whole—to give college entry exams more weight than they were ever intended to have would clearly work against [the student who tests poorly]. Those same pressures are distorting the admissions process, corrupting education generally and slanting the field toward students whose families can afford test preparation classes."

3. Staples argues that most schools determine merit through testing.
4. The National Association for College Admission Counseling suggests a more holistic view of merit, where students are evaluated with test scores "as one in a range of factors that include grades, essays, and so on" (para. 4).
5. A syllogism that presents the main points of Staples's argument might look like this:

   Major premise: Colleges should admit and give aid to the best-qualified applicants.

   Minor premise: Tests are an inadequate measure of scholastic merit.

   Conclusion: The obsession with admissions tests is damaging education.

   Based on their own experiences and observations, students may wish to dispute Staples's conclusion.
6. Students may question whether it is possible to quantify and treat equally such measures as essay grades.

Summary of "Hamilton College to End Merit Scholarships in Favor of Need-Based Aid," Associated Press, p. 136

This text is an Associated Press news story based on a Hamilton College (New York State) press release, detailing the school's decision to stop offering merit scholarships and instead put that money toward need-based aid for low- and middle-income families. The news story portrays this announcement as a groundbreaking decision by Hamilton College and states that the school "is believed to be the first school to entirely abandon its merit scholarship program" (para. 10).

At Issue: Sources for Developing a Logical Argument, p. 137

1. As stated in the summary, this news story seems to praise Hamilton College's decision, primarily because it quotes a school leader who believes the decision is a win for lower-income families. Ask your students, however, if this slant is the fault of the AP or just due to the fact that the quoted educator is in favor of Hamilton's decision.
2. As students think about whether other colleges and universities will be able to follow Hamilton College's lead, remind them that Hamilton is a private college with a small number of students. Also direct them to the part of the news story that explains the average tuition students pay and how much the need-based aid helps (para. 8).
3. In the third paragraph, the story states that Hamilton College's announcement "comes at a time when colleges have been criticized for using their resources to lure high-achieving students—many of whom don't need the money to attend college." Later on, readers learn that there are other schools that have made similar changes to their financial-aid policies (10). Still, there

is very little explanation of the debate that surrounds merit-based aid. See if your students agree that the bias in this news story could be tempered by including more background or context.

Summary of "Merit-Based Scholarships for Incoming Students," Lewis & Clark College, p. 138

This Web page from Lewis & Clark College in Oregon gives some concrete examples of the kinds of merit-based scholarships offered at one particular university. The scholarships are awarded based on GPA, SAT/ACT scores, and class rank. They are awarded to students who focus on certain disciplines. There is no discussion of financial need or income levels for eligibility.

At Issue: Sources for Developing a Logical Argument, p. 141

1. The awards recognize outstanding achievement—either in academics generally or in specific areas of study. Several scholarships specify GPA, SAT/ACT, and class ranking requirements. There is no mention of financial need or of preference given to the family's income. Scholarships are differentiated by area of study and by preference given to students who demonstrate leadership, character, and so on.
2. The named scholarships that are described on this Web page appear to come from private trust funds and endowments or are otherwise provided by private donors. Several of the scholarships do not disclose their source.
3. On the question of whether merit-based scholarships take aid away from needy students, see what your students can infer, based on the other texts they have read in this section. There is no direct connection, according to the Web site, between the school's privately funded sources of financial aid and the funds allotted for need-based aid, but some students may infer a connection.

Exercise 5.11, p. 142

This exercise asks students to complete a template as a deductive argument in favor of merit-based scholarships. A sample response is provided; the given text is in boldface.

Template for Writing a Deductive Argument

Merit-based scholarships make sense for society as well as for students. As a rule, society should encourage good students to work hard and be rewarded for that good work by receiving help with the burden of paying for college. **Everyone benefits when** the country's best students have access to the best universities. **For example,** if students are already excelling in science, math, music, or art, they should be able to attend the best schools and further their abilities with the most experienced faculty. **By identifying good students and providing them with merit-based scholarships,** these students will see that hard work pays off, allowing them to choose the school that's right for them—be that a state university or a private university. **Therefore,** merit-based aid should continue as long as it is not taking away from funds that are dedicated to need-based scholarships. **Not everyone**

agrees with this position, however. Some people argue that merit-based aid only gives money to students who already come from wealthy families and could afford to go to elite institutions anyway. **This argument misses the point. When colleges give merit-based scholarships,** they are rewarding student achievement, regardless of that student's income or family background. Further, the funding for merit-based aid does not take money away from need-based scholarships, since the two come from different sources. **For this reason, colleges should provide merit-based scholarships** so that talented students are rewarded for their hard work; however, in no case should schools offer merit-based aid at the expense of need-based aid.

Exercise 5.12, p. 142

This exercise asks students to complete a template as an inductive argument against merit-based scholarships. A sample response is provided; the given text is in boldface.

Template for Writing an Inductive Argument

Today, many students cannot afford to go to college. Tuition at both public and private universities has skyrocketed. **In addition, books and** room and board have also become more expensive. **To meet these costs, some students** have decided to go to less expensive colleges or universities—often the schools that were not necessarily their top choices but are more affordable or offer better aid packages. **Other students** have been forced to delay college until they can save up enough money to meet their families' suggested contribution. **In addition, some colleges have less money for financial aid packages. This means that when they give merit-based scholarships, they** essentially devote more money to students who, in many cases, can already afford college without assistance. **Those who favor merit-based scholarships, however, argue that** the best and brightest students should be awarded for their achievement, not punished for their family's income level. **Although this may be true, in today's financial environment,** it is the low- and middle-income families who *are* being punished for their income level, as many of the families who exceed the requirements for need-based aid simply do not have enough money to pay high college costs. **As a result, it is clear that** universities must make need-based aid a priority and phase out merit-based aid so that the students who need assistance can get it.

Exercise 5.13, p. 143

This exercise asks each student to interview several of his or her classmates and instructors about merit-based scholarships and then to revise the drafts of the paragraphs they wrote in Exercises 5.11 and 5.12, accordingly.

Teaching tip: When students are interviewing one another, remind them that they should be jotting down the reasons that their interviewees either agree or disagree with merit-based scholarships. These notes should provide the students with specific observations or opinions that they can then use as support in their paragraphs. You may also want to remind students to write some of the more salient comments down word for word and quote them in their revisions.

Exercise 5.14, p. 143

This exercise asks students to put all their reading and discussion to work by constructing an essay that is either for or against merit-based scholarships. Students are instructed to refer to the readings on pages 128–141 and to use primarily inductive or deductive reasoning while arguing their points. Remind students that they'll need to document any sources they use, and be sure to discuss your expectations for source documentation (and refer students to Chapter 10, for documentation help).

Exercise 5.15, p. 143

This exercise asks students to return to the essays they wrote for Exercise 5.14 to see if they committed any logical fallacies. If their essays contain any fallacies, they should underline them, correct them on a separate sheet of paper, and then revise their drafts accordingly.

Teaching tip: Oftentimes finding fallacies in one's own work can be difficult, so you may want to suggest that students exchange papers and identify logical fallacies in one another's work.

Exercise 5.16, p. 143

Finally, this exercise asks students to go back to Chapter 1 and review the four pillars of argument. Then students should return to their own essays and be able to identify these four elements in their own work. If anything is missing, they should revise accordingly.

Teaching tip: If students have trouble with this exercise, you may suggest that they first return to one of the essays on pages 128–141 and identify the four pillars of argument there; then, with this practice, students can return to their own work with a fresh eye.

CHAPTER 6

Rogerian Argument, Toulmin Logic, and Oral Arguments

This chapter helps students to identify and write three major forms of argument—Rogerian, Toulmin, and oral. For each form, the chapter first explains the structure and writing; then includes a sample student essay, labeled with each of the form's major elements; and concludes with a list that distills the pattern of each form's structure of argumentation. The At Issue topic for this chapter is distance learning; since most universities now offer a variety of online courses, the growing debate about distance learning is likely to pique student interest—some may even have personal experiences to share.

Teaching tip: Because Rogerian, Toulmin, and oral arguments differ significantly, don't try to cover all three in one class period. In fact, if you want students to learn the nuances of each form, teach one a day, and have students compare and contrast the forms; this approach will ensure that students can differentiate one form from another.

Understanding Rogerian Argument, p. 146

Challenging the notion that argument must be confrontational, psychologist Carl Rogers suggested that by finding common ground, by considering so-called opponents more as colleagues, and by searching for cooperation, a writer or speaker is more likely to find a mutually agreeable solution.

Teaching tip: Ask students to consider one unsuccessful argument they've recently made and to identify why it was unsuccessful; it's likely that the argument failed because students were too combative or unwilling to see the merit of a different perspective. Then have students write about how their argument differed from a Rogerian approach, and ask them to consider whether or not making a Rogerian argument would have led to a more successful outcome.

Structuring Rogerian Arguments, p. 147

Noting the differences between Rogerian argument and traditional argument, the text here gives the example of writing to the manufacturer about a broken camera. In the example, the camera breaks a week after its warranty expires, and a store can do nothing for the consumer. Stressing the interest the company has in maintaining consumer satisfaction and, thus, purchasing loyalty, the letter is not confrontational but cooperative.

Exercise 6.1, p. 148

This exercise asks students to choose an At Issue topic from any chapter in the book and write a sentence stating an opinion on the issue. Students should then attempt to plan a Rogerian argument by (1) listing two areas of common concern they might share with someone who holds the opposite position, (2) summarizing the main concerns of someone who holds the opposite position, (3) summarizing their own views, and (4) writing a sentence that explains how their views might benefit individuals (including the opposition) or society in general.

For example, a student might choose to write about the bottled-water debate discussed in Chapter 1 and favor drinking tap water. He or she might list the environment and health as two shared concerns. Then, he or she might summarize the opposing argument as follows: drinking bottled water is safer than drinking tap water, and with the increase of recycled material in packaging, the impact that bottled water has on the environment is minimal. In contrast, the summary of his or her own view might focus on the weight of water, use of fuel for transportation and manufacturing, the lack of benefits from drinking bottled water, and the potential contamination of bottled water. The final point might focus on the importance of protecting the environment and of maintaining clean tap water for all.

Writing Rogerian Arguments, p. 149

Rogerian arguments are typically used to address controversial issues in a quest for compromise. The text also suggests that while Rogerian arguments may produce an entire essay, they may also function as part of a more traditional argument—for example, as the refutation sections of a more traditional argument. Here the chapter also contains a useful feature that explains how a Rogerian argument can be structured.

Sample Student Essay: "Do the Olympic Games Need Permanent Host Sites?" p. 150

Modeling a Rogerian argument, this student author argues in favor of establishing permanent host sites for the Olympic Games "in countries that embody the basic values that are symbolized by the games" (para. 1).

Identifying the Elements of Rogerian Argument, p. 153

1. The writer anticipates that most readers will agree on the importance of supporting host nations, athletes, and the spirit of unity and peace fostered by the Olympic Games. He could have also suggested that most readers support human rights and find fault with oppressive regimes. Further, he might have pointed out that the bidding wars to host the games are not in the spirit of the games' message of unity.
2. In the essay's second paragraph, the author discusses the inefficacy of boycotts during the 1980 and 1984 Olympic Games: they had no consequence on political policy and ultimately punished the athletes. Opinions about the essay's acknowledgment of those who disagree will be mixed, but point students to the essay's second paragraph (reader's views), the end of the third (which students may suggest contains some adversarial language, perhaps), and the conclusion, where the author does acknowledge disagreement.
3. Students should point to the essay's use of *we* to build rapport. However, students may point to the strong language in the essay's third paragraph as adversarial.
4. The conclusion advocates for permanent host sites but also suggests that those sites are in everyone's best interest because they would be chosen to reinforce the spirit of the games; the conclusion advances the notion that a host country's politics affect everyone's perceptions of the games.
5. Instead of considering opposing viewpoints and focusing on compromise, the writer of a traditional argument would likely advance his or her argument with support for only his or her thesis. The second paragraph, where the author introduces common views of the problem, would likely be shunted to a segment on counterargument and refuted; the point of the refutation would be to account for and dismiss the opposition's argument as insufficient.

Understanding Toulmin Logic, p. 153

Philosopher Stephen Toulmin noticed that formal logic rarely accounts for the arguments waged in everyday life. In *The Uses of Argument* (1958), Toulmin names and defines the structure of these everyday arguments, which have three main parts: **claim** (usually stated as a thesis), **grounds** (evidence to support the claim), and **warrant** (the stated or implied inference that connects a writer's claims to his or her grounds).

Teaching tip: Remind students that Toulmin logic is useful for constructing arguments but that a sound argument using Toulmin logic can be made only if students avoid the logical fallacies covered in Chapter 5.

Constructing Toulmin Arguments, p. 154

As Toulmin observed, arguments require more than a claim, grounds, and warrant. The full model that he identifies begins with but builds onto these elements. The text identifies and defines seven elements of a Toulmin argument: claim, reason, warrant, backing, grounds, qualifiers, and rebuttals.

Teaching tip: Because this argument structure will be new to most of your students, it is helpful to give several in-class examples of arguments you have already covered in class. For example, consider returning to the debate about bottled water (Chapter 1) or media violence (Chapters 2 and 3) to find topics for which students can build Toulmin arguments.

Exercise 6.2, p. 155

This exercise asks students to choose an At Issue topic, by looking through the text's table of contents, and constructing a Toulmin outline for the topic. The text provides a list of the Toulmin elements and lines on which to write. As suggested above, using examples from chapters already covered as a class can teach these concepts and reinforce those previously covered.

Topic:	bottled water
Claim:	We should drink bottled water.
Reason:	because it is cleaner and safer than tap water
Warrant:	It is good to have safe, clean water to drink.
Backing:	(supports the warrant) evidence about the effects of polluted water and about the safety of bottled water
Grounds:	(supports the claim) personal experience that bottled water tastes better than tap; easily contaminated public water
Qualifiers:	Some bottled water is only purified tap water.
Rebuttals:	need refutation of environmental concerns—that is, the waste of bottles; need refutation of the relative cleanliness and safety of tap water

Writing Toulmin Arguments, p. 156

This portion of the text compares Toulmin arguments with the classical model and suggests that Toulmin's focus is more realistic and useful in its consideration of opposing arguments. Unlike the classical model, which presents ideas as absolute facts, the Toulmin model concedes that these are opinions even though they advance a particular argument. A list shows where in an essay each element of Toulmin argument occurs; a sample student essay follows.

Sample Student Essay: "Our Right to Burn or Burning Our Rights?" p. 157

Modeling a Toulmin argument, the student author argues against amending the Constitution to prohibit the desecration of the American flag; elements of the argument are labeled in the essay and in the margins of the text.

Identifying the Elements of Toulmin Argument, p. 160

1. While answers will vary, students should suggest a claim such as the following: Flag burning should remain protected under the freedom of speech. The grounds for the argument can be worded as follows: Flag burning is an important and symbolic means through which a citizen can criticize the government. The warrant can be stated as follows: It is un-American to restrict this expression of criticism for one's government.
2. Opinions about this student author's inclusion of backing will vary, but some students may point to the following as other backing that could have been included:
   - The author could discuss other countries, such as China, that do restrict the political speech of its citizens and press.
   - The author might consider the Iranian government's censorship of protest following Iran's 2009 elections.
3. Opinion about the qualifier will vary, but students are likely to suggest that it does not limit the argument in any meaningful way; rather, it seems to reinforce the argument. The author might have qualified the argument to account for particular reasons for desecrating the flag—perhaps conceding that flag-burning means something only when burnt in protest or suggesting that sometimes desecration is not a productive means for criticizing one's government, as its statement is often ambiguous or ineffectual if a citizen is seeking real change.
4. Student responses will vary, but students are likely to offer other objections for rebuttal, such as the following:
   - Flag burning is an unproductive means of protest.
   - Flag burning is disrespectful to the country.
   - Flag burning encourages criticism from other countries.
   - Flag burning encourages hostility toward our country.
5. Once they understand the Toulmin model, students generally like that it provides a rubric for a well-planned and easy-to-follow argument with prescribed elements and locations for the elements. Other students may suggest that these qualities are also disadvantages because they make arguments feel formulaic, and they seem to discount more nuanced approaches—particularly, in accounting for others' perspectives, as the Rogerian argument does.

Understanding Oral Arguments, p. 160

Like written arguments, oral arguments have an introduction, body, and conclusion; they also address and refute opposing points of view. However, there are differences in presentation because the audience listens rather than reads. The text suggests that students use transitional phrases ("my first point," "let me sum up," etc.) to guide their audience; use simple, direct language; repeat key information; and include visuals.

Planning an Oral Argument, p. 161

This portion of the text suggests some tips for constructing a more effective oral argument; choosing a good topic, knowing one's audience and time limit, identifying the thesis statement, preparing speaking notes, using visual aids, and practicing are a few of the suggestions offered.

Teaching tip: Consider drawing these tips into classroom conversation by having students identify topics that might work as oral arguments; ask students to consider each numbered tip and the way they might account for it in an oral argument on the topics they've identified. This type of practice planning will help them as they prepare to write and deliver their own oral arguments.

Here the text also discusses in greater detail how to choose and prepare visual aids; since preparation may cause anxiety for some students, spend some time brainstorming about how to make visual aids, stressing that neither handmade posters nor computer programs like Microsoft's PowerPoint are the only options.

Exercise 6.3, p. 164

This exercise asks students to select three At Issue topics that they might deliver as an oral argument and to list three possible visual aids for each.

Teaching tip: Repeatedly drawing from one topic for in-class examples may help students to see how they can argue in different ways. Here, we again draw from the bottled-water debate.

Visuals for an oral argument in favor of drinking tap water:

- Large bag full of bottles representing one week of bottled water consumption for one person
- Handout of statistics about bottled water's effect on the environment
- Graphs about the drinkability of tap water in the United States
- A diagram displaying the resources consumed to make bottles for water
- A chart comparing regulations of tap water (many) with the regulations of bottled water (few)

Delivering Oral Arguments, p. 164

Delivery is one of the most important parts of oral argument; the text offers students several helpful pointers to consider before delivery, including speaking slowly and clearly, moving purposefully, and accepting some degree of nervousness.

Teaching tip: Since most students will not have had extensive experience speaking in public, the thought of delivery will frequently cause anxiety. Help prepare students to speak in front of their classmates from the beginning of the semester—consider using introductory ice-breaking activities to acquaint students with one another, require students to speak in class once a week as part of their participation grade, or actively build speaking activities into your lesson planning (such as group work that includes a presentation of the group's discussion or findings).

Writing an Oral Argument, p. 167

You might acknowledge that many people first fully write out arguments they intend to present orally and then prepare speaking notes from their full-text versions—this may be a good suggestion to emphasize in class, particularly for first-time speakers with fears. The text also includes an outline for an oral argument.

Sample Student Essay: "An Argument in Support of the 'Gap Year,'" p. 168

Modeling the typical organization of an oral argument (outlined on p. 167), this student author argues in favor of a "gap year"—working or studying abroad for a year before attending college or taking a year off during college.

Identifying the Elements of an Oral Argument, p. 173

1. For transitions, students will likely indicate the final sentence of the first paragraph ("As the rest of my speech"), the second sentence of the third paragraph ("This slide shows"), and the first sentence of the final paragraph ("After considering the benefits").

   Teaching tip: Consider asking students if these transitions are clear enough or where and how students might add additional transitions.

2. Opinions about the author's use of simple, direct language will vary; the author's topic sentences are particularly clear and direct. Some students may point to the fifth paragraph as ripe for simplification; the author reintroduces a scholar she mentioned at the beginning of the speech by last name only, which should be clarified again for the audience. Students may also point to specific words like *suitability* and *warranted* (para. 5) for simplification.

3. The argument does repeat key information; importantly, the author's thesis names three specific reasons for supporting a gap year—reasons that she then repeats in the topic sentence of each paragraph following. Perhaps the author could structure topic sentences to repeat the previous key idea as she announces the next—for example, paragraph 4 might begin as follows: In addition to increasing student's options while in school, a gap year may also help students gain admission to a better school.

4. The speaker identifies the opposing arguments as "parental concerns about 'slackerdom' and money." Although she addresses them, the writer could more fully refute them than she does here by, for instance, discussing how some of the resources listed on Slide 4 include guidance on setting goals, providing structure, and obtaining funding.

5. Answers and opinions will vary, but some may suggest including a more detailed handout, photos of gap-year projects, or a testimonial excerpt from a "gapster."

6. Students could have a number of questions for the speaker; this would make a good class exercise.

Reading and Writing about the Issue: Is Distance Learning as Good as Classroom Learning? p. 174

Returning to the debate on distance learning raised at the outset of this chapter, this section collects three argumentative essays, two Web pages, and two photographs responding to this debate. Each essay and image is followed by an At Issue section with several questions about structure; you will find here a brief summary of each written argument and sample responses to the questions.

Teaching tip: Try beginning this section with a classroom debate about distance learning. Because this issue directly affects students, a lively debate will encourage students to think through argumentation—to raise claims and provide evidence of their own—before reading the opinions of others. As you may have students who have tried distance learning, this debate will also give them an opportunity to reflect on and speak from experience. As students debate, you might make a list of pros and cons on the board, laptop, or transparency; you may want this list in a reusable form, as one reading in this section ("Frequently Asked Questions about eLearning," p.182) contains a pro-and-con list to which you might compare and contrast the one you've generated in class.

Summary of "Online Education Rivals 'Chalk and Talk' Variety" by Sandra C. Ceraulo, p. 175

Sandra Ceraulo, an instructor wanting to take courses in information technology but unable to commute to evening classes, decides to take a course online. Beginning with this anecdote, Ceraulo argues in favor of offering online courses because of the freedom they allow students to control their learning experience.

At Issue: Sources for Using Alternative Approaches to Argument, p. 176

1. Ceraulo announces her thesis at the end of paragraph 5, when she writes: "The lesson seems clear: Online courses can provide as good an education as traditional classes." Student summaries of her thesis should suggest that she equates distance learning with traditional learning. It's likely that students will suggest that Ceraulo needs to describe her own experience of the course and her surprise about its success before arguing in favor of distance learning.

2. A "chalk and talk" lecture refers to a traditional instructor's classroom practice of lecturing to students and writing important points from the lecture on the chalkboard. Unlike the online lecture posted in its entirety for students to access and revisit at any time from any place, the chalk and talk method requires students' presence at a particular place and time to hear a lecture and take notes, forcing students to rely on notes taken in class or on the instructor's distilled chalkboard notes.

3. Ceraulo does use Rogerian techniques at the start of her essay. She begins by acknowledging that her audience may be skeptical of online learning and concedes that she used to share their view: "Like many people whose formal education was based entirely on 'chalk and talk' lectures, I was skeptical about the value of online education."
4. In short, Ceraulo points to different styles of learning as the reason that online courses are not for everyone; she suggests that those who like a "hands-on" educational experience or direct access to a professor will not benefit from online learning.
5. In paragraph 8, Ceraulo suggests that the technological proficiency of the instructor and staff is the most important factor in determining the quality of the online course.
6. Advantages named by Ceraulo:
   - Convenience for students (para. 3)
   - Natural flow of discussion on discussion board (3)
   - No commuting time (3)
   - Ease of scheduling (7)
   - Truly self-directed study (7)
   - Comfort with workplace technology later in life (9)

   Other advantages:
   - Ability to think through ideas in writing
   - Record of class proceedings to which one can later return for review
   - Written commentary from classmates and instructor, to which one can later return

Summary of "The Sensuous Classroom: Focusing on the Embodiment of Learning" by Suzanne M. Kelly, p. 177

Suzanne Kelly, an instructor of women's studies, argues that bodies make the classroom. She suggests that part of the classroom experience is sensual and performative and that the learning environment requires human contact and interaction. For Kelly, in a women's studies classroom where women's bodies are central to theory, she suggests that a physical classroom is a necessity.

At Issue: Sources for Using Alternative Approaches to Argument, p. 179

1. Anecdotes frequently capture a reader's interest, give the reader something to relate to, and establish the author's credibility through experience. Some may argue that anecdotes detract from the import of an argument because they establish a conversational or too intimate tone.

Teaching tip: In Chapter 1, Tom Standage's "Bad to the Last Drop" begins with an anecdote. Consider asking students to compare the use of this tactic in each essay and to comment on which author's use seems more effective and why.

2. For Kelly, classroom learning provides a multisensory experience. She suggests that students perform in relation to one another and that the tone of their voices and their affect and gestures inform their learning from and with one another.
3. Kelly suggests that the body is particularly important to a women's studies course; that is, theoretical discussions of the body require the presence of the actual human body (para. 8). Student opinions will vary, and either position is supportable. However, if students do not consider how an online course may affect discussions about the body (in theory and in reality), ask students to consider how the anonymity of a bodiless classroom may also be freeing for some students. To some degree, Kelly's argument is essentialist, as it claims we are and must be our bodies.
4. Student opinions will vary; however, students are likely to follow Kelly's logic and draw analogies to other classes. Some may suggest that literature classes require reading texts aloud to experience the work; others might argue that mathematics requires hands-on instruction and in-person direction and troubleshooting, and still others may suggest that foreign-language classes require a traditional classroom for speaking exercises and pronunciation correction.
5. Kelly's concluding anecdote is self-reflexive, highlighting a moment that makes her own classroom body visible to her through the eyes of a student. For Kelly, this recognition reveals the centrality of her body to a student's reception and understanding of the course material, as the student was contrasting Kelly's lively classroom antics to "constraining lectures" her friend experienced in law school (18). Some may argue that to better support her thesis, Kelly should have chosen an anecdote that related to a specific moment in the classroom when students' bodies became central to learning. Others might suggest that she should have included research about how classroom learning surpasses distance learning or how particular types of material are best covered in a traditional classroom setting.

Summary of "Calling a University 'Virtual' Creates an Actual Oxymoron" by Marilyn Karras, p. 180

Marilyn Karras, a features editor for the Salt Lake City *Deseret News*, argues that distance learning does not match university learning. She maintains that degrees earned online are not the equivalent of degrees earned in traditional universities; she argues that an online degree is to a traditional university degree as an equivalency certificate is to a high school diploma (para. 7).

At Issue: Sources for Using Alternative Approaches to Argument, p. 181

1. Because the word *virtual* means "in effect but not in actual fact" (para. 2), Karras considers it an apt term to "define the high-tech transfer of information" that one perceives as the effect of an online university while in actual fact no transfer occurs.

2. Karras views *virtual education* as an oxymoron because she believes that *education*, by definition, cannot be virtual, or attained in effect but not in fact; education is attained only in fact, through the acquisition of facts.

3. In paragraph 5, Karras argues that a university education offers debates, discussion, exchanges of ideas among peers and professors inside and outside the classroom, while virtual education, which isolates each student in a room with a television or computer, cannot provide that type of interaction.

4. Some students will think Karras's argument in favor of an actual—not virtual—university is elitist. Drawing from what they've learned in Chapter 5, some students may suggest that Karras's reasoning in the G.E.D. analogy is unsound, while still others may think about the Toulmin logic covered earlier in this chapter and point out that Karras's warrant—that an online education is not rigorous enough to be equivalent to a university degree—is elitist.

5. Student opinions about the status of a virtual degree and the status of a traditional university degree will vary, but ask students to consider all the essays they've read as they respond to this question.

   Teaching tip: Remind students to practice their oral argument skills by providing a point in support of a thesis ("yes, university degrees should have the same status as a virtual degree" or "no, they should not") and evidence to support that point.

6. In Karras's essay, the claim is that a "virtual" university is not the same as a traditional one. For support she cites the facts that a "university education involves, among other things, debate, discussion and an exchange of ideas among classmates and professors, both inside and outside the classroom. Stimulating independent thinking is one of its primary objectives" (5) and that students who fail to graduate from high school can receive a certification, but without meeting the requirements, cannot receive a diploma (7). The warrant is that the distinction between a traditional secondary education and a virtual one matter. The writer makes the case that such distinctions do and should matter more than what is being claimed by advocates of virtual education.

Summary of "Frequently Asked Questions about eLearning," eLearners.com, p. 182

This excerpt from the eLearners.com Web page offers a list of pros and cons to help students determine if distance learning is right for them.

At Issue: Sources for Using Alternative Approaches to Argument, p. 183

1. Because the site does promote distance learning, students may suggest that the pro and con lists are unbalanced. Ask students to compare the language on the two lists—while there are *will* and *can* on the pro list, *may* and *possibly* dominate the con list. Essentially, the strong verbs on the pro side encourage students to try online learning, while the weak verbs on the con side do not equally discourage students from online learning. Further, the points on the pro side are much stronger than the points on the con side.

2. After noting the disparity between the two lists, students are likely to offer more negative comments about distance learning than positive ones. Here are suggestions for both categories.

   Negative:

   - Connection problems
   - Lack of technical support
   - Lack of interest among other distance learners; no fruitful online conversations
   - Lots of writing
   - Inability to access physical college resources: library books, support services
   - Time-management problems
   - Possibility of a poor online instructor—late with responses, posts, etc. (without the pressure of face-to-face encounters, instructor may short-change students)

   Positive:

   - Online conversations, beyond class time, by means of postings and email
   - Easy-to-refer-to written responses from classmates and professor

3. Students may note isolation, delay in feedback, and need to learn new software as the top three arguments against distance learning. Students may refute the isolation argument by suggesting the possibility of increased online contact with peers, which may rival or surpass interaction with peers in a traditional classroom. They might also argue that in a traditional classroom students also wait for feedback, and sometimes that feedback is offered only orally, making it less effective in the long run. Finally, students might argue that while learning new software can be difficult, it's great experience for the workplace, where they are likely to encounter similar software or to be asked to learn new software.

4. Students may note equality, pace of learning, and writing rather than speaking in class as the top three arguments in favor of distance learning. Students may refute the idea of equality by arguing that because students do not know one another they are less likely to sensor their responses to one another, leading to brutal honesty. Additionally, some students' ideas will still be commented on more than others, undercutting the notion of equality. Refuting the argument

in favor of self-determined learning pace, students may argue that it can lead to procrastination and complicates finding another student to chat with on specific concepts. Finally, students may suggest that the amount of writing they are forced to do is actually an argument against distance learning. Lacking tone and gestures, written comments may also be misconstrued unless students spend much time carefully planning comments before posting.

Summary of "Distance Learning," Naugatuck Valley Community College, p. 184

This screen shot from the Naugatuck Valley Community College Web site encourages students to try distance learning. The college bills distance learning as "flexible," with "high quality" programs that are affordable.

At Issue: Sources for Using Alternative Approaches to Argument, p. 184

1. This Web page is an informative advertisement that encourages students to enroll in distance-learning courses at Naugatuck Valley Community College.
2. The audience for this page is the prospective student. The language of it frames an argument for convenience as well as quality and affordability. It addresses the student with "your learning schedule." The image is clearly intended to be that of a student.
3. The Web page's treatment of distance learning is not balanced. The page promotes only positive benefits of distance learning. It does not address any potential negative consequences, such as whether the lack of traditional interaction with other students and professors could diminish the quality of the educational experience.
4. Since the previous question focused on balance, students may be inclined to address the Web site's biases. To be more balanced, the Web page should offer counterarguments and refutations. It might also provide evidence for its assertions—arguing that online education "often demands more time" is a subjective assessment that is not reliable without proof. Generally, the argument would be more effective if it included support for each of its statements.
5. Responses should focus on how Karras would critique this Web page.

   Teaching tip: When asking students to imagine how one author would respond to another, encourage students to identify specific arguments in the two pieces that are in conflict. For instance, students might point to the conflict between the Web page's suggestion that online education "often demands more time" and compare it with Karras's argument that students miss out on the debates and idea sharing that occur inside and outside the classroom in a university setting.

At Issue: Sources for Using Alternative Approaches to Argument, p. 185

1. Students will likely notice that the instructor seems isolated from her students. Students may draw from what they've learned about visual arguments in Chapter 3 and suggest that the technology, rather than the person, is the central figure in the photo. They may also suggest that the photo creates a feeling of isolation, even claustrophobia, with the technology facing the corner of the room and no students visible. From the picture, some students may suggest that peer interaction is lost; others may suggest that the photo underscores how little space distance learning demands.
2. Because the picture shows a student in pajamas and in bed with a laptop, students will likely focus on the ease and comfort of distance learning.
3. ***Teaching tip:*** Require students to focus their answers by drawing evidence from the essays you've covered. Consider requiring students to cite one of the authors in their response; even orally, this practice in citation can later help students with integrating quotations in their writing.

PART

3

Writing an Argumentative Essay

CHAPTER 7

Planning, Drafting, and Revising an Argumentative Essay

Both Chapter 7 and Chapter 8 are dedicated to the writing process, reminding students how the various steps of planning, structuring, drafting, and revising apply to argumentative writing. The opening section of this chapter helps students to find ways to choose and narrow their topics, and it gives helpful tips on topics to avoid. As for its thematic content, Chapter 7 begins with an At Issue on whether college campuses should "go green," and each of the exercises relates to this theme, as does the sample student essay at the end of the chapter.

Choosing a Topic, p. 190

You may want to find out what "going green" initiatives are taking place on your college campus or in your town—or even ask students to do this research. They can then incorporate what they find into class discussions or work in the various exercises. This work may help students to tailor their writing to campus-related issues and make the work more useful.

Exercise 7.1, p. 191

This exercise is a brainstorming activity, of sorts. It asks students to consider the At Issue information about going green (p. 189) and then to list ten possible topics they could write about in an essay. After making this list, students should pare it down by considering what interests them, which topics they know something about, which they care about, and which they have an open mind about. Ideally, these criteria should help them when choosing topics for other papers as well. Topic selection is key to a successful argumentative essay because students write their best papers when they are interested in their topic and are invested in convincing readers of their position.

Thinking about Your Topic, p. 191

You may want to supplement this brief section by introducing your students to some techniques for freewriting or brainstorming. Ask your students what they've done for invention in the past, and generate a list of options on the board. Remind them that whether they make a bulleted list, freewrite, or create a visual (for example, a web, "mind map," or chart), what is important is that they find a technique that works for them.

Exercise 7.2, p. 192

This exercise asks that students choose from the list of topics they generated in Exercise 7.1 and practice brainstorming. You may suggest that they try at least two different ways of brainstorming to see what works for them. From this brainstorming session, students should be able to make informal outlines of what they would cover if they were writing a paper on going green, and the outline structure on page 192 shows them a possible way to arrange their information.

Exercise 7.3, p. 193

This exercise asks students to make an informal outline, similar to the one on page 192, based on the information and ideas they brainstormed. Remind them that they do not have to follow the outline given but can create their own, based on what they'd want to write about in their own papers.

Taking a Stand, p. 193

After generating a topic, brainstorming, and drafting a brief, informal outline, students should have a rough thesis statement in mind. This statement can change, of course, based on information they find, but in order to draft, they should have a rough idea of what they want readers to understand about their topic. The thesis should also provide a way to organize their papers. It is important that students understand that thesis statements should be *debatable*, not factual or merely preference based.

Teaching tip: Most students will have already heard about thesis statements (see Chapter 1). Many students have a hard time with thesis statements and, as a result, hate thinking about them. But you might help them by reminding them that a good thesis statement is not merely a task for the writer; instead, it also provides a goal for readers by defining exactly what the paper is about and what they should understand from reading the paper.

Exercise 7.4, p. 193

This exercise provides useful practice with thesis statements, based on the information and ideas students generated in the earlier exercises, and asks students to consider which of their possible thesis statements is most promising.

Understanding Your Audience, p. 194

One of the most important aspects of argumentative writing is understanding the audience. This section prompts students to consider a likely audience for their paper and then to tailor their writing and information to that audience. This assignment can be tricky for students because when they're writing papers for a class, there often isn't a direct audience beyond the instructor. You might overcome this difficulty by reminding students that, in peer-review and small-group situations, they will be reading one another's work, so they really will have an audience. This fact might help them to think about what fellow students already know about going green, why students may be skeptical about their ability to be green while in college, and so on. Or to help them think about possible audiences outside the class, you might suggest that students can later use the information they include in their papers for letters to the editor in the school paper or even a letter to school administrators.

Exercise 7.5, p. 194

This exercise has students reconsider the thesis statements they drafted and decide how various audiences might respond to these statements. It might be helpful to brainstorm a list of possible audiences, either as a class or in small groups, so that students have a variety of possible audiences to choose from.

Gathering Evidence, p. 194

The next step of the writing process is to collect evidence (though you may remind students that, in some cases, they'll need to collect a bit of evidence, commentary, information, or other research even earlier in order to get through the brainstorming and thesis-writing steps).

Kinds of Evidence, p. 195

It is a good idea to remind students of the kinds of evidence they can use in a paper—and this section gives them examples of what counts as good evidence.

Exercise 7.6, p. 195

This exercise, which asks students to consider what evidence they might use to support their thesis statements from Exercise 7.4, can be opened up for class or small-group discussion.

Criteria for Evaluating Evidence in Your Sources, p. 195

By reminding students that their sources must be accurate, relevant, representative, and sufficient, this section helps them to decide exactly what sources are useful for their paper and, more important, *why* they should be trusted. You might also want to remind students that it's important to consider these criteria for Web sources as well—as many students will want to do some of their research online but don't always consider if certain Web sites are legitimate and trustworthy. For more information on this issue, see Chapter 8.

Detecting Bias in Your Sources, p. 196

Sometimes students assume that any source that has a hint of bias should not be used in a paper, but this section gives you a chance to talk about bias in class and figure out when and how overtly biased sources can be used. The bulleted list provided in the text suggests how to detect bias; it may take students some practice in order to catch on. Consider bringing in a few examples of slanted language or a written text that presents only one side.

Exercise 7.7, p. 197

This exercise can be a challenge for some students, as it can be difficult to detect our own biases. You might help them by having them consider what values, beliefs, or experiences lead them to feel the way they do about going green and about the environmental movement. For instance, students who grew up in a town that did not offer curbside recycling may be more biased against a college recycling program because they think it will take too much time and effort.

Exercise 7.8, p. 197

This exercise is most useful if your students are actually going to write a full-length paper on the topic of going green on college campuses. It asks them to gather evidence, look for bias in the sources they find, and document each source carefully.

Refuting Opposing Arguments, p. 197

As we mention in the responses to the essays in Chapter 5, it is important that students' papers speak to the opposing sides of the argument in a way that refutes these opposing points. In doing so, students may choose to defuse the either/or fallacy implicit in many arguments by simply finding and explaining common ground between the opposing opinions, or sides. Or students may acknowledge the strengths of an opposing viewpoint while also pointing out its shortcomings. The essay "Putting a Plague in Perspective" provides a good example of how one author refutes opposing arguments in an informed and fair manner.

Exercise 7.9, p. 198

Summary of "Putting a Plague in Perspective" by Daniel Halperin, p. 198

This essay takes aim at U.S. current and proposed policies on the AIDS epidemic. Halperin acknowledges that the global epidemic "requires continued attention" but argues that many other public-health issues in developing countries are being ignored as a result of the attention to AIDS (para. 1). Halperin contrasts the amount of money spent on the AIDS pandemic with the amount that the

United States has dedicated to safe-water projects, nutrition, and other preventable causes of death overseas. He also argues that in Africa H.I.V. tends to be more of a problem in the wealthiest and more developed countries, leaving countries such as Senegal, Congo, Ethiopia, and Nigeria to fend for themselves for basic needs like clean water and medicine to prevent illnesses such as diarrhea. In the end, he calls for the United States to rethink its global health priorities.

Identifying the Elements of a Refutation Argument, **p. 200**

1. Halperin believes that it is important for the United States to contribute to overcoming the AIDS epidemic in Africa but says that this effort shouldn't allow us to lose sight of other global health-related causes that also need attention and funding. Make sure that your students understand that Halperin is *not* against American assistance with the AIDS epidemic but he considers it dangerous and unfair to focus merely on one disease.
2. Halperin starts his essay by refuting the position that the United States should provide even more foreign assistance to fight AIDS; such a position misses the mark, he says. After this opening statement, Halperin spends the rest of his essay supporting his point by arguing that increased funding for AIDS means less funding for other preventable diseases. Students may have a difficult time knowing just what position Halperin is refuting, so you may want to ask them what debate Halperin is engaged in and what the opposing opinion might sound like. This coaching should lead students back to Halperin's opening paragraph.
3. Your students should be able to identify multiple ways that Halperin supports his thesis. He states that the United States should have a broader view of its foreign health assistance because
   - focusing so much attention on the AIDS pandemic takes money away from the treatment of other preventable disease (para. 3, 4)
   - often the countries where AIDS is most prevalent are also the most wealthy and developed, leaving poorer countries with AIDS underserved (4)
   - many millions of African people die from malnutrition, pneumonia, diarrhea, and other preventable diseases, which are easily cured (5)
   - sometimes communities have extra medication for AIDS but lack basic medicine and treatment for diseases that are easier to treat (9, 10)
   - there isn't already a global fund for things like safe water, antibiotics, and so on, while the AIDS cause gets much more attention (12)
4. You may ask your students to think again about the means of persuasion they learned earlier in the semester. Halperin establishes his credibility, or *ethos*, several ways. He establishes himself as an expert on U.S. spending on foreign health assistance, he understands the politics behind such spending, he is intimately familiar with the AIDS crisis and has specific information about individual countries, and he visited villages in poor African countries while he was the United States Agency for International Development's H.I.V. prevention adviser in 2005 and 2006.

Revising Your Thesis Statement, p. 200

This brief section reminds students that their thesis statements should be not only debatable, as discussed earlier, but also specific. You might suggest that they ask *how?* and *why?* in response to their thesis so that, as the example shows, they can add more information and support, making the statement more compelling.

Exercise 7.10, p. 201

This exercise has students practice making their thesis statements stronger and more specific by considering possible refutations to counterarguments. They should return to the thesis statements they crafted in Exercise 7.8 and revise them by acknowledging and refuting the most important opposing argument.

Teaching tip: Your students will likely need some help with this exercise, and it may be a good idea to have them put their revised statements on the board so that all students can see the variety in how such theses can be structured. It will also be useful to explain that the individual parts of their thesis statements can provide a structure for the upcoming essay.

Understanding Essay Structure, p. 201

Planning an essay's structure can be one of the most important parts of the writing process. Students who are unsure how to organize or structure their paper often lack one of the four main components of an argumentative essay: thesis, evidence, refutation, and concluding statement. This section helps them to think of these four elements as sections of their essays, and you should encourage them to consider the order in which they present these four elements. In some of the example essays, such as Halperin's, the refutation comes first, and in other essays throughout the book, the thesis statement is delayed until further on in the essay. Naturally, students need to understand *why* certain arguments should be structured in certain ways, and the goal is to get your students to consider the best way to organize their own argument. Have them once again consider their readers—what readers know, what they will need to know upfront, what their objections will be, and so on.

Using Induction and Deduction, p. 202

Just as students should consider their argument's structure, so they should also think of the argument in terms of inductive and deductive reasoning. Will they be using a deductive argument, built on major and minor premises that add up to a conclusion? Or will they use an inductive argument, presenting a series of observations that, taken together, lead to an inductive leap by which they arrive at a conclusion?

Constructing a Formal Outline, p. 202

Students should consider which kind of argument they will build throughout the paper and then construct their formal outlines accordingly.

Exercise 7.11, p. 203

This exercise asks students to continue working with the material they've collected (their thesis, evidence, and so on) by constructing a formal outline for their paper. You may consider giving them suggestions on various outline strategies—a numbered list, a bulleted list, a combination of Roman numerals and letters, and so on. Then encourage them to find an outline strategy that works for them.

Preparing to Write, p. 203

As students consider what will go into their papers, they should also be thinking about how they can use the three means of persuasion—logical, emotional, and ethical appeals. Each of these appeals will make them appear more credible to readers and will make their arguments more balanced.

Establishing Your Credibility; Maintaining Your Credibility; Being Fair, p. 203

This section helps students establish themselves as writers that their readers can trust. To do so, students must demonstrate their command of the material and their reasonableness. Among the ways students can accomplish both goals is to establish common ground with readers (remind them of the Rogerian style of argument) and to maintain a reasonable tone (tell them not to rely too much on emotional language).

Teaching tip: When students are passionate about their argument or are writing about a controversial topic, it can be difficult for them to remain fair, to not distort or exaggerate evidence, and to not quote out of context. The section "Being Fair" reminds them of that, and you may want to stress that for readers fairness often equals credibility.

Writing Your Draft, p. 206

Finally, it's time for students to draft their essays. This section revisits the basics of essay writing, such as following the structure of an argumentative essay, using transitions, connecting various points in the essay with coordination and subordination, defining terms, using clear language, and showing confidence in their own mastery of the material. You might have students skim this section in preparation for writing their drafts and then return to this section later for suggestions on what and how to edit.

Exercise 7.12, p. 208

Quite simply, this exercise asks each of your students to draft an essay of his or her own, incorporating the thesis statement, outline, supporting evidence, and so on, from earlier exercises.

Revising Your Argumentative Essay, p. 208

As the final component of the writing process, revision is an essential step that allows your students to mold their drafts into complete, thorough, and convincing arguments. It is important to establish the difference between revising and editing: the former involves more significant changing and restructuring of the essay, and the latter refers to superficial changes in grammar, spelling, or formatting. When it comes to revision, one thing most students ask is *how* to revise. The sample questions in this section are useful, then, as they have students consider matters such as how much supporting evidence they've used, whether they've consulted a wide variety of sources, or how they've attempted to refute opposing arguments.

Getting Feedback, p. 209

One of the most effective strategies for revision is to get feedback from trusted peers. Often, when writers are asked to evaluate their drafts, they have a hard time being objective and determining if their argument is clear. This section instructs students on the various forms of valuable feedback they might get—from instructors, from the college's writing center, and from their peers.

Teaching tip: A good way to help students practice getting feedback is to have them work in groups that go through the revision questions supplied in the previous section on pages 208–209. You might also want them to consider the kinds of feedback they can give beyond answering the provided questions: students can summarize for the writer what each paragraph is about, they can evaluate whether the argument is well supported or convincing, they can suggest information to add or background that might be helpful, and they can even provide an opposing viewpoint to which the writer may need to respond.

Exercise 7.13, p. 210

This exercise directs students to read one another's drafts and then give feedback. You may have them exchange drafts in class, email drafts, or combine the two methods (have them jot down feedback on emailed drafts and then bring the marked-up drafts to class to discuss with each other).

Adding Visuals; Editing and Proofreading; Choosing a Title, p. 211

At the final stages of drafting, students should consider how they can further strengthen their argumentative essays by adding visuals (compelling photos, charts, maps, and so on), by editing and proofreading for smaller details, and even by choosing a title. These are processes that students might not consider, so you might want to explain why they should be looked at as part of the overall argument of their essays.

Student Essay, "Going 'Green,'" p. 212

This sample student essay provides a model for students to use as they think about planning, drafting, and revising their own work. We have included the model on the topic of the chapter so that students can clearly connect the topic of the paper to the examples that have been used throughout the chapter.

Exercise 7.14, p. 216

This exercise asks students to incorporate a visual. As with including textual sources, visuals should be used to support and strengthen students' positions and not merely decorate the paper.

PART 4

Using Sources to Support Your Argument

CHAPTER

8

Evaluating Sources

Since so many of your students are engaged in online social networking, this chapter's thematic focus—the debate about whether data on these sites should be "fair game" for employers—is likely to pique their interest. The chapter opening introduces students to this debate with some background information and useful statistics, which will be further developed by a series of readings later in the chapter. Like the chapters preceding it, this chapter, of course, also focuses on skill development: students will learn to evaluate print and online sources for objectivity and credibility.

Teaching tip: Consider asking students to evaluate the content on their own social networking sites and the content on the sites of others. You might ask them to look at the site as a prospective employer and to consider what aspects of self-disclosure might raise flags. A more involved assignment might ask students to evaluate their friends' sites, find the most and least employable person based on the information disclosed, and write about why these sites position their friends as such. Either assignment begins the process of evaluating sources, as it encourages students to use the critical-thinking skills they have been developing, to explore their own opinions about social-networking sites, and to begin thinking about good and bad sources.

Evaluating Print Sources, p. 220

With questions for students to ask about the sources they encounter and with tips to help students evaluate the sources, this section introduces five major criteria for evaluation: accuracy, objectivity, credibility, currency, comprehensiveness. Subsections define and explain each criterion in some detail: An **accurate** source is factual and free of error; even errors in spelling can raise doubts about a source's credibility. **Credibility,** which refers to trust of an author, relates to accuracy, objectivity, and currency; a credible writer is an accurate writer, who looks at facts objectively and at the most current information on a particular topic. Credibility also involves the reputation of the author and of the author's sources; here the text suggests students consider the scope of an author's expertise by looking at book reviews or at Amazon.com for a list of other works the author may have written. **Objectivity** also relates to credibility; while it is virtually impossible to find a wholly unbiased argument, objective writing explores data on all sides of an issue and reveals rather than hides its biases. **Currency,** particularly important in writing about science or technology, asks students to consider how recently the information has been written. Finally, students should consider the **comprehensiveness** of a source—that is, the depth of an author's exploration of a subject and the scope of the author's research.

Exercise 8.1, p. 225

This exercise asks students to read and evaluate three sources for use in writing a three- to five-page argumentative essay; in their evaluation, students should consider accuracy, credibility, objectivity, currency, and comprehensiveness. The sources, found on pages 226–231 of the text, are listed and briefly summarized and evaluated below.

- **"Stay Informed on Facebook's Third-Party Privacy Policies" by Michael Gregoris, p. 226** Published in the opinion section of the University of Western Ontario's student newspaper, the article contends that Facebook users are relatively uninformed about how the site uses their information. He argues that in our desire to reconnect, we're overlooking the consumer-driven mentality underwriting the site, an insidious prospect for the author. (**Unacceptable source**—citation missing or specious, opinionated; see evaluation in Exercise 8.2 for further detail.)
- **"How Sticky Is Membership on Facebook? Just Try Breaking Free" by Maria Aspan, p. 227** Published in the *New York Times*, this informative article is based on interviews with several relevant sources—mainly those working in technology fields—about the difficulty of removing information from Facebook; the author even interviews and quotes a spokeswoman for the site. (**Acceptable source**—citation sound, interviews expert, informative, less biased.)
- **"What Was Privacy?" by Lew McCreary, p. 230** This short article published in the *Harvard Business Review* begins with an anecdote about how one man lives "off the grid" and questions what privacy means in an age of technology. (**Acceptable source**—credible, informative, accurate; students may question brevity and relevance and suggest it's unacceptable because it does not mention social networking per se.)

Exercise 8.2, p. 231

Drawing on the reading and thinking that students did in Exercise 8.1, this exercise asks students to write a one- to two- paragraph evaluation of each of the sources, offering evidence to support each point. A sample evaluation of each article follows.

- **"Stay Informed on Facebook's Third-Party Privacy Policies" by Michael Gregoris, p. 226** While Gregoris's article is acceptably current, it is also both opinionated and written by a student, not the most credible source. Accuracy is also questionable, as neither the author nor the Web site he cites provides a source for allegations about the CIA's links to Facebook (para. 4). Further, the Web site he does cite is a .com that links to a biased political-interest group called Common Ground Common Sense. Finally, the article is not a comprehensive look at Facebook's privacy policy, as it offers little in the way of research.

- **"How Sticky Is Membership on Facebook? Just Try Breaking Free" by Maria Aspan, p. 227** The source in which the article appears is generally credible. The author reports with objectivity. The report is also current. Aspan's choice of interviewees underscores her credibility; not only does she interview a spokeswoman for Facebook (8), but she also focuses on interviewing professionals in technology fields, such as the director at a biotech consulting firm (4), a software engineer (22), and an online community developer (27).
- **"What Was Privacy?" by Lew McCreary, p. 230** Students will likely first recognize the source, the *Harvard Business Review*, as conferring immediate credibility and accuracy to the article. Since the reporting is informative and the issues are timely, the article is both objective and current. Because of the article's brevity, its focus only on defining *privacy*, and its lack of evidence, it does not score well on comprehensiveness. The story of one person's attempt to live off the grid also limits the article's scope (1, 2).

Evaluating Web Sites, p. 231

This section of the chapter reviews the key criteria for evaluating print sources (accuracy, credibility, objectivity, currency, comprehensiveness) and applies them to Internet sources. The textbox "Using a Site's URL to Assess Objectivity" (p. 235) helps students decipher domain names. The textbox "Avoiding Confirmation Bias" (p. 235) alerts students to the tendency people have to accept, without critical interrogation, information that supports their own beliefs.

Teaching tip: Recalling the first tip of this chapter—the suggestion to have students assess their own social-networking sites—now ask students to use the criteria outlined in this chapter to assess their favorite news sources. Consider turning this assessment into a short writing assignment so that students practice organizing and writing this type of evaluation; additionally, having students focus on sites that they visit regularly encourages students to personalize—to apply what they are learning to their own lives outside the classroom.

Exercise 8.3, p. 237

This exercise asks students to evaluate three online sources for accuracy, credibility, objectivity, currency, and comprehensiveness. A summary and an evaluation of each source are provided here.

- **"The Importance of User Education in Privacy" by Jonathan Kleiman, p. 238** This article comes from an independent, consumer-interest group focused on issues pertaining to Facebook. The article, a blog post that opens with a personal anecdote, briefly discusses privacy settings on the site and asks for responses. Since the site belongs to an interest group dedicated to analyzing Facebook, its objectivity and credibility are questionable. Students should consider the ease with which one can post to this site and how the largely unregulated ability to post affects the site's accuracy. Certainly, the information is current and comprehensive, but because this is a user-interest blog (likely not written by professionals in a technology-related field or insiders at Facebook), the comments are also questionable.

- **"Facebook Principles," an excerpt from Facebook's Privacy Policy Statement, p. 239** From the Facebook Web site, this excerpt rivals the previous in bias, as it is a corporate author dedicated to promoting use of the site; it cannot be objective. Since the page is attached to the site, it is necessarily current and accurate; however, comprehensiveness and credibility, too, are questionable, given the company's self-interest.
- **"A Flashy Facebook Page, at a Cost to Privacy" by Kim Hart, p. 242** This article from *WashingtonPost.com,* the online version of the *Washington Post* newspaper, is written by a staff writer who, by association, is credible. Hart writes about the questionable security of Facebook, where information is so easily garnered through thousands of site-sponsored applications. She draws support from researchers investigating the potential for greater security breeches. Hart's research is from elite institutions such as Indiana University, the University of Virginia, and Carnegie Mellon University, so it seems credible and comprehensive. The article is recent, informative, and research centered rather than argumentative.

Exercise 8.4, p. 244

This exercise asks students to read a blog post and series of comments before answering a number of questions about those posts. You will find here a brief summary of the blog post and comments (identified by poster's name) as well as suggestions for discussing each question and sample responses.

Summary: Posted on a reputable legal blog, this post is both informative and argumentative in its discussion of whether employers using Facebook as a background check face legal risks. Arguing by the post's end in favor of employer disclosure of the practice, the author first explains the extent of the practice and then offers opinions by other legal professionals about the debate.

Brief explanations of comments from five readers, with varying degrees of credibility: The first comment, from "birdy," offers no way to verify credibility; birdy raises the question of how employers are getting information via Facebook when privacy settings are controlled by users. Carol Shepherd, the second to comment, suggests that even a profile picture, visible to all regardless of privacy settings reveals bases for discrimination: gender, age, race, body type, and attractiveness, for example. Third poster Jason Morris reports that he posted the blog to his company's employment-screening Web site. A comment by Bob Maxwell points to his expertise, as he mentions the FCRA (Fair Credit Reporting Act). The final poster, Monica Dunham, identifies herself as a researcher on the topic, which points to her assessment of the site's credibility.

1. To determine the accuracy of Elefant's information, students could most easily go to the original posting, at http://legalblogwatch.typepad.com/legal_blog_watch/2008/03/do-employers-us.html. (Or simply Google the author and title of the selection to find the post.) There students are able to click on the hyperlinked sources that Elefant cites, such as the article from *Financial Week.*

This might be a good opportunity to discuss the purposes of citing sources and the methods that professional researchers use, such as MLA citation style. You might also refer students to the information earlier in the chapter to help them determine the objectivity, currency, and comprehensiveness of the sources she uses.

2. While there is an "About the Bloggers" page that contains fairly substantial information about primary posters' qualifications, it's not necessarily possible to determine if these posters are respected in their respective fields.
3. Because of its comfortable use of legalese and deference to reputable professionals and sources (for example, *Financial Week*), the blog is likely written for professionals in the field of law.
4. If the author of the primary post is listed and searchable in "About the Bloggers," there is more than enough information to confirm that the post is a suitable source. In fact, because of the reputation lent to the site by its primary bloggers, it's arguable that any post should be considered a suitable source.
5. The first comment notes how privacy settings on Facebook must be carefully adjusted in order to prevent others from viewing one's profile. (Default settings for the site may allow more to display than the individual would like or is aware of.) The poster describes specific identifying traits that could be used for purposes of discrimination. The third poster adds the information that professionals are sometimes hired to screen potential employees. The final post notes that the screening process may vary by the kind of employment the person is seeking.

Exercise 8.5, p. 247

This exercise asks students to read an excerpt from an online journal and then to locate and label the information that enables a reader to determine its suitability as a source; you'll find a brief description and evaluation of the source here.

The Web page is the homepage of the *Electronic Journal of Human Sexuality*, an online humanities journal of peer-reviewed articles. The journal's board of editors all hold doctorates. Students should point to the credentials of the consulting editors and the peer-review process as confirmation of the publication's accuracy and credibility. In the journal's mission statement, the phrase "all aspects of human sexuality" points to the comprehensiveness of the source while the fact that the journal continually publishes new articles points to the currency of its information. While each academic author published in the journal likely argues for a particular idea or approach, the inclusion of multiple authors and multiple viewpoints testifies to the journal's overall objectivity. (While most academics would agree that peer-reviewed journals are committed to some degree of objectivity, some students may point to both California and San Francisco as seats of liberal bias and argue against the publication's potential for objectivity.)

CHAPTER

9 Summarizing, Paraphrasing, Quoting, and Synthesizing Sources

For many students, the very idea of research—of finding sources, interpreting them, and then distilling them into useful information—is a daunting task. This chapter helps to simplify the process by having students break research into steps. First, they need to clearly understand the sources they find; second, they should identify and choose the quotations and ideas that they'll need to incorporate into their work. You'll want to advise students to summarize general ideas and information, to paraphrase more developed information, and to quote word for word the most salient ideas. The text provides examples of all three kinds of citations and reminds students to use direct quotation only when absolutely necessary.

The thematic content of this chapter continues from Chapter 8—whether social-networking sites like Facebook should be "fair game" for employers to look at. All the sample sources and data, as well as the essays and exercises, pertain to this issue. Because of their familiarity with the debate that surrounds social-networking sites, it's a good time to remind students that "common knowledge" about such sites can be summarized briefly and does not require documentation. Also, you may want to encourage students to consider, for every writing assignment, what their readers already know about the topic and how much background to provide for them.

Summarizing Sources, p. 250

This is a good opportunity to discuss with students the reasons for summary. It is important for researchers and writers to get a sense of the work that others have done on a subject. There's no reason for students to think that they have to invent an entire subject on their own. You can point out that it is actually much easier and much more efficient for students to see the work that others have done. Students must, however, be able to position themselves in relation to a source. Rather than simply summarizing the work of another, they must then be able to take the next step and distinguish that writer's ideas from their own and discuss how and why they would employ the summary.

Exercise 9.1, p. 251

This exercise asks students to provide a two-sentence summary of the given paragraph. Next, they should edit their summaries down to one sentence. Remind students that their two- and one-sentence summaries should convey the main idea of the paragraph as well as provide proper documentation for the source.

> *Two-sentence sample summary:*
>
> Social-networking sites like MySpace and Facebook, while open to the public, are still somewhat private mediums. Therefore, while employers and universities are legally allowed to look at someone's Facebook or MySpace account, it is still not ethical to do so (Hall [page number]).
>
> *One-sentence summary:*
>
> While it is legal for employers and universities to look at someone's Facebook or MySpace account, it is unethical for them to do so because social-networking sites are still regarded as somewhat private mediums (Hall [page number]).

Paraphrasing Sources, p. 251

Sometimes students don't really grasp the distinction between summarizing and paraphrasing and think that paraphrasing is merely a long summary. In some cases, it might help to make a sports analogy when comparing the two: A summary is like recounting a football game by giving just the score and saying which team won; in contrast, a paraphrase is like giving a play-by-play of the game, providing more details about each pivotal point. In this way, quoting is like showing the highlight reel, where fans actually get to go back to the original action and see it and hear it firsthand. This analogy distinguishes not only the ways students can interact with sources but also the ways each interaction has a different purpose.

Exercise 9.2, p. 253

This exercise gives students practice paraphrasing and directs them to return back to the paragraph by David Hall in Exercise 9.1. Students should paraphrase the excerpt by Hall and then consider how their paraphrases are different from their summaries. Here are sample responses.

> *Paraphrase:*
>
> It is time for some decision to be made regarding a person's privacy on the Internet. Social networking sites like MySpace and Facebook are, in practice, considered somewhat private and should be treated this way by everyone. Opponents of this idea say that anyone—even employers and universities—are within their legal

rights to look at someone's Facebook or MySpace page, and in some ways, that's true. There is no law prohibiting employers or universities from visiting these sites, which are part of the public domain. However, the fact that this practice is legal does not necessarily "make it ethical" (Hall [page number]).

Paraphrase vs. summary:

A paraphrase is a more thorough presentation of the paragraph, following its main points fully and acurately. The example follows Hall's ideas in order, and when the paraphrase does borrow a phrase from Hall, it is presented in quotation marks.

Exercise 9.3, p. 253

In this exercise, students are directed to read the provided paragraph and circle any distinctive words or phrases they might want to quote. Students should then write a paraphrase, incorporating these words or phrases. Remind them, again, that each paraphrase needs proper documentation. You may have students discuss what words or phrases got their attention and why. Possible choices and an example paraphrase follow.

Distinct words and phrases: "responsibility and caveat emptor," "let the buyer beware," "potential consequences," "outside viewers," "lighthearted presentation of one aspect of a person," "aware of the downsides"

Paraphrase:

When it comes to privacy on social-networking sites, there are two important guidelines: "responsibility and caveat emptor" ("Beware" [page number]). This means, first, that people should carefully and responsibly describe themselves and their friends; similarly, employers and others must access this information with open minds. Second is the idea "let the buyer beware," which means that everyone using Facebook needs to realize the effects of sharing information even if material on Facebook is only a "lighthearted presentation of one aspect of a person" ("Beware" [page number]). Facebook can be valuable, but users need to understand its negatives ("Beware" [page number]).

Quoting Sources, p. 254

It is useful to remind students that choosing a good quotation is a crucial skill. A writer may make a point in particularly striking language or in a wonderfully concise way, and so that might make for a good quotation. Quoting is also a good way to bring authority to a student work. Accuracy is important when quoting, as is including information on the source of the quotation.

Exercise 9.4, p. 255

This exercise presents three paragraphs and asks students to choose particular words and phrases they'd want to quote if using this source in an argumentative essay. Ask why they chose the words and phrases they did. Underscore that they should limit quoting and that, in some cases, it is more effective to quote only brief phrases rather than long passages.

Exercise 9.5, p. 256

This exercise has students read an essay by Alison George and highlight its most important ideas, draft a summary of one paragraph, and paraphrase another paragraph. Students should properly document for their summaries and paraphrases. Consider having students do this work individually and then have them come together to compare their work in small groups. Here is a summary of the essay.

Summary of "Things You Wouldn't Tell Your Mother" by Alison George, p. 256

Alison George looks at the recent phenomena of social-networking sites and explains how the information that users post on these sites can be used against them by employers, universities, or other outside viewers. Because Facebook and MySpace users are often open with what they post on these sites, there is a danger that they will be judged according to what they share—photos, intimate information, political opinions, or even off-color jokes. George explains that there are ways for users of these sites to control what information is available to the general public—by adjusting their privacy settings, being more careful with what they post, or even prioritizing information that appears in an online search of their name. Ultimately, George encourages readers to think about their "multiple identities online" and be smart about what information they share and who they share it with.

Working Source Material into Your Argument, p. 258

Now that students have had practice summarizing, paraphrasing, and quoting, it's important to help them work this material into their essays. This section gives students tips for how to introduce source material with identifying tags and how to smoothly incorporate others' phrases and ideas into their sentences.

Teaching tip: Many students have a tendency to use "drop quotes," meaning that they don't introduce a quotation or indicate that it's from an outside source. Instead, they just drop the quotation into the text of their essay and let it stand on its own, without comment. This approach often distorts meaning and can confuse readers, who don't know who is speaking or how to interpret the quotation. You should emphasis that you don't want each student to constantly write, "Alison George said," at the beginning or end of every quotation. Instead, encourage them to change things up and try different approaches.

Exercise 9.6, p. 261

This exercise has students return to what they wrote for Exercises 9.1 and 9.3 and add identifying tags that blend the source information into their own words. They should vary the tags that they use, integrating the borrowed material sometimes into the beginning of a sentence, sometimes into the end, and sometimes as a full sentence or so. Remind them to include proper documentation, whether as part of the signal phrase or in parentheses.

Synthesizing Sources, p. 261

The final section of this chapter has students consider how they can combine summary, paraphrase, and quotation to form a synthesis—a piece of writing in which students interact with their research sources while also presenting their own ideas. In some cases, these sources provide support for a student's thesis, and in other cases they provide a counterpoint. The excerpt in the text comes from a sample student essay and should help your students blend sources smoothly into their own writing.

Teaching tip: You may remind your students that researched, argumentative essays are in many ways like a conversation. Students need to represent the people who have gone before them and who have specific expertise; at the same time, students need to add their own ideas and reasons for those ideas. In this way, summary, paraphrasing, and quoting not only bring their readers up to speed on the issue (in this case, the debate about privacy and social-networking sites) but also give writers themselves something to build on when presenting their own perspective. In short, remind students that their research should allow them to acknowledge the discussion that has gone before them and then to insert their own stance on the subject.

CHAPTER 10

Documenting Sources: MLA

Although many students receive a crash course in MLA-style documentation in high school, they generally come to college writing classes with some degree of anxiety about documenting their sources—particularly, as they learn of the severe consequences for academic dishonesty. And, as we all know, teaching documentation is tedious—as instructors, we're forced to focus on punctuation, spacing, and indentation, on teaching the nuts and bolts of a source rather than its content. To make your job easier, this chapter contains a formatting guide with examples for most of the sources (periodicals, books, Internet sources) your students are likely to cite in their research essays. The chapter ends with a well-documented sample student essay that uses a variety of these sources so that students have another example of MLA-style documentation for in-text citation and a works-cited page. Since this chapter acts as a handbook for citation, there are neither At Issue readings nor exercises.

Teaching tip: Finding good sources and integrating and documenting those sources well can be a daunting task for students. Consider scheduling a class appointment with the reference librarian; most university libraries offer in-library class research sessions that focus on helping students negotiate the physical and virtual spaces of their campus library. Another useful activity is a library scavenger hunt. In an antiquated form, this project sent students to locate obscure sources and facts from the cobwebbed corners of the library's second basement; today's version of the hunt can ask students to find a variety of print and electronic sources based on their own research topics. Provide a general list of eight to ten types of sources for students to find; to practice documentation skills, require students to type or handwrite their finds as a works-cited page.

Students will likely ask you about online documentation machines like EasyBib and NoodleTools—some universities even subscribe to documentation services. Regardless of one's opinion about the sites or services, the end product is only as accurate and precise as the information entered by the student. Be sure to tell students that these sites are not a fail-safe; remind them to attend to the details of correctly entering all source information and to double-check every source entry—particularly, the more complicated entries.

Using Parenthetical References, p. 265

This section of the text offers a brief explanation of the rules and exceptions for parenthetical references, including the rule for using long quotations.

Preparing the Works-Cited List, p. 266

This section of the text offers a brief explanation of the rules for preparing a list of works cited and includes a bulleted list of common rules for abbreviation, punctuation, and formatting.

Periodicals, p. 267

This section offers a brief explanation and one or two examples of how to cite the following periodical sources:

- Journals
- Magazines
- Newspapers
- Editorial, letter to the editor, or review
- Political cartoon or comic strip
- Advertisements

Books, p. 269

This section offers a brief explanation and one or two examples of how to cite the following textual sources:

- Books by one author
- Books by two or three authors
- Books by more than three authors
- Two or more books by the same author
- Edited book
- Translation
- Revised edition
- Anthology
- Work in an anthology
- More than one essay in the same anthology
- Section or chapter of a book
- Introduction, preface, foreword, or afterword
- Multivolume work
- Article in a reference work

Internet Sources, p. 271

This section offers a brief explanation and one or two examples of how to cite the following Internet sources:

- Entire Web site
- Document within a Web site
- Online video
- Blog post and blog comments
- Podcast
- Message from an email discussion group
- Online book
- Part of an online book
- Article in an online scholarly journal
- Article in an online magazine
- Article in an online newspaper
- Article from a library database

Legal Case; Government Document, p. 273

These sections of the text offer brief explanations about citing a court opinion or a government document found in print or online.

Sample Student Essay: "Should Data Posted on Social-Networking Sites Be 'Fair Game' for Employers?" p. 274

Arguing that social-networking sites should be fair game for potential employers, this student author asserts that we must recognize that the Internet has redefined our notions of *public* and *private*. She advocates thoughtful, responsible online posting that avoids applauding indiscretion or risqué self-construction. The essay cites seven sources and includes a works-cited page.

CHAPTER

11 Avoiding Plagiarism

Perhaps one of the most vexing issues in any writing class, plagiarism is something you want your students to understand—and avoid—in both their college careers and their professional lives. Academics and professionals often insist that *any* unattributed borrowing is plagiarism. Misunderstandings about plagiarism are especially common now due to our online culture: resources are easy to find, and text can easily be cut and pasted by students who forget (or don't choose) to document their sources. This chapter helps students recognize and avoid the many forms of plagiarism, and it reminds them why plagiarism is a serious matter. The At Issue readings at the end of the chapter help you to relate discussions about plagiarism to Internet sources, campus life, and even broader issues of ownership and intellectual property; with this more expansive discussion of plagiarism, students see how difficult yet necessary defining plagiarism is.

Understanding Plagiarism, p. 282

This section gives students various definitions of *plagiarism* and acknowledges the difficulty of determining whether something is plagiarized intentionally or unintentionally. Most important, students are reminded to document any information they take from sources, including direct quotations; summaries or paraphrases of someone else's original ideas; someone else's opinions, judgments, and conclusions; and statistics or other data from charts or graphs in a source. **Common knowledge** is the term given to familiar quotations or phrases, broadly known information, and the writer's own ideas or conclusions; these do not need to be documented.

Teaching tip: You'll want to spend some time helping students understand what information they need to document and what information or ideas they don't need to document. The concept *common knowledge* can be difficult to grasp, but remind students that if information is available to the public and appears in a variety of sources, then it is considered common knowledge. Whether information is common knowledge or not may depend on a writer's intended audience. For instance, common knowledge in the advertising world may not be so "common" when a student writes an analysis of advertising campaigns for his composition class. When in doubt, students should err on the side of caution and document rather than not document their sources.

Exercise 11.1, p. 284

This exercise asks students to consider a series of statements and say whether each requires documentation or not. Students should also be able to explain, more important, *why* they would or would not need to document these statements. Sample responses are provided below.

1. No documentation necessary: In most cases, this statement would be common knowledge, though if the writer wants to name specific awards that Goodwin has won, then he or she may need to cite sources.
2. No documentation necessary: This fact is common knowledge and can be found in a variety of sources or simply by looking at the book.
3. No documentation necessary: For those who are familiar with the controversy surrounding Goodwin's book, this statement is common knowledge; it may also be considered common knowledge because it is information that's available in several sources.
4. No documentation necessary: This statement reflects the writer's own opinion on the book's controversy.
5. Documentation needed: This statement uses a direct quotation, either from another source or from Goodwin herself, so it must be documented.
6. Documentation needed: This statement uses a direct quotation from Goodwin herself, so it must be documented.
7. Documentation needed: While this is not a direct quotation, the information in this statement is either a summary or a paraphrase of a source that needs to be documented.
8. Documentation needed: This statement is likely not the writer's original idea but is based on information that the writer found in an outside source, so it needs to be documented.
9. Documentation needed: This statement gives information about Goodwin's response to the allegations, so it is information that the writer could not have had without the help of an outside source.
10. Documentation needed: This statement is likely derived from a source that then lists *who* believes Goodwin's "reputation as a historian" was hurt. The writer needs to attribute the information, as it is not his or her original idea.

Exercise 11.2, p. 285

This exercise directs students to read an editorial and decide what information they would need to document and what they would not need to document. In each case, students should underline two sections of text in the editorial and note why they should or should not be documented. This is a good exercise to share in small groups, because it encourages students to process the information used in the editorial and then consider the *kind* of information it is, not just what it is says.

Summary of "Cheaters Never Win" from the *Austin American-Statesman*, p. 285

Providing an up-to-the-minute look at plagiarism, this article discusses the ease with which students plagiarize by means of the Internet—from buying whole term papers to finding and using information without documentation. The article also provides insight into the ways plagiarism is punished at certain schools and explains the many ways students "lose out" on their education by taking the easy road of plagiarism.

Teaching tip: Before discussing this editorial with your students, you might want to refresh your memory on your own school's plagiarism policy. You may also want to photocopy your department's description of plagiarism (if there is one) or even try to have your students draft a definition of *plagiarism* for the class.

Two excerpts that need documentation:

- **Student Judicial Services at the University of Texas defines plagiarism as "representing as your own work any material that was obtained from another source . . ."** (para. 5). This statement includes a direct quotation from the University of Texas and needs to be documented.
- **The Center for Academic Integrity found last year that more than 70 percent of college students admitted to having cheated at least once . . .** (6). This statement needs to be documented, because the information is taken from another source and is not simply the writer's own knowledge or opinion.

Two excerpts that do NOT need documentation:

- **If you think that's an exaggeration, do an Internet search of "free term papers." You'll find cheathouse.com, Cheater.com . . .** (2). This statement is the writer's own words and work, based on an online search. The information does not come from someone else's work.
- **Strict disciplinary action should follow students who are caught . . .** (7). This statement expresses the writer's opinion and, therefore, does not need documentation.

Revising to Eliminate Plagiarism, p. 287

When students think of revision, they rarely think of it in terms of preventing plagiarism. But revision is a good time for students to take a second look at the information and ideas they're including in their papers and decide what needs to be documented, if it isn't already. The text explains the guidelines that guard against plagiarism and gives examples that ignore the guidelines.

Exercise 11.3, p. 289

This exercise has students read a paragraph from a researched paper and two sources on which it is based. The assignment is to make specific changes to the provided paragraph by referring to the source material. At the end of the exercise, you might discuss with students *why* these changes should be made, how the changes clarify meaning, and how the revised paragraph avoids plagiarism.

Reading and Writing about the Issue: Where Do We Draw the Line with Plagiarism? p. 292

While the issue of plagiarism is often looked at as a classroom issue, this set of readings and questions helps students think of the issue in broader terms. Some articles *are* focused on academic plagiarism and policies, but other articles (by Shafer and by Goodwin) look at how plagiarism can be an issue in newspaper and book publishing. The Posner article takes a more humorous look at the history of plagiarism on college campuses, in history books, and even in film and theater. The goal is for students to think of how plagiarism links to issues of attribution, ownership, and even copyright, how plagiarism has implications beyond the classroom. Ideally, this discussion will also encourage students to choose not to plagiarize and to realize that attributing information will improve their own credibility as writers.

Summary of "Sidebar: Comparing the Copy" by Jack Shafer, p. 293

This article from *Slate* compares opening passages from four different news stories about mad cow disease. The first paragraph is from a Bloomberg News article, the second is from the *New York Times* (and lifts passages from Bloomberg without attribution), and there are two other opening passages from the Toronto *Globe and Mail* and the *Omaha World-Herald* with very different wording. This compilation should help students see the ways that attributions are necessary even in the news world, and it reminds them that when they do their own writing it's best to take a different approach and word things in a unique way so that they avoid plagiarizing. Following the article is a list of questions for your students to consider.

At Issue: Sources for Avoiding Plagiarism, p. 296

1. **Passages in the *New York Times* story that are too close to the original Bloomberg News story:**
   - Both Bloomberg and the *New York Times* article have similar phrasing, such as "to resume imports of Canadian cattle" and "after an appellate court . . . because of mad cow disease" (para. 2, 5); "The first shipments from Canada may arrive / could arrive at U.S. / American slaughterhouses" (3, 6).
   - Both sources use the same quotation from Mike Johanns, they set the quotation up in the same way, and both say that Canadian and U.S. officials "are coordinating how to certify animals for shipping" (3, 6).
   - Both stories write about the U.S. courts ruling "in favor of the government, which argued / had argued that Canadian cattle / cows under 30 months of age don't /did not pose a risk of mad-cow disease."

2. We do not include all of the similarities, but here are some starting points: The first paragraphs of the *Globe and Mail* story and the *New York Times* story both include the information that Canadian cattle imports will resume. The fourth paragraph of the *Globe and Mail* story discusses the U.S. appeal court panel decision, as does the last paragraph of the *New York Times* story. The first paragraphs of both the *Omaha World-Herald* story and the *New York Times* story report that Canadian cattle will be able to be imported into the United States shortly. The fourth paragraph of the *Omaha World-Herald* article and the third paragraph of the *New York Times* story quote Agriculture Secretary Mike Johanns.
3. Student's findings for question 2 should prepare them to answer this question. See if they agree that the Toronto and Omaha stories are "starkly different" from the Bloomberg story; have them justify their responses by referring to earlier information in this chapter.
4. For this question, students are likely to go back to the articles and compare *exact wording*. Remind them that they should also consider where the articles summarize or paraphrase similar information without attribution, because plagiarism is not just lifting text word-for-word. You might remind students that the original source is the conference call with the agriculture secretary. Do the articles make it sufficiently clear that the call is the source of the information?
5. Students should support their conclusions about the *New York Times* and plagiarism by citing copy from the four excerpts as well as from earlier Chapter 11 text that describes plagiarism. Do students think the *New York Times* story represents significant plagiarism? Is it intentional? What might be the restrictions for reporting on news from a conference call? How could such plagiarism be avoided?

Summary for "How to Fight College Cheating" by Lawrence M. Hinman, p. 297

Hinman discusses what he calls "disturbing" evidence that an increasing percent of high school and college students cheat or plagiarize (para. 1). He says that, while students have always cheated, it has become easier to do so with the availability of sources, and even "term-paper mills," online (5). The response from teachers and administrators has been to fight this development with more technology, by turning to plagiarism-detection software and the like. But Hinman says this strategy is not enough. Instead, he poses three main ways to combat cheating and plagiarism: professors who work more closely with students in order to see the process of their thinking and working, students who have a better sense of integrity and responsibility, and students who are willing to come forward and confront academic dishonesty.

At Issue: Sources for Avoiding Plagiarism, p. 298

1. Hinman admits that students have always cheated, but that, before the Internet, students had to plan ahead to cheat. They could order a term paper and

have it faxed, have someone else write one for them, or draw on the collection of papers that many fraternities and sororities kept on file. But now students can order a paper online and have it printed out immediately, ready for class the next day. Hinman also mentions that cutting and pasting research sources is very common now, as students take sentences and paragraphs from Internet sources, even if not plagiarizing a whole paper.

2. Student responses will vary, of course, but each student should understand that Hinman thinks good teaching is the best way to prevent cheating and plagiarism. His subsequent points come from this assertion.

3. *Hinman's view of plagiarism-detection sites:*
   - Hinman calls antiplagiarism services "the academic equivalent of mandatory urine testing for athletes" (para. 4). He admits that these services can catch students, but they don't prevent students from cheating.
   - Instead, he states that each side will continue to construct "more elaborate countermeasures to outwit the other" so that the situation will "undoubtedly continue to spiral" (5). Clearly, according to Hinman, other measures must be taken on the preventive side.

4. Hinman outlines several ways that "good teaching" can combat cheating and plagiarism:
   - Professors need to change their curriculum, not allow it to fall prey to "routine, lack of interest and overwork" (6).
   - Professors need to know their students and give them assignments that require regular interaction with their professors (6–7).
   - Professors should help students develop work that is "a meaningful development of their own interests" (7).
   - Professors need to be familiar with their students' writing so they can detect inconsistencies as a sign of plagiarism (7).

5. *Hinman's additional remedies:*
   - Hinman states that instructors need to "encourage the development of integrity" in their students (8). This includes a "sense of responsibility about one's intellectual development" and an understanding that cheating is "inconsistent with one's identity" (8).
   - Teachers must encourage students to see academic dishonesty as something that hurts all students, not just the cheater. Students who plagiarize often do get good grades, and their cheating can take scholarships, recommendations, and admission spots away from qualified students (9). Students who know about cheating must be willing to confront it (9).
   - Ask your students whether these seem like possible remedies or if Hinman is being overly idealistic. Also ask them who Hinman puts the burden on (the teachers) and see if they think that is fair.

6. To help your students identify opposing arguments and possible rebuttals by Hinman, consider asking them what objections *they* have to Hinman's article. What limitations do teachers face with class size, curriculum requirements,

and time limits that might make Hinman's advice difficult? Might readers argue that Hinman needs to put more responsibility and blame on the students who cheat? Could readers counterargue that plagiarism penalties must be more severe in order to deter such cheating?

Summary of "The Rules of Attribution" by Deborah R. Gerhardt, p. 299

By opening with an anecdote about creative writing and copyright infringement, Gerhardt portrays plagiarism rules as a code of honor for writers. She says that many students and young writers in general aren't taught these rules of the game and, therefore, don't understand how these rules differ from the kind of copying and borrowing they see elsewhere in society. She focuses on young fiction writer Kaavya Viswanathan, who was accused of plagiarism in her novel *How Opal Mehta Got Kissed, Got Wild, and Got a Life*. Gerhardt maintains that Viswanathan is one of many young writers who aren't abiding by plagiarism rules simply because no one took the time to explain them. In many other areas of culture—music, theater, movies, even government documents—"borrowing" or using earlier works for inspiration are accepted practices. In writing, however, the expectations are different, and Gerhardt says instructors need to take more time to teach students about plagiarism.

At Issue: Sources for Avoiding Plagiarism, p. 301

1. Gerhardt asks, "Why do smart students commit plagiarism?" (para. 1). She answers this question at the end of the same paragraph, after comparing the "rules of plagiarism" to the rules of the game (basketball), when she states, "I fear that too often we send our high-school writing stars to college and graduate school without teaching them the academic and legal rules that govern their creative work." In other words, smart students plagiarize because they aren't familiar enough with the rules to know that they're plagiarizing.
2. Gerhardt clearly places the blame for plagiarism on instructors (as well as on editors and advisers, in the case of young published writers like Viswanathan). See if your students think this is a fair assessment of the situation.
3. Gerhardt likens student writers to student basketball stars in paragraphs 1 and 3. She states that basketball players learn the rules of the game, and that these rules are taught repeatedly throughout the years, not just one time and then forgotten. Gerhardt believes that students need to be more familiar with the rules of writing and plagiarism and that these rules must be taught over and over again, to remind students of expectations and limitations. See what your students think of the basketball/writing comparison. Do students need to practice obeying the rules, or is plagiarism something altogether different from learning the rules of basketball? You might ask them if they've needed time to learn what plagiarism is and how to avoid it; answering in the positive would support Gerhardt's analogy.

4. In our society as a whole, students are constantly exposed to recycling of objects and ideas, according to Gerhardt. She provides various examples of what things are often borrowed or recycled, especially in entertainment. See if students think that this common practice in society as a whole may have led them to be more relaxed about plagiarism in their own writing than they should be. Also be sure to ask them if this is a strong point in the article.

5. Gerhardt references this student, Kaavya Viswanathan, throughout her article, and uses her as an example of college students who don't know the rules of plagiarism. In Viswanathan's case, she had taken information for a novel from another writer whom she admired, but for your students the issue of plagiarism usually comes up in an academic setting—research papers, argumentative writing, and so on. See what they think are the parallels, and ask if this comparison is strong enough in Gerhardt's article.

   Teaching tip: In recent years, the issue of copyright and plagiarism has come into the spotlight—especially, in the case of James Frey's *A Million Little Pieces,* which was an Oprah's Book Club selection. Frey's book became a scandal after he admitted that much of the book's content was not truly autobiographical (it had been billed as nonfiction/ memoir) and he was accused of lifting material from other authors. Students may be familiar with this instance or other similar mainstream stories of plagiarism. How do they feel about the ethics of copyright and truth telling? How does the way they feel relate to ethics and plagiarism in their own work?

Summary of "The Truth about Plagiarism" by Richard A. Posner, p. 302

Posner laments the fact that most people define *plagiarism* simply as copying or borrowing without attribution. Such practices are commonplace in our society, Posner states, and it is for this reason that many students are confused as to why some forms of plagiarism are wrong. Posner cites examples of how theater, literature, music, and other fields constantly endure borrowing and reinvention—all without any attribution to the original source. He says that students must be better educated about *academic* plagiarism because such copying "disrupt[s] the system of student and scholarly evaluation" (para. 4). The writer also posits a more useful definition of plagiarism as that which is copied without acknowledgment so as to be deceptive (12).

At Issue: Sources for Avoiding Plagiarism, p. 304

1. Posner says that plagiarism is usually seen as "the capital intellectual crime" (para. 1), "fraud" (3), "copying" (6), and a form of theft (6). But Posner believes that there need to be distinctions between these various definitions. For instance, plagiarism and copying are not the same, according to Posner; he proposes that plagiarism be "confined to literal copying, and moreover literal copying that is not merely unacknowledged but deceptive" (12).

2. Posner argues that plagiarism committed by students and professors is the most serious. In paragraph 4, he supports this view by stating that, students and professors who plagiarize "disrupt the system of student and scholarly evaluation." In other words, some forms of plagiarism are not as harmful, but in an academic setting, plagiarism robs students of the process of learning and developing. See if your students have arguments against this view and the plagiarism hierarchy Posner creates in this article, or if they agree.
3. In paragraphs 7 and 8, Posner gives many examples of alluding to, copying, and borrowing that occur in theater, literature, art, and movies. Students will likely be familiar with several of his examples and may comment on nonacademic "plagiarism."
4. In paragraph 16, Posner says that even judges conceal their original thinking and, instead, appeal to their predecessors for "rules and principles." Posner is arguing that, just as those who interpret the law build on the ideas of others, so do writers; all writers, as Posner would argue, build their ideas on others' ideas, so the idea of a "universal moral law" against copying is simply unfair.
5. Posner says that the demand to punish plagiarists is a backlash against the postmodern idea that journalists and historians are not truthful and instead rely on relativism when approaching the facts of news or history. In these disciplines, punishing plagiarism is a way to gain back credibility (18).
6. See if students agree that Posner upheld this claim in his essay, and find out why they think he did or didn't. Then, to answer the second part of this question, you might consider telling students a bit about copyright and ownership throughout history or even in other countries (for instance, in the nineteenth century in the United States, it was common for writers to lift whole passages and storylines from other writers, or to reprint, without citation, newspaper excerpts or other published writing). Ask students how our thoughts on individualism and originality might be a more modern-day, American concern and how this might spill over to what Posner believes is an unfair comparison of plagiarism to copying.

Summary of "How I Caused That Story" by Doris Kearns Goodwin, p. 305

Goodwin published this article in *Time* in response to a much-publicized discussion about leaving quotation marks off attributed passages in her book *The Fitzgeralds and the Kennedys*. Here, Goodwin explains how her extensive research and ten-year-long process of writing the book led to some confusion over source material. She concludes her response by stating how much she values good, honest scholarship and says that, with new technological capabilities, she's found a new "process of research and writing that minimizes the possibility of error" (para. 7).

At Issue: Sources for Avoiding Plagiarism, p. 306

1. Most of Goodwin's essay is an explanation of how research material from other sources made it into her book without quotation marks. She explains

that her 900-page book involved extensive primary and secondary research, included approximately 300 books, and resulted in more than 3,500 footnotes. Over the course of researching and writing, which took ten years, she states that she confused some phrases from outside sources with her own notes, leading her to put them in the book without quotation marks.

2. Students have been told not to plagiarize and therefore might be harsh on someone who has neglected to use quotation marks where they were needed. On the other hand, students are likely to be astonished by the extensive number of sources, pages, and footnotes involved in Goodwin's endeavor and, as a result, may be more understanding.
3. Goodwin opens by establishing her *ethos* with readers. She identifies herself as a wife and a mother and as a historian, all of which roles she takes seriously, she says. Then she describes an incident involving overlooked quotation marks, and she explains how the error occurred and how she took great pains to correct the error and move on. This admission demonstrates that Goodwin *does* take her work seriously and, most important, that she is willing to admit wrongdoing when necessary. This builds trust with the readers, leading them to believe that she's more likely to admit wrongdoing again, if she *had* done something wrong.
4. Goodwin's writing style in this article is definitely intended to make the piece seem like a personal letter to her readers—a way to sit down with readers one on one and explain where she's coming from. Her tone is thoughtful, sincere, forthright, and even apologetic about the issue. Some students may think this approach builds trust, while others may think it sounds too soft.
5. Much of the plagiarism debate involves *intent*—see if students think Goodwin's plagiarism was willfully deceptive or not.

Summary of "Copy This" by Carolyn Foster Segal, p. 307

Segal's article is a somewhat humorous take on the issue of plagiarism in the writing class, and she begins with the statement, "Technology has raised the crafty business of plagiarism and its detection to a whole new level." She goes on to recount the various experiences she's had involving students and plagiarism, and she explains how, as an instructor, she tries every year, in every course, to dissuade students from cheating. In contrast to other writers in this set of readings, Segal defines plagiarism as *theft* that hurts the students who cheat, their fellow students, and even their professors.

At Issue: Sources for Avoiding Plagiarism, p. 310

1. Segal's definition of *plagiarism* appears in paragraph 5, when she states that "it is theft, plain and simple . . . of another writer's ideas, work, time; it is theft of their fellow students' time; it is theft of their own time, honor, and education; and it is theft of my time." Segal's essay is centered on how her experiences

with students have shaped her view of plagiarism. More specifically, she states that because the majority of her students *do* try to do their best and turn in their own work "plagiarism by the few [is] all the more appalling" (para. 6). See what other examples of Segal's experiences your students notice.

2. Posner states that plagiarism cannot simply be called "theft" because that makes it a crime and equal to copyright infringement. Instead, Posner argues that plagiarism is "literal copying that is not merely unacknowledged but deceptive" (para. 12). In contrast, Segal argues that plagiarism *is* theft, not in a legal sense, but in more of an ethical sense. Segal describes her own methods for preventing plagiarism, and in paragraph 4 she says that "even an emphasis on the process of writing . . . does not stop some students." In many ways, Segal's personal experiences stand in stark contrast to Hinman's view that teachers need to work more closely with students and follow their writing process—as if this method alone will end plagiarism (7). Segal is basically saying that no matter what preventive measures a professor takes, there will still be students who try to cheat. See if your students agree and why.
3. In paragraph 6, Segal acknowledges that most students do not plagiarize; she argues that "they are honest, love writing, and want to learn how to do it better," and she states that their hard work "has made the plagiarism by the few all the more appalling to me." The subsequent anecdotes she gives, then, are designed to earn the support and sympathy of her readers. Ask students for their responses to these anecdotes and see if they are frustrated, like Segal, with students who choose to plagiarize.
4. Some of the students may think Segal's tone is a bit too sarcastic or that she expresses too much frustration in her essay. If this is the case, you may want to remind students of the ways that Hinman says plagiarism hurts honest students—by taking away from them scholarship money, recommendations, and admission to certain programs (9). Some students may say that Segal should have included anecdotes about students who did their own work though it was difficult and saw the rewards. Such examples might have made Segal sound less harsh.

Exercise 11.4, p. 311

This exercise asks students to compose a one-paragraph argument in which they take a position on where to draw the line with plagiarism. Students should fill in the given paragraph structure with their own words. Here is a sample response with the given text in boldface

Template for Writing an Argument about Plagiarism

To many people, plagiarism is theft; to others, however, it is not a simple issue. For example, some define plagiarism as merely borrowing; **others see it as** copying another's words or ideas. **Another thing to consider is** whether the person who plagiarized did so deceptively and with the intent of defrauding readers. **In addition,** we must realize that borrowing or copying are common in other areas of society, such as in music, movies, or even literary plots. **Despite these differ-**

ences of opinion, plagiarism is often dealt with harshly and can ruin careers and reputations. All things considered, it is important to note who was involved and what the circumstances were surrounding any incident of plagiarism, and the label of "plagiarism" should be reserved for willful cases of fraud.

Exercise 11.5, p. 311

This exercise asks students to discuss the issue of plagiarism in small groups. The goal is to have them think about how they'd define plagiarism and to consider who is involved in plagiarism—who commits plagiarism (who doesn't) and who are its victims. Finally, students should draft a paragraph that summarizes the key points of their discussion.

Teaching tip: In this discussion, have students think back to the readings. Do students think that there is a difference between copying a plotline for a movie and quoting paragraphs of research in a paper without documentation? How is a person's intent a factor?

Exercise 11.6, p. 311

Finally, in this exercise, students are directed to draft an argumentative essay "Where Do We Draw the Line with Plagiarism?" By narrowing their focus to a specific group, the students will be able to more effectively address the often-unwieldy topic of plagiarism. Students should also address whether plagiarism always has a negative effect. In their essays, they should refer to At Issue readings and be sure to document their sources.

Exercise 11.7, p. 311

This exercise asks students to think foundationally about the arguments they wrote for Exercise 11.6 by now reviewing the four pillars of argument discussed in Chapter 1. Students should establish whether their own argument includes these pillars, add anything that is missing, and then label the essay by identifying these parts.

Writing Assignments: Avoiding Plagiarism, p. 312

This section allows you to take the concept of plagiarism a bit further by having your students draft either a causal argument (see Chapter 13) or an argument by definition (see Chapter 12). Each of these suggestions has students engage with the At Issue essays while considering both their opinions on the plagiarism issue and the ways they can present these opinions through different styles of argumentation.

PART 5

Patterns and Purposes

CHAPTER

12

Argument by Definition

Because precise word choice is important to any argument, there are times when the definition of key terms becomes central to making an argument. An argument that rests on a particular definition of a word or idea is frequently called an *argument by definition*. Focusing on explaining, developing, and structuring arguments by definition, the chapter also includes a sample student essay entitled "Why I Am a Nontraditional Student" and an At Issue section on whether *Wikipedia* is a legitimate research source.

Teaching tip: For many students, the notion that a single word can incite and sustain an argument might be a hard sell. Consider asking students to think about scenarios in their own lives when the definition of a particular word—such as *curfew* or *grounded*—became the linchpin in a parent's or guardian's argument. For a resistant class, this line of inquiry might prompt students to offer other examples from their own lives, underscoring the text's focus on *practical* argument.

What Is Argument by Definition? p. 316

As the introduction to this chapter notes, an **argument by definition** depends on defining a particular word or idea in service of your argument. To provide concrete examples for students, the text offers a bulleted list of questions that rely on defining a term in a particular way. Perhaps the best example to begin with is the one implied at the end of the first: "Is graffiti art?" Most students will understand that *art* is a subjective term with various definitions and that the artistic quality of graffiti is also arguable. Accordingly, the text explains that a writer must first define *art* and then argue that graffiti fits the definition.

Returning to the text's focus on practical application, the section introduces the idea that any social or legal dispute involves argument by definition and gives several contentious terms as examples: *sexual harassment*, *political refugee*, and *illegal alien*. Because of its contemporary resonance, you may also want to introduce the term *marriage* here, although the term does appear as a word for students to define in Exercise 12.2 (p. 325). Finally, this section asks students to consider how our thinking and, as such, our language changes over time.

Teaching tip: Ask students to consider how and why language changes. For many students, particularly for first-year students, the idea that language both reflects and affects ideology is a relatively new and complex concept; argument by definition provides a good opportunity to ask students to think about the importance of language generally and specific words in particular.

Developing Definitions, p. 317

Outlining the major approaches to developing an argument by definition, this part of the chapter explains dictionary definitions (also called formal definitions), extended definitions, and operational definitions. **Dictionary,** or **formal, definitions** traditionally classify and differentiate one item from others in its class; these are objective and descriptive definitions and are quite useful for concrete terms. By contrast, **extended definitions** are useful for abstract terms and often rely on relevant examples to develop that definition; reinforcing this notion, the text points to the effectiveness of Thomas Jefferson's twenty-five paragraphs of examples of King George's tyranny. **Operational definitions** focus on how something acts or works. The text suggests that researchers, particularly those in the natural and social sciences, rely on operational definitions so that they can carry out their work.

Structuring an Argument by Definition, p. 318

As in previous chapters focused on forms of argumentation, such as Chapter 6's definition of oral forms of argument, this section offers a bulleted list for structuring an argument by definition.

Sample Student Essay: "Why I Am a Nontraditional Student," p. 319

This student author begins his essay with the formal definition of *nontraditional student* used by the National Center for Education Statistics. He wants to show the insufficiency of that definition. Working against this definition, the author provides evidence that shows the problems with the definition most universities use for his situation and at the essay's close offers a new definition of the *nontraditional student.*

Grammar in Context: Avoiding *Is Where* and *Is When,* p. 321

This textbox focuses on a common problem that student authors experience when writing arguments by definition—that is, the use of the phrases *is where* and *is when*. The box explains clearly that any form of *to be* requires a noun to follow.

Exercise 12.1, p. 322

This exercise asks students to read "The Wife-Beater" by Gayle Rosenwald Smith and to answer questions in response to the essay; a brief summary of the essay and sample responses to the questions follow.

Summary of "The Wife-Beater" by Gayle Rosenwald Smith, p. 322

In this brief essay, Smith questions the use of the term *wife-beater* as the conventional name for "the skinny-ribbed white T-shirts" (para. 4) worn by both men and women. After surveying the construction of the stereotype and interrogating the term's disturbing associative image and the unflinching use of it, particularly by wearers under twenty-five, Smith wonders if the current trends in fashion reveal a violent return to male dominance (11).

Identifying the Elements of an Argument by Definition, p. 324

1. Students should express the thesis as the author's dissatisfaction with the term *wife-beater* for an article of clothing that could, she argues, have a less-charged name.
2. Smith suggests that the use of the term (a) advances a stereotype (6–7) and advocates a violent image of men (14–15), (b) reinforces violence (9–10), and (c) unjustly discounts the very real family violence occurring each year in the United States (13–14).
3. Smith introduces the dictionary definitions of the term in paragraphs 7 and 8. Offset from the text by space preceding and following, the two numbered definitions that Smith includes draw attention to the connection between domestic violence and the term for the shirt. Smith's definition focuses on the effects of the term, the cultural icons who lend it popularity, the levity with which it suggests we view domestic violence, and our unchallenged assumptions about masculinity. Smith's definition goes beyond the literal one in the dictionary and includes a cultural aspect of the shirt, tying domestic violence to it.
4. When considering possible objections to her definition, students should point to paragraph 10, where she mentions other sources that argue the term stems from popular cultural figures, not the practice of domestic violence (ironically, each figure she mentions is also associated with domestic violence), and to paragraph 11, where Smith asks rhetorically: "Am I reading too much into a fashion statement . . . ?"
5. Note that the original essay does not include an image. We have included an iconic image of Marlon Brando as Stanley Kowalski to make sure that students understand what the term *wife-beater* refers to. You might ask them about popular contemporary manifestations of the shirt by entertainment figures such as Kid Rock and others.

Exercise 12.2, p. 325

This exercise asks students to write a one-sentence definition of the following words and then to compare their definitions with those in a dictionary. Sample definitions follow.

- *Terrorism* is any threatening or violent act perpetrated to induce fear and terror in a victim and dominance in the perpetrator; frequently *terrorist* acts are large-scale and for political ends.

Teaching tip: Because the Bush Administration popularized the phrase *war on terror* as a national movement, students are likely to make associations to 9/11, Iraq, and Guantanamo more readily than to other instances of terrorism like those perpetrated by the KKK, Timothy McVeigh, the Animal Liberation Front, or those who bomb abortion clinics. Be aware that an in-class discussion could lead to stereotyping and/or racist or ethnic assumptions that you may need to address in class; the largely white perpetrators of the second list may help students to dissociate the stereotype of the nonwhite, non-American terrorist, as it points to a lineage of largely white, American, and male terrorism.

- A *comic book* is a narrative text made up of a series of frames of cartoon drawings.
- A *cell phone* is a mobile telephone that relies on wireless communication to receive and transmit phone calls.
- *Marriage* is a legal and sometimes religious union between two people.

  ***Teaching tip*:** Because of the recent and continuing debate over a constitutional amendment defining *marriage* as a union between a man and woman, a discussion may spark student debate. Consider engaging students in a debate about whether or not marriage should be defined by the U.S. Constitution; in addition to focusing on definition, a discussion of this word is a good way to remind students of the skills needed for an effective oral argument (Chapter 6) and a good way to reintroduce the logical fallacies (as discussions about marriage are frequently rife with them) discussed in Chapter 5. You might also consider a structured debate that asks a few students to act as unbiased moderators who point out the fallacies and remind students of the types of evidence and support needed to make a good argument.
- A *blog,* or *weblog,* is usually a site on which a particular author or group expresses opinions.
- A *union* is a joining together of things or people for a common good or goal.

Exercise 12.3, p. 325

This exercise asks students to choose one of the terms they defined in Exercise 12.2 and to write a paragraph-length argument with two or three examples supporting their definition. Here is a sample paragraph defining *marriage.*

> For our society, *marriage* has largely been defined as a legal and religious union between a man and a woman; however, this definition points to a lineage of compulsory heterosexuality and Judeo-Christianity in our culture. Unlike the American society of earlier centuries, not all parties in twenty-first century American marry in a religious setting, nor does societal practice harshly censor and ultimately restrict the expression of homosexuality as it once did. We might even recall an older lesson, that of our colonial forebears who came to this country largely to escape religious persecution. Are we not compromising a couple's First Amendment right by persecuting the nonreligious who choose to marry in civil ceremonies when the definition of *marriage* maintains a religious component? Further, defining *marriage* as between a man and a woman implicitly recalls that objections

to homosexual marriage are rooted in religious belief, another trouncing of the First Amendment. And, more important, marriage is fundamentally a state-determined and state-recognized union—one needs to first procure a license from the state in order to marry. Accordingly, when our law is largely rooted in the separation of church and state, it seems we legally need to redefine marriage as a state and/or religious or spiritual union between two people regardless of sexual preference or gender; all other definitions are clearly *un*lawful.

Exercise 12.4, p. 325

This exercise asks students to read a poem by Nikki Grimes, to identify the characteristics of a "good poem" according to the author, to suggest additional characteristics for inclusion, and to write a paragraph in favor of their own definition of a "good poem." Here are a list of characteristics Grime identifies, a list of other potential characteristics, and a sample paragraph.

Characteristics of a "good poem" for Grimes:

- Celebrates language (line 3)
- Takes you on a short journey (3–4)
- Touches your heart (4)
- Turns on your imagination (5)
- Or tickles your funny-bone (5–6)

Other possible characteristics of a "good poem":

- Makes you think
- Creates a vivid image
- Complicates our understanding or offers a new way of seeing
- Is original, not a cliché
- Creates an experience for the reader
- Questions a timeless truth or belief

Sample paragraph:

While Grimes's definition of a "good poem" is a good starting point, she overlooks the need for a good poem to make a reader think or to complicate our understanding of the world. By her definition, a limerick is a good poem, but many would not be willing to concede such; accordingly, her definition is too broad, too encompassing—we might call it the definition of a poem but not of a "good poem." In contrast, a good poem has the complexity of a riddling Sphinx or a vintage wine and can carry with it the depth of a bottomless abyss or can traverse the expanse of the universe in a single word. Lest one argue that this definition is elitist, I suggest that a good poem is inclusive, not exclusionary. The original beauty of its words touches any reader by experience while meditative rereadings complicate our ways of understanding or seeing the world; indeed, a good poem touches all and makes each of us a better reader.

Exercise 12.5, p. 325

This exercise asks students to examine two pictures (p. 326) that define *courage*, to write a paragraph defining *courage*, and, if desired, to find an image supporting their definition of the term. Here are a brief description of each image and a sample paragraph defining *courage* from a different perspective.

Top picture: A stark image, the picture contains the silhouette of a firefighter holding a hose, backlit by the yellow-orange flames of fire filling the rest of the frame; the photo uses only the colors black, yellow-orange, and red.

Bottom picture: This image uses only blues and whites and features penguins diving from the edge of a glacier. The quotation used as a caption ascribes courage to these flightless birds.

Sample paragraph:

Courage is born of compassion and integrity; it is the ability to show compassion when others will not and the capacity to remain true to one's own sense of purpose when others cannot. Courage is both a trait one possesses and a capability one embraces. Courage can be a single action or a state of being: just as it compels a bystander to run to the aid of an accident victim, so it also daily compels the social worker to fight for her client's rights. In some ways, it is the daily display of compassion and integrity that truly defines the courageous, for courage becomes a quality of character rather than an isolated heroic display, a trait rather than a single action. Although courage is certainly seen in isolated actions, the greatest displays of courage—like those of Gandhi and Martin Luther King Jr., Rosa Parks, and Mother Teresa—are displays of one's fundamental character.

Reading and Writing about the Issue: Is *Wikipedia* a Legitimate Research Source? p. 327

Because anyone can add and edit entries in *Wikipedia* and because entries frequently contain errors, many instructors—and in some cases, college departments—question *Wikipedia*'s legitimacy as a research source.

Summary of "A False *Wikipedia* Biography" by John Seigenthaler, p. 328

Seigenthaler's essay discusses his own defamatory *Wikipedia* biography that recast his work for Robert Kennedy as involvement in his assassination plot. While the specious biography remained online for four months, Seigenthaler worked to no avail to find the person responsible for defaming his character and found that the current new media laws seem to protect everyone but him.

At Issue: Sources for Developing an Argument by Definition, p. 330

1. Students should list Seigenthaler's objections to everything originally posted to *Wikipedia* about him except for the sole correct fact—that is, he "was

Robert Kennedy's Administrative Assistant in the early 1960s" (para. 4). (The piece by Seigenthaler in *Practical Argument* predates the posting of the Seigenthaler biography currently on *Wikipedia.*)

2. Seigenthaler contacted the founder of *Wikipedia* (7), found the defamer's IP address (10), contacted the user's Internet provider by email (10) and phone (12), and consulted an attorney because the Internet provider (BellSouth) was required to protect the user's identity (13).
3. Students will likely identify the illegitimacy of *Wikipedia* as a research source as the point Seigenthaler wants his story to make.
4. Seigenthaler mentions the Web site's enthusiastic supporters (5, 16) and funding as a nonprofit foundation (16) as potential arguments in defense of *Wikipedia,* but he does little to advance these points as counterarguments. He could point to the thousands of error-free postings, the revolutionary potential of giving free access to information, and even the protection Internet users are afforded by law as other counterarguments.
5. Some students may argue that the essay is not an argument because it has no thesis statement or a concluding statement about what should happen to *Wikipedia;* others will argue that Seigenthaler's essay is an argument that points to the problems of new media enabled by Congress (18).
6. Seigenthaler's concluding anecdote reminds readers that gossip has long been considered evil. The metaphor suggests that like feathers flying out with no hope of returning to their original containment, the proliferation of gossip cannot be wholly undone; Seigenthaler positions *Wikipedia,* far-reaching and rife with potential for gossip, as an analog.

Summary of "Anonymous Source Is Not the Same as Open Source" by Randall Stross, p. 331

Stross's article discusses the problem anonymity presents for credibility, a problem that *Wikipedia* founder Jimmy Wales rejects. Informative but critical, Stross explores the growing problem of anonymity on the site when the site's mammoth growth leaves little potential for accountability.

At Issue: Sources for Developing an Argument by Definition, p. 334

1. Students should suggest that *Wikipedia*'s philosophy maintains that collectively interested parties will work to perfect the information for a particular entry and that this collective is as reliable, perhaps more so, than a single, traditionally credible source.
2. Students should suggest that in paragraphs 7–10, 12, 21, and 28, Stross seems most concerned about the credibility of the authors and entries. Referring to the "Wikipedian hive" in paragraph 11, Stross constructs an unflattering and perhaps dehumanized image of worker bees whose efforts are superfluous.
3. Responses will vary, but many students may not understand the terms *anonymous source* and *open source,* and for that reason will suggest that Stross define

them. Point students to paragraphs 23, 24, and 27, and ask students if they can glean a definition of *open source* from the context. Also, to reinforce the skills covered earlier in this chapter, consider asking students to define these terms in this article and how and where students might insert these definitions to strengthen Stross's argument.

4. Student opinions about whether or not *Wikipedia*'s strengths outweigh its weaknesses will vary; Stross outlines *Wikipedia*'s strengths in paragraphs 14 through 19.

5. Some students may point to the rapid development of technology and how it is daily changing the shape of education and the workforce, while others may point to America's "rugged individualism" by suggesting that single-author works will never seem strange in an individualistic culture.

6. Stross refers here to the "featured article status" mentioned in paragraph 26, a status afforded to less than one thousand articles that have been pristinely polished and verified, a status that for Stross would upgrade *Wikipedia* to a newer, better version of itself, what he wittily calls Version 1.0.

Summary of "About the *EoE*," *Encyclopedia of Earth*, p. 335

This selection from the *Encyclopedia of Earth* provides some welcome background on the site. (We had never used it or heard of it previously.) The page explains the need for the encyclopedia, those behind it, the source of its content and its scope, the editorial and publication process, and its intended objectivity. It concludes with an explanation of its relationship to *Wikipedia* and the larger Earth Portal site.

At Issue: Sources for Developing an Argument by Definition, p. 340

1. The *Encyclopedia of Earth* differs from *Wikipedia* in that, although it may include content from *Wikipedia*, the content of *EoE* is scrutinized by those with "core areas of expertise" and rewritten if necessary. All material is then reviewed prior to publication in *EoE*.

2. Only credentialed experts are able to add and edit material in *EoE*.

3. *EoE* has a substantive policy on objectivity (see p. 338). They strive for neutrality and attempt to be as inclusive as possible when considering sides of a dispute. They also attempt to acknowledge when a controversy exists.

4. As discussed in the response to the first question, *EoE* limits content from *Wikipedia* to that which has been reviewed by experts.

5. Students may point out that *EoE* should be much more reliable than an open site such as *Wikipedia* because of its review standards. For that reason we think it is likely to be more reliable in its particular subject area. However, *Wikipedia*'s breadth of content probably makes it a better general purpose encyclopedia than *EoE*. Students, however, should understand that the content in *Wikipedia* is often not reviewed by experts.

Summary of "Wikiphobia: The Latest in Open Source" by Neil Waters, p. 341

Waters, a professor of history at Middlebury College in Vermont, recounts the national and international media attention he and Middlebury received after the history department passed a brief, two-point policy forbidding students to use *Wikipedia* as a source.

At Issue: Sources for Developing an Argument by Definition, p. 343

1. Students are likely to find the history department's policy unfair, as most are likely avid users of *Wikipedia*. To an academic, like those in the history department at Middlebury, the policies are likely to make sense.

   Teaching tip: Ask students to recall the rules for evaluating online sources covered in Chapter 8. You might consider having students use these criteria for evaluating pages of *Wikipedia* or to compare an entry in *Encyclopedia Britannica* with an entry on *Wikipedia*. If your objective is to disprove *Wikipedia*'s validity, you may want to preselect at least a few pages that you know are erroneous. This project would also work well in a small group.
2. *Wikipedia* is such a widely used source that most Internet users are familiar with it. It continues to grow widely. Recently studies have analyzed the quality of the information in it as compared to traditional encyclopedias; *Wikipedia* came out surprisingly well.
3. Student opinions about whether or not Waters oversimplifies the issue of using *Wikipedia* will vary; however, students might point to some of the following as additional points Waters could have included as arguments against *Wikipedia:* the problems of citing articles that contain flaws, the likelihood that those writing about history do so with outdated knowledge, and even the idea that historians presently attempt to tell a story from multiple and varied viewpoints—which *Wikipedia* and other encyclopedias are not likely to include.
4. Students should identify paragraphs 4 and 5 as those containing arguments in favor of *Wikipedia;* they should point to sentences 4–8 of paragraph 5 as well as sentences 2–4 of paragraph 6 as refutation.
5. In summarizing Waters's reasons for thinking that *Wikipedia* is not an acceptable research source, students should describe *Wikipedia* as open source and as containing erroneous information.

Summary of "Wikipedia with Caution," Stanford Daily, p. 344

This editorial from the Stanford University newspaper suggests that the Middlebury history department's policy regarding *Wikipedia* is "a bit overzealous" (para. 7). While the editors agree that *Wikipedia* should not be cited in an academic paper, they believe a policy that bans the source should be replaced with a less formal, cautionary note.

At Issue: Sources for Developing an Argument by Definition, p. 345

1. Students should suggest that the editorial finds the policy forbidding the use of *Wikipedia* overzealous and note that, according to the Stanford editorial, the site is perfectly useful, with caution, for a definition or as a first-glance resource. The editors do agree, however, that *Wikipedia* should not be cited in serious academic work.

   Teaching tip: This might be a good time to remind students of the chapter's larger theme, and to ask them how and where *they* would define *serious academic work*.

2. Students' definitions of *acceptable source* might specify, for example, information from a peer-reviewed journal article or a government database; work by a professor or a professional in the field; and a writer whose credentials are verifiable.
3. Students should suggest that an "example" is a single instance to support a particular point, while an "authoritative source" is used to develop, hone, or refine an idea or argument.
4. Student opinions will vary; encourage students to give support and reasons for those opinions.

Summary of "Revision History of 'Global Warming' [in *Wikipedia*]," p. 346

This image shows a list of revisions performed to a single entry on global warming over the course of a few days.

At Issue: Sources for Developing an Argument by Definition, p. 347

1. The excerpt lists the reviser's screen name as well as the time and date of each revision. For each change offered, the reviser specifies a reason for the change; revisions also discuss appropriateness of sources offered by other revisers.
2. Some students will point to the discussion of source validity and seeming attention to detail as indicators of the attention paid to the site. Other students, however, may note the minimal substantive changes that seem to occur given the number of revisers listed.
3. Students may describe the material as impressive, suggesting that site revision and improvement are continual and unending. For some, that suggestion will increase the source's credibility.

Summary of "Global Warming (Differences between Two Revisions)" (Visual Image), p. 348

This image shows the actual in-text revisions performed to a single entry on global warming in one day.

At Issue: Sources for Developing an Argument by Definition, p. 349

1. The revision reveals only a minor change in wording at the beginning of the passage. Some may argue that the change is less specific than the original version.
2. Student opinions will vary.
3. Student responses will vary.

   Teaching Tip: Do your own search the night before teaching this particular exercise. Bring printed examples of versions to compare in class (small groups would limit the amount of examples you need to provide), or, if you have access to a computer lab, allow students to compare versions online.
4. Again, student opinions will vary.

   Teaching tip: Ask students to consider the nature of the revision and whether or not it improves the article. Also, since this is the last entry in the At Issue section, consider asking students to support their opinions with evidence from the other articles they have read.

Exercise 12.6, p. 350

For this exercise, students fill in the blanks to create their own arguments. A sample response follows with the given text in boldface.

Template for Writing an Argument by Definition

Many people are questioning the use of ***Wikipedia*** **as a legitimate research source. A** ***legitimate source*** **can be defined as a source that** has a reputable author and always cites credible and verifiable information. **According to this definition,** ***Wikipedia*** is not a legitimate research source because its authors are anonymous and information presented as fact is not always credible or verifiable. **Not everyone agrees, however. Some people say that** *Wikipedia* is just as reliable as other encyclopedias. **Others say that** the information is consistently monitored by knowledgeable and interested parties. **Although these points make sense, it is clear that** the anonymity of *Wikipedia* authors does affect one's ability to view the site as just as reliable as print encyclopedias or other verifiably authored and expert-reviewed texts. **In conclusion,** ***Wikipedia*** should not be considered a legitimate source for citation in college research papers.

Exercise 12.7, p. 350

This exercise asks students to interview two or three instructors about their opinion of *Wikipedia*'s legitimacy and to revise the draft from the previous exercise to include these opinions.

Exercise 12.8, p. 350

This exercise asks students to write an argument by definition on the topic of whether *Wikipedia* is a legitimate research source; defining *legitimate research source* should be the central focus of their argument.

Exercise 12.9, p. 351

This exercise, like the one concluding the previous chapter, asks students to think foundationally about the arguments they are forming by reviewing the four pillars of argument discussed in Chapter 1. Students should review their own argument to check for the inclusion of these pillars, add anything that is missing, and then label the essay by identifying these parts.

Writing Assignments: Argument by Definition, p. 351

This chapter ends by offering three writing assignments. The first asks students to consider whether college instructors should have *academic freedom*, the second asks students to consider whether *community service* should be required for graduation, and the third asks students to rate the service and food at a college eatery by defining terms like *excellent*, *good*, *bad*, or *poor*.

CHAPTER 13

Causal Argument

This chapter introduces students to **causal arguments**—arguments that are concerned with the causes and effects of events or situations. In some cases, these arguments attempt to find the reasons for a given outcome, and at other times, such arguments consider the possible outcomes. For instance, an essay that addresses the question, Why don't more Americans vote? may look at the reasons behind low voter turnout—causes such as distance to the polling station, interest in the issues, ease of registering to vote, apathy toward or disillusionment with politics, and so on. On the other hand, to answer the question, Do single-sex schools improve students' academic performance? an essay could look at the possible outcomes of single-sex education to trace if, and how, these environments contribute to academic success.

This chapter's readings and discussion focus on the question, Will Lowering the Drinking Age Solve the Problem of Binge Drinking among College Students? The At Issue box at the start of the chapter provides useful background information regarding current laws that set the legal drinking age at twenty-one, and it explains a bit about the debate over changing these laws. Like many of the other At Issue themes in this book, this issue will spark much discussion among your students, as it affects them directly. However, keep the discussion profitable by looking at causes and effects overall rather than at personal anecdotes from the weekend.

What Is Causal Argument? p. 354

As the introduction to the chapter notes, causal argument depends on linking causes to outcomes or on identifying the consequences of an argument. To provide concrete examples for students, the text offers a bulleted list of questions that ask for causes. These questions offer topics for full papers for students to investigate at greater length.

Exercise 13.1, p. 354

This exercise directs students to look at the visuals and consider what causes and effects they'd discuss if they were creating a causal argument about one of the given statements (p. 354). The statements are provided here in boldface with possible answers.

- **Guns don't kill people; people kill people.**
    - Causes: availability of guns; American attitudes toward guns; laws that allow for self-defense; incorrect use and storage of guns; drugs, gangs, and poverty in certain areas
    - Effects: crime rates; gun accidents in homes with children; changes to legislation involving gun control; laws that seek to deter criminals from engaging in gun-related crimes; school shootings
- **Caution: Cigarette smoking may be hazardous to your health.**
    - Causes: addictiveness of nicotine; advertising that entices young people to smoke; legislation that led to this warning by the surgeon general
    - Effects: smoking as a cause of cancer, emphysema, or other lung disease; issue of secondhand smoke (hazardous not just to smokers' health but also to the health of others); current debates about smoking in public places
- **Friends don't let friends drive drunk.**
    - Causes: drunk-driving rates among teenagers; binge drinking; drinking on campuses; underage drinking; availability of alcohol
    - Effects: setting the legal drinking age at twenty-one; formation of groups such as Mothers Against Drunk Driving and Students Against Drunk Driving; ad campaigns that urge responsibility; crackdown by law enforcement for DUIs and DWIs

Understanding Cause-and-Effect Relationships, p. 357

To encourage your students to consider the complexities surrounding cause-and-effect relationships, have them list all the possible factors that cause a certain situation and/or list the possible outcomes of a given event or action. In this way, students can move beyond simple black-and-white, two-sided notions of argumentation and follow debates through from beginning to end. Remind them to think of the various factors that impact a certain problem or issue, and ask them to consider the issue from various perspectives. Doing so will help them brainstorm for topics for their causal-argument essays. In response to the question, Why don't more Americans vote? the diagram in the text (p. 358) simulates brainstorming and gives possible reasons for low voter turnout.

Teaching tip: As your students look over the diagram, ask them to note groups of people who might be associated with each of the causes given (students, parents, working people, people who rely on public transit); as a result, students may realize that their own lists of causes and effects should incorporate various points of view.

Main and Contributory Causes, p. 357

Within the category *causes*, not all factors are equal. Instead, for any outcome, there is usually a main cause and a series of secondary, contributory causes. Students have practice identifying these in Exercise 13.2.

Exercise 13.2, p. 358

This exercise directs students to look back over the diagram (p. 358) and consider which are the main and contributory causes and why. Students should also address whether all the factors listed on the diagram are causes, and if they should suggest other causes. Have students consider, as well, which cause they would focus on and what support they would use if they were to write a paper explaining why so many Americans do not vote.

Immediate and Remote Causes, p. 358

Sometimes the causes of a certain outcome are not easily identifiable. To identify a cause-and-effect relationship more clearly, it is important to understand immediate and remote causes. An immediate cause is the most obvious cause of a given outcome—the one that occurs right before an event. The example in the text is of a political scandal that becomes news the day before an election and seemingly upsets the election results. In reality, that outcome may have been affected by one or more remote causes, factors that occurred further in the past but had a more significant impact.

Exercise 13.3, p. 359

For this exercise, students are asked to identify and answer a series of questions about the remote and immediate causes on the diagram (p. 358). It may be a good idea to have them list the various causes under the headings *remote* and *immediate*, then to create the headings *main* and *contributory* to see which overlap.

Causal Chains, p. 359

The example in the text uses a causal chain to explain why some Americans do not vote. Understanding how one event or phenomenon leads to the next can help students establish an outline that leads readers from a thesis statement to a conclusion. The example also suggests key words for causal arguments (p. 360).

Exercise 13.4, p. 360

This exercise has students fill in the blanks of several causal chains. Possible examples are provided below, with the given text in boldface.

1. **Restaurants should be required to list fat and calorie content on their menus. If they do so,** customers will be aware of the nutritional value of the foods offered. **As a result,** customers can stay within their recommended caloric and fat intake each day. **Eventually,** people will learn which foods have lower fat and calorie values and will develop healthier eating habits.
2. **Abstinence programs should be instituted in high schools. One immediate result would be** a more public debate among parents, students, educators, and health-care professionals on the role of morality and health in public education. **This could bring about** a more nuanced look at current sex-ed programs and the question of whether abstinence-only is a beneficial or detrimental policy. **This in turn might lead to** a compromise between those who advocate teaching abstinence-only and those who advocate teaching safe sex. **Ideally,**

the result would be young people who hear both sides and are able to make an informed decision about sex.

3. **Taxes on cigarettes should be raised. If this step is taken, the first result would be** more income for state and local governments. **Another possible effect might be** that smokers may try harder to quit, in order to avoid the steeper cost of supporting a cigarette habit. **In a few years' time, the outcome might be** that the income on cigarette taxes is able to cover the cost of health care for those who suffer from smoking-related illnesses.

Post Hoc Reasoning, p. 360

As students consider causal chains and the overall cause-and-effect relationships of social and political issues they encounter, it is only fair to remind them that not every event that precedes another is a cause. Seeing all preceding events as causes means falling into the logical fallacy of *post hoc* reasoning, which is described in Chapter 5. The excerpt provided in Exercise 13.5 gives students examples of *post hoc* reasoning.

Exercise 13.5, p. 361

This exercise asks students to read the included essay by Nora Ephron and to identify the cause-and-effect relationships she discusses. Second, students should list several plausible causes for each effect, as Ephron's take is really just a humorous look at *post hoc* reasoning.

Summary of "The Chicken Soup Chronicles" by Nora Ephron, p. 361

In this brief article, Ephron relays a series of *post hoc* arguments to illustrate the shortcomings of some cause-and-effect thinking. Be sure to remind students that Ephron's is a humorous article, meant to illustrate *post hoc* reasoning—not an *actual* argument by the writer.

Cause-and-effect relationships Ephron discusses:

- Ephron says that because she got a cold even after eating chicken soup—the tried-and-true preventative—chicken soup actually *causes* colds (para. 1).
- She argues that the rise in breast-feeding has led to increased allergies in children (2).
- She reasons that the rise in computer technology has led to a decline in the quality of screenplays (3).
- In her most outlandish example, she argues, through a hastily constructed causal chain, that hand-washing leads to memory loss (4).

Other plausible causes for each effect:

- Ephron neglects to mention that a virus could have caused her cold; that close contact with someone sick could have given her this virus; that chicken soup—as a cure—is merely folklore, and that if she had already been infected, nothing would have prevented her from getting sick (1).

- Ephron looks at two developments that occurred simultaneously and essentially says that one caused the other. She says that recently breast-feeding has become more popular and regarded as a healthier option that may even prevent some childhood allergies. Also, she says that recently more children have been diagnosed with allergies so that breast-feeding must *cause* allergies. She neglects to mention that doctors may just be able to diagnose allergies earlier; that better medicine and education have led to a better understanding of allergies; or that more parents see allergies as a serious threat to their children's health and are, therefore, more willing to have them treated (thereby raising the number of children with allergies, compared with years ago) (2).
- Ephron links screenplays with the ease of writing on the computer. She neglects to mention that she's evaluating the quality of current movies against the standards of the 1930s (the movies she cites as good are from this decade), does not discuss how new categories of movies have evolved, and oversimplifies the process of writing a high-quality movie, as if it only involves the ability to put pen to paper or type on a computer (3).
- Ephron states that, for hand-washing to be effective, people should wash for the same amount of time it would take to sing "Happy Birthday." But Ephron admits that she forgets where she read this piece of advice and concludes that the practice of hand-washing leads to memory loss. Clearly, there are many other causes of memory loss—illness, old age, injury, or trauma (4).

Structuring a Causal Argument, p. 362

This section begins with a useful overview for your students to consider when they organize causal arguments. While there is, of course, leeway in how a causal argument is organized, most follow the progression that's given: Introduction (including thesis), Refutation of opposing arguments, Evidence (first point in thesis), Evidence (second point in thesis), and Conclusion.

Summary of Student Essay "Texting: A Boon, Not a Threat, to Language," p. 363

In response to popular opinions about texting and its effects on language, Kristina Mialki argues that texting is actually a creative use of the English language and has the power to make communication more effective and enticing. She says that texters often "spend hours each day engaged with language" (para. 4) and that texters "continually [play] with words and [come] up with new ways of expressing themselves through language" (5). Her ultimate conclusion is that texting "is keeping the language alive" (1).

Teaching tip: While there is no exercise that works directly with this sample student essay, you may consider the following activity:

- After students read through the essay, have them construct a rough outline of its structure.

- Have students consider how Kristina arranges the components listed under "Structuring a Causal Argument" on p. 362. Why might she have chosen this arrangement?
- Ask them if they, as readers, think they were more likely to agree with Kristina's causal argument because of the way she organizes her paper. What additional suggestions do they have for strengthening her argument?

Grammar in Context: Avoiding "The Reason Is Because," p. 365

This text box includes guidance on integrating support into a causal argument. As with all grammar instruction, it is important to tie grammatical usage to student work. Grammar taught in isolation from student work is much less likely to benefit students.

Exercise 13.6, p. 365

This exercise asks students to read the essay "U.S. Needs an Educated Citizenry" by Marjorie O. Rendell and then to answer a series of questions. Here is a summary of Rendell's piece, followed by possible answers to the questions.

Summary of "U.S. Needs an Educated Citizenry" by Marjorie O. Rendell, p. 365

Using a quotation from Benjamin Franklin as a springboard, Rendell argues that American citizens have disengaged from the democratic processes that sustain this country. She states that more needs to be done to create a knowledgeable citizenry and then to inspire that citizenry to participate in their communities and government. In order to have more educated and informed citizens, Rendell states that American public schools must "once again make civic education the cornerstone of public education" (para. 9). Ultimately, Rendell says that it is the duty of citizens to maintain and sustain their government, to keep it accountable, and to keep it moving forward. And she states that to face the challenges of the next generation, citizens have to "rise to the challenge of serving their communities and the nation" (17).

Identifying the Elements of a Causal Argument, p. 367

1. In paragraph 4, Rendell argues that only a third of Americans trust their federal government and are, therefore, not engaged in sustaining the republic that Ben Franklin and other founding fathers helped create. Ask your students how Rendell strengthens her causal argument by going back to one of the earliest "causes" of our nation—the sentiments of the founders of the nation.
2. Citizens distrust the government → Citizens withdraw from participating in government → Declining participation by citizens causes a decline in the quality of governance → Citizens further disengage from their communities and the nation.

3. Rendell says that the lack of involvement and even the disillusionment many citizens face come from a lack of knowledge. Citizens need to know how they could and should engage in the democratic process and be "productive citizens."

4. *Recommendations Rendell makes for how to solve the problem she discusses:*
   - American citizens need to be more informed about how "citizen participation benefits democracy" (para. 6).
   - We "must recognize the role that public schools . . . must play in training young people for active citizenship" (7).
   - Civic education needs to be "the cornerstone of public education"—a "joint commitment on the part of individual schools, as well as policymakers at every level" (10).
   - Students need to be educated about how to participate in their "communities, government and society" (12).
   - Schools should promote civic engagement both in the classroom and also through service-learning projects (14).
   - States and the federal government should "include civics on mandated assessments" to be sure it's being taught in schools and isn't edged out by other subjects (15).

5. Rendell argues that an informed and active citizenry will be able to answer national challenges from "energy dependence to the rising deficit to the wars overseas" by rising to the challenge and serving their communities and the nation as a whole.

6. In her closing statement, Rendell refers to the earlier quotation by Ben Franklin and says we can "keep the Republic" only if America's public schools return to teaching civics and active citizenship in their classrooms.

Reading and Writing about the Issue: Will Lowering the Drinking Age Solve the Problem of Binge Drinking among College Students? p. 368

Sometimes causal arguments sound too academic or removed from our students' everyday lives. This At Issue section seeks to help students understand how causal arguments work by drawing on a subject that they likely know a lot about and have strong opinions on, as well. Some of the writers in this At Issue argue that the drinking age should be lowered—that doing so would reduce binge drinking problems and be a fairer way to treat eighteen- to twenty-one-year-olds as adults—and others argue that the drinking age should remain at twenty-one or even increase to twenty-five in an effort to ensure that those consuming alcohol act in a responsible and safe way. However your students feel about this issue, they will find in this At Issue articles, editorials, and even a position paper that rely on causal arguments.

Summary of Amethyst Initiative's "Statement," p. 369

This statement, issued by the Amethyst Initiative, calls on elected officials to reconsider the current drinking age laws by supporting a "dispassionate public debate" over the effects of these laws and to "invite new ideas" about the best ways to prepare young adults for making decisions about alcohol. This is a petition, of sorts, by more than a hundred college presidents who say that the current drinking age of twenty-one is "not working" and that it actually encourages binge drinking and disrespect for the law.

At Issue: Sources for Developing a Causal Argument, p. 370

1. Students should compose a thesis statement such as the following: "The current legal drinking age of twenty-one is not working, so it's time to rethink this law."
2. Paragraph 5 argues that adults under twenty-one are able to vote, sign contracts, serve on juries, and enlist in the military but they are told they aren't "mature enough to have a beer." To refute this argument, students might argue that the listed rights all involve civic duty or responsible engagement in society; drinking does not fall into this category. Students can further refute the argument by pointing out that it oversimplifies the situation when it says those under twenty-one just want to have "a beer"; clearly, the issue is about binge drinking and drunk driving.
3. The statement does not explicitly call for lowering the drinking age. Instead, it argues for a "dispassionate public debate" and a reconsideration of the current laws (para. 7).
4. The statement asks elected officials to
   - support a public debate over the effects of the current drinking age, twenty-one (7)
   - "consider whether the current 10% highway fund incentive encourages or inhibits that debate" (7, 8)
   - "invite new ideas about the best ways to prepare young adults to make responsible decisions about alcohol" (7)

   In exchange, the college presidents say, "We pledge ourselves and our institutions to playing a vigorous, constructive role as these critical discussions unfold" (8).
5. You may want to remind your students of the ways that authors establish *ethos,* or credibility. In this statement, the college presidents simply set themselves up as knowledgeable and experienced in regard to the issue of drinking (they know the history behind the laws, and they can list ways that the current laws are "not working"). Because they pledge their support, they indicate that they are trustworthy and willing to follow this debate through.

Summary of "Amethyst Initiative's Debate on Drinking a Welcome Alternative to Fanaticism" by Radley Balko, p. 371

Opinionated from the opening sentence on, the article by Balko expresses his take on the recent discussion about the drinking age and the ways that certain groups, including the Amethyst Initiative, are encouraging public debate about the issue. Balko provides background on how the drinking age was first set at twenty-one and includes studies by economic researchers and various organizations, either denouncing or backing the current law. In the end, Balko argues that an open, honest debate about the drinking age *is* necessary and that it's foolish to dismiss the people behind the Amethyst Initiative—especially, given their experience with college students.

At Issue: Sources for Developing a Causal Argument, p. 373

1. Student responses to this question will vary depending on how effective they think a delayed thesis statement would be. Many students have been taught to include a thesis statement up front, but using Balko as an example, you might show how a delayed thesis statement can be an effective rhetorical choice.
   - Your students should be able to identify Balko's thesis at the end of the essay, in paragraph 15. Here, Balko argues that "the nation's policy makers would be foolish to dismiss" the concerns expressed by the Amethyst Initiative, as they have "collectively spent thousands of years with the very young people these laws are affecting" (para. 15).
   - Have students express this argument in their own words, and then ask them why Balko may have delayed his thesis until the end of the article. Most likely he did so to build readers' support for his position. Writers often use this technique if the issue is one their readers will already feel strongly about. See if your students think the delayed thesis is an effective strategy, and ask them if there are hints earlier in the essay that indicate Balko's position without stating it directly (such hints are necessary when the thesis is so delayed).
2. *Summaries of problems regarding higher drinking age:*
   - Balko states that any time something is prohibited, the restriction leads to overindulgence.
   - Balko states that the current drinking age is flouted by college students, and it forces underage drinking underground.
   - Because drinking underage is illegal, Balko says those under twenty-one are less likely to seek medical help if someone needs treatment from over-drinking.

   See what other examples your students can list as problems that the current law causes. For instance, students may argue that the current law mystifies alcohol (as Balko states later on, in paragraph 14), or they may say that students are more likely to find themselves in compromising situations since drinking is forced underground and out of the comfort of public spaces.

3. *Balko on the Amethyst Initiative:*
   - In paragraph 3, Balko discusses the Amethyst Initiative, saying that the group calls for "a new national debate on the drinking age." He also states that the group of college presidents "say the federal minimum drinking age has contributed to an epidemic of binge drinking, as well as other excessive, unhealthy drinking habits on their campuses."
   - Balko accurately characterizes the group's position—that it is asking for a public debate—but omits other considerations that the group calls for (in the last section of the statement). Also, because of the tenor of Balko's article, it seems as if Amethyst's position is to change the drinking age from twenty-one, when the group never explicitly states this goal.
4. Other than Miron and Tetelbaum, Balko does not cite others to support his position.
   - Miron and Tetelbaum's research indicates that the studies that look at the number of highway fatalities after the drinking age was raised to twenty-one use some inappropriate data (9).
   - Miron and Tetelbaum also state that there are other considerations for the decrease in highway fatalities, such as medical advancements and better safety standards in cars (10, 11).
   - Ask what other support students would like to see, or if there are other potential causes for lowering the number of fatalities linked to drinking.

   Teaching tip: Ask students to identify the *kinds* of causes Balko is using in his article—such as major and contributory causes, or immediate and remote causes.
5. *Inflammatory vs. neutral language:*

   Balko's article is slanted from its opening sentence, so it is useful to see how your students respond to his style. Do they feel attacked, do they mind his sarcasm, or do they feel he was unfair to his opponents? If they do object to his slanted language, have them select a few lines that include inflammatory words and then rewrite them to sound more neutral. This exercise will help them in their own work—especially, when they're writing about something they feel strongly about.

Summary of "Alcohol and Those under Twenty-One Don't Mix" by Joanne Glasser, p. 374

Joanne Glasser is the president of Bradley University, and she writes this article in response to the current discussion surrounding minimum drinking-age laws. While at Bradley, she says she's been determined to toughen the enforcement of underage drinking laws. Glasser both presents information in support of her argument and refutes those who say that lowering the drinking age will reduce binge drinking and its associated problems.

At Issue: Sources for Developing a Causal Argument, p. 375

1. *Glasser's refutation of the university presidents:*
   - Glasser first mentions the Amethyst Initiative's position in paragraph 3, and refutes it in paragraph 4, when she states, "I vehemently disagree that lowering the drinking age would make college campuses safer."
   - This statement seems to be the first part of Glasser's thesis but not her whole thesis. Instead, in the remaining part of the article, Glasser argues that colleges and universities must make more of an effort to "combat the misuse of alcohol" (para. 16) by developing more preventive policies (10), educating students (12), and instituting stronger penalties for violations (13).
   - Ask your students whether Glasser's thesis was clear enough or if it should have been more explicitly stated.
2. *Glasser's data:*
   - The National Highway Traffic Safety Administration report regarding lower numbers of drinking-related highway fatalities (6);
   - A 2005 Harvard University study that found binge drinking is lower in states with tough laws on "high-volume sales" (7);
   - Two University of Minnesota researchers who stated that a higher drinking age reduces alcohol consumption (8);
   - A statement by a "leading expert on the misuse of alcohol," Henry Wechsler of the Harvard School of Public Health, who says that lowering the drinking age would not "reduce the misuse" of alcohol (9);
   - An American Medical Association statement that says lower drinking ages led to fewer alcohol problems, providing strong support for keeping the current drinking age (10).
   - Ask your students if the preceding data are facts or if they seem taken out of context or plucked from statements to arbitrarily support the writer's opinions.
3. *Glasser's anecdotes in paragraphs 1 and 5:*
   - In both instances, Glasser uses the anecdotes to gain her readers' support through *pathos* (appealing to emotion).
   - See if your students think both anecdotes are effective. Also ask if Glasser's conclusion about the twenty-two-year-old's death is fair or if it hurts her overall argument.

Summary of "Raise the Drinking Age to Twenty-Five" by Andrew Herman, p. 376

This argument may seem surprising, given that Herman is a college student, but in this article, he states that the only way to reduce alcohol-related injury, assault, accidents, and deaths is to increase the drinking age to twenty-five. This change will reduce the availability of alcohol to those who are underage (because they will have fewer connections to those who can legally drink), and it will require Americans to wait until they're more mature before they are legally allowed to drink. Herman also refutes those who advocate lowering the drinking age, and he cites various studies to support his argument that college students simply cannot handle the responsibility of drinking.

At Issue: Sources for Developing a Causal Argument, p. 377

1. Students may be surprised that a college student, like them, would not want to have free rein and to lower the drinking age. How might this very fact make him more credible in their eyes? Do they take his thoughts more seriously, or do they dismiss him? Remind them that even if they don't agree with him, they can still find his position credible.
2. *Common ground:*
   - Herman is writing to college students—to his peers—and so he opens with a discussion about going back to school and the prevalence of alcohol on college campuses. This beginning draws students into his article and helps readers see Herman as one of them.
   - Herman uses inclusive language such as *our* and *we*. In this way, he identifies himself with his readers and, at the same time, puts the burden on them to take responsibility and overcome the abuse of alcohol on campus.
   - Throughout his article, Herman describes common scenarios that his readers would be familiar with—from the college party scene to the regularity of dangers associated with alcohol (rape of someone they know, death of a loved one, and so on). These scenarios play on *pathos* but also remind students of stories they've heard or of people they know who've been negatively affected by alcohol. Therefore, readers are more likely to agree with his position.
3. In paragraph 14, Herman acknowledges the position of those who want to lower the drinking age. They state that "gradual transition to alcohol" will reduce alcohol abuse. Herman counters this argument by saying those under twenty-one already misuse alcohol, so it seems unwise to "grant free rein to those individuals to do it legally" (15). He also compares lowering the drinking age to a parent who observes his child abusing the neighbor's dog and then buys a dog for the child without altering his dangerous behavior. This analogy seems like a stretch, and your students will likely think it is a bad comparison. Ask them which kind of logical fallacy this might be, and challenge them to come up with a better refutation.

Summary of "Save Us from Youth" by Bradley R. Gitz, p. 378

Drawing on the argument that laws should be based on consistency, Gitz argues that the drinking-age debate should not center on questions of maturity or responsibility but should be evaluated for consistency. He states that because people are considered adults at eighteen—able to vote, serve in the military, and engage in other "consensual adult behavior"—then they must also be allowed to drink; or, conversely, those other rights need to start at twenty-one to be consistent with current drinking laws. Above all, for Gitz, consistency is the key concern in the debate.

At Issue: Sources for Developing a Causal Argument, p. 379

1. *Gitz's thesis:*
   - Students should identify and compose a thesis similar to the following: To be consistent with other legal rights of adulthood—such as voting, serving in the military, and engaging in consensual adult behavior—we must either allow those between eighteen and twenty-one to drink, or we must raise the legal age of other rights of adulthood to twenty-one.
   - Make sure your students are clear—while Gitz seems to advocate lowering the drinking age, he also allows for the possibility of increasing the age people have to be to do other things like vote and so on. What's most important is consistency.
   - Ask students: How does this argument fundamentally change the debate about college students and alcohol?
2. See if your students were confused by the Emerson quotation, and ask them who Gitz's ideal audience is. How might Gitz be using Emerson to establish his own credibility? How might using Emerson's quotation distance him from readers? What other strategies for introductions could be more effective?
3. Most of Gitz's argument is based on logic: if we allow people certain rights of adulthood at eighteen, how is it logically consistent to deny them one particular right of adulthood (drinking) until twenty-one? In paragraph 5, Gitz puts this into moral terms, saying that current laws are unethical if they are not consistent. Ask your students why Gitz might include this *ethos* appeal, when everything else in his article is based on concrete logic. How might his use of the phrase "morally acceptable" make his argument seem weightier?

Summary of "There's No Benefit to Lowering the Drinking Age" by Robert Voas, p. 380

As the title of this article clearly states, for Voas there is no merit to the idea of lowering the drinking age. He calls the debate "extremely frustrating" and says that those who advocate changing the law do so based on "glib conjecture and self-selected facts" (para. 2). Voas goes point by point to refute the main arguments his opponents make, and at the end he reveals that he has studied the issue of drunk driving for nearly forty years and has been involved in public health and behavioral health for fifty-three years (11).

At Issue: Sources for Developing a Causal Argument, p. 381

1. *Voas on Gitz:*
   - In paragraphs 4 and 5, Voas tackles Gitz's argument that if adults of eighteen are allowed to be in the military, they should also, according to the principle of consistency, be allowed to drink. Voas argues that "going to war and being

allowed to drink" have nothing in common, and he states that the reason the military recruits young people is that they are not yet physically and mentally developed, so the military can mold them into soldiers. He also states that the last thing platoon leaders and unit commanders want is for young soldiers to be allowed to drink.

- See if your students think this is a strong enough refutation. And what do drinking and going to war have in common, if anything?

2. *Voas's attitude toward opponents:*
   - Throughout his article, Voas is very dismissive of those in favor of lowering the drinking age. He says their arguments rely on "glib conjecture and self-selected facts" (para. 2). He also states that they "ignore or manipulate the real evidence and instead rely on slogans" (3).
   - In contrast, Voas sets himself up as *the* authority on the issue—one who has spent years in research and who promotes the facts (2, 11).
   - Ask students what they think of Voas's dismissive—even, at times, condescending—tone. Is it warranted? Were they put off by it? And why might he be justified in his frustration, as he indicates in paragraph 2?
3. *Voas's credentials:*
   - Voas states that he has been "studying drinking and driving for nearly forty years and [has] been involved in public health and behavioral health for fifty-three years" (11). This background establishes him as an expert on the issue, not just a person who's frustrated by the current debate about lowering the drinking age. See if students would have liked to know this before they read his argument; where would they have had him disclose this information about his experience?

Exercise 13.7, p. 382

This exercise directs students to fill in the blanks to create a causal argument in which they take a position on whether or not to lower the drinking age. A possible response is provided below, with the given text in boldface.

Template for Writing a Causal Argument

In 1984, the federal drinking age was raised to twenty-one. Since that time, there have been many positive results, such as lower numbers of alcohol-related crashes. **However, there have also been some negative effects. As over 100 college presidents who favor reconsidering the federal drinking age point out,** with the legal drinking age set at twenty-one, many college students take their drinking underground, leading to more binge drinking and alcohol abuse. **MADD and others, however, argue against lowering the drinking age, noting that** doing so will only make alcohol abuse on college campuses legal. **Granted,** there is some risk in lowering the age back to eighteen, and there may at first be a backlash as eighteen- to twenty-one-year-olds acquire alcohol legally. **Still,** if we allow citizens at eighteen to serve their country in the military, to vote, to sign contracts, and to be consenting adults, we have to be consistent and allow them this other right of adulthood. **For these reasons,** public officials, college administrators, parents, teachers, and the public should engage in an honest debate about how to best transition the drinking age from twenty-one to eighteen.

Exercise 13.8, p. 382

This exercise has groups of two or three discuss their own experiences with drinking in high school and in college and determine whether or not they think current drinking laws cause or exacerbate an interest in alcohol. You will want to be sure to keep students focused in this exercise on relating their observations to the debate in these articles—whether or not it would be best to lower the drinking age, raise it, or keep it the same. What you *don't* want students to do is simply recount humorous or even damaging stories from weekend adventures. At the end of their discussion, the groups should draft a paragraph that explains their position on the issue, based on their experiences.

Exercise 13.9, p. 382

Now students have a chance to compose a causal argument of their own that answers the question, Will Lowering the Drinking Age Solve the Problem of Binge Drinking among College Students? Students should begin by considering a list of *all possible causes* of binge drinking, then determine which factors are most to blame. Finally, they should consider whether lowering the drinking age would have a positive or negative effect on the problem. They may include the paragraph they composed for Exercise 13.8, if they like. Students should also cite information and ideas from the readings in this chapter and document each source in their essay.

Teaching tip: Before they compose their essays, remind students, once again, about the kinds of causes included in causal arguments. For their essays, they can identify some of the contributory causes or even what appears to be the immediate cause of binge drinking, but eventually they should pin down what they think is the major cause or even, in some cases, the remote cause. You may also want them to review the tips for "Structuring a Causal Argument" on page 362.

Exercise 13.10, p. 383

This exercise, like those concluding the previous chapters, asks students to think foundationally about the arguments they formed for the previous exercise by reviewing the four pillars of argument discussed in Chapter 1. Students should review their own argument for the inclusion of these pillars, add anything that is missing, and then label the essay by identifying these parts.

Writing Assignments: Causal Argument, p. 383

This section allows you to take the concept of causal argumentation beyond the At Issue theme of drinking-age laws. In these three activities, students will look at how causal arguments may allow them to encourage fellow students to live healthier lifestyles; students can investigate how pictures of celebrities in popular magazines are causal arguments in visual form and will consider how they impact readers' self-esteem; and, finally, students will look at why children's lives are more structured now than they were years ago. Of course, these are just a few examples of the kinds of causal arguments that are possible, but they give your students more freedom to consider how cause-and-effect relationships can help them construct strong arguments about these and other current social and cultural issues.

CHAPTER 14

Evaluation Arguments

Evaluation arguments, which express an opinion about the quality of an idea or thing, are commonly found in everyday life and will probably be a familiar form to your students. Students have likely read online consumer opinions about a product at Amazon.com or have read film reviews at Rottentomatoes.com; students themselves may have written abbreviated evaluation arguments on their Facebook or MySpace pages. This chapter's At Issue selections focus on an equally familiar subject—that is, the Harry Potter phenomenon. The question addressed by those selections is, Do the Harry Potter Books Deserve Their Popularity?

Teaching tip: Since this chapter is focused on Harry Potter and most, if not all, of your students will be familiar with the books or movies, consider asking students to freewrite about their experiences with the texts, to narrate their favorite or least favorite scene, to tell the story of their first encounter with the texts, or to tell the story of why they've avoided the books or movies. Asking students to explore their memories about the texts in writing will prepare them for work later in the chapter and may naturally lead them to evaluative language. Consider having students return to this freewrite after they've completed Exercise 14.2 (p. 386), which introduces students to a list of evaluative words. Ask students to scan their freewrite for evaluative language. This teaching tactic can make arguments by evaluation seem less unfamiliar by reinforcing the notion that students already know how to make evaluative assessments and incorporate them into their writing.

What Is an Evaluation Argument? p. 386

The text suggests that students constantly make decisions about positive and negative qualities—whether thinking about an upcoming party or selecting clothes or electronics to purchase. This section of text also provides a bulleted list of the kinds of questions that lead students to write an argument by evaluation.

Teaching tip: Consider having students make a list of things they evaluated in the time between waking and class; possibilities might include choosing something to wear, taking or not taking a shower, eating *x* and not *y* for breakfast or lunch, and so on.

Exercise 14.1, p. 386

This exercise asks students to make a list of ten topics suitable for evaluation arguments. Ideas that students may suggest include standardized testing, the effect of course caps, most useful or useless required college courses, scholarships, tuition, dorm conditions, television shows or movies, best or worst toothpaste, brands of ice cream, pizza, or fast food.

Exercise 14.2, p. 386

This exercise asks students to choose one word from each pair of words in the following box (p. 387). They should then use each word in a sentence that evaluates a service at school. Example responses follow:

- Campus medical services here are *superior* to those at other universities.
- Financial aid is *useful* to many students.
- The library is an *inefficient* place to conduct research because online sources have rendered it outdated.
- Wireless Internet services are highly *effective* on this campus.
- The campus email system is *successful* in meeting student needs.
- Counseling services are *deserving* of increased funding because of the number of students they serve.
- Admissions is one of the most *important* services on campus.
- Greek life is *trite* as it replicates sororities and frats all over the country.
- Late transportation on campus is *predictable.*
- The study abroad program is *interesting* because it offers a lengthy list of places to study.
- Because of their age and dilapidation, the dormitories are *depressing.*

Making Evaluations, p. 387

Here the text provides a bulleted list of words commonly used to wage evaluative arguments; the section is brief.

Criteria for Evaluation, p. 387

As this part of the chapter suggests, it is not enough to determine the quality of an idea or thing in an evaluation argument; writers must also explain the criteria by which they formed the value judgment. Importantly, the text distinguishes criteria supporting positive judgments from those supporting negative ones by suggesting that when making a positive judgment writers reveal how an idea or object meets or exceeds criteria, while when making a negative judgment they reveal how the object fails to meet particular criteria. Usefully, this section concludes with a list of questions about an example subject—each question points to a different criterion for evaluation.

Exercise 14.3, p. 388

This exercise asks students to select a topic listed for Exercise 14.1 and to list five possible criteria for an evaluation argument on the topic. For example, students might choose *standardized testing* and list the following five criteria for evaluation:

- Usefulness in measuring an individual student's learning
- Fairness to all students
- Scores necessary for federal funding of schools
- Effect of test prep on the rest of the curriculum
- Relationship of high scores on standardized tests to readiness for college

Exercise 14.4, p. 388

For this exercise, students partner to consider the criteria by which they evaluate their college textbooks, determine the most important criteria, and evaluate *Practical Arguments*, their course text.

Teaching tip: For a positive evaluation, students might imagine their evaluative arguments as blurbs for the back of their textbook.

Structuring an Evaluation Argument, p. 388

As in previous chapters on forms of argumentation—such as Chapter 6's coverage of Rogerian, Toulmin, and oral argument and Chapter 12's work on argument by definition—this section shows the structure of an evaluation argument as a bulleted list.

Summary of Student Essay "Not Just a 'Girl'," p. 389

Following the structure just outlined, this student author makes an argument about Jig, the female character in Ernest Hemingway's short story "Hills Like White Elephants"; she is frequently seen as a sexist representation of women typical of Hemingway's work. Unlike most critics, this student writer suggests that Jig is a "complex, sympathetically drawn character" (para. 1).

Teaching tip: Appendix A (p. 713) offers a brief discussion of literary arguments, which students may find useful to read in conjunction with this sample essay—particularly, if you will require students to write a literary argument.

Grammar in Context: Comparatives and Superlatives, p. 392

Since comparatives and superlatives are frequently used in writing evaluation arguments, this textbox provides examples of correct and incorrect usage likely to appear in student writing for this chapter.

Exercise 14.5, p. 393

This exercise asks students to read a newspaper editorial entitled "Do We Have the World's Best Medical Care?" and to answer questions about it; a brief summary of the editorial and sample responses to the questions follow.

Summary of "Do We Have the World's Best Medical Care?" *Kalamazoo Gazette*, p. 393

This editorial draws from a study comparing health care in the United States with that in 190 other countries, offers seven criteria for evaluation, and explains how and why the United States falls well below the best.

Identifying the Elements of an Evaluation Argument, p. 395

1. Students should identify the final sentence in the first paragraph as the editorial's thesis statement; their restatements of that thesis should focus on how health care in the United States provides neither timely nor effective care.
2. Student opinions will vary, as evaluation requires them to make value judgments. Require students to explain their reasons for choosing a particular criterion.
3. In the *Access* section, the author suggests that while waits for specialists or elective surgery are shorter in America, getting care on nights or weekends is more difficult than in other nations and waits are generally longer to see one's own doctor. While the study ranked quality of care in the United States first, care for the chronically ill, protection of patients, and meeting patient's needs and preferences lowered the U.S. rating to last (among five). Additionally, surgical and medical mistakes occur more often in the United States than in other countries. Finally, the survival rate for several diseases is the best in America; however, the author refutes that ranking by quickly noting that the survival rate for several other diseases is worse in the United States than elsewhere.
4. The editorial concludes that the United States certainly does not offer the world's best health care but resolves that the knowledge of its failures accompanied by the country's political and economic power means that it should be able to reach that ranking.

Reading and Writing about the Issue: Do the Harry Potter Books Deserve Their Popularity? p. 396

Since the publication of the first Harry Potter book, *Harry Potter and the Sorcerer's Stone*, in 1997, fans have been mesmerized and critics have been questioning the book's merit. Advocates of the series laud the stories as imaginative, while detractors have criticized everything from their poor writing to their central theme. As the textbox at the outset of this chapter (p. 386) explains, more than twelve years later, their popularity (and marketing) has only continued to grow. While the franchise continues in film, video games, and a host of consumer products, so does the debate over whether or not the books deserve all the attention.

Summary of "An Epic Showdown as Harry Potter Is Initiated into Adulthood" by Michiko Kakutani, p. 397

In this book review of *Harry Potter and the Deathly Hallows*, the final book in the Harry Potter series, Kakutani largely applauds J. K. Rowling's achievements with the series. Calling her ability to negotiate such an intricate seven-volume plot

"Dickensian" (para. 10), Kakutani offers little criticism of the final tome other than suggesting it has "some lumpy passages of exposition and a couple of clunky detours" (2).

At Issue: Sources for Developing an Evaluation Argument, p. 399

1. Student thesis statements for Kakutani's review should mention Rowling's ability to blend fantasy and reality to create a new world for the reader.
2. Students should list the following positive statements by Kakutani:
   - "monumental, spellbinding epic" (2)
   - "good, old-fashioned closure" (2)
   - "astonishingly limber voice" (3)
   - "she manages to make Harry both a familiar adolescent [. . .] and an epic hero" (9)
   - "magpie talent"; "effortlessly mixes up allusions" (9)
   - "created a world as fully detailed as L. Frank Baum's Oz or J. R. R. Tolkien's Middle Earth" (10)
   - "so minutely imagined [. . .] it qualifies as an alternate universe" (10)
   - "Dickensian ingenuity and ardor" (10)
3. Students should suggest that Kakutani evaluates the book and series based on a number of criteria; they might list the book's ability to transport readers to another world, the artistry of the narrative, the author's ability to give voice to characters to match the craft of renowned children's texts.
4. *Kakutani's adjectives:*
   - Monumental; spellbinding; good old-fashioned; heart-racing, bone-chilling; lumpy; clunky (2)
   - Limber; youthful; philosophical; somber (3)
   - High-spirited (4)
   - Familiar; epic; magpie; mythic (9)
   - Alternate; passionate; fervent; breadcrumb; jigsaw-puzzle; Dickensian; important (10)

   While the adjectives do not all have positive connotations, most of them do; the inclusion of less positive adjectives suggests the reviewer attempted to write a more objective evaluation of the text, by recognizing that even a generally praiseworthy book is not perfect.

   Teaching tip: To ensure that everyone in your classroom knows what an adjective is, consider having students define the term and search for a few together as a class. While some students may find this juvenile, others may welcome the refresher.
5. In paragraphs 9 and 10, Kakutani compares the Harry Potter series with other children's books or characters from other texts; her comparative evaluation is positive, as she likens Rowling's craft to that of renowned author Charles

Dickens and suggests that she created detailed, imagined worlds that match those of fantasy masters L. Frank Baum and J. R. R. Tolkien.

Summary of "We're All Still Wild about Harry" by Carlie Webber, p. 400

Carlie Webber opens with a quick précis of the Harry Potter books. Harry, raised by his ordinary (if not affectionate) aunt and uncle, finds his destiny when he attends a school for wizards. Webber argues that "these books are not focused on mischief and adventure. Instead, they explore good, evil, love and death" (para. 6). She argues that it is the characters' humanity that comes through in difficult situations that makes the books stand out. The characters are not intended to be perfect role models, and that is one of the reasons for their appeal.

At Issue: Sources for Developing an Evaluation Argument, p. 402

1. Webber says that the books are so compelling because Rowling builds on the "literary tradition of the hero's journey" (para. 9), a tradition that includes Star Wars and the Lord of the Rings books.
2. Rather than evaluating the books as literature, Webber asks why they are compelling. Her answer is that "readers take joy in watching Harry and his friends grow" (10).
3. Byatt might agree with Webber that the books are compelling but might not feel as Webber does that the characters are "painfully real" (10).
4. Given her effusive praise of the series, it is clear that Webber, like many other adults, is a fan of the Harry Potter books.

Summary of "Harry Potter and the Childish Adult" by A. S. Byatt, p. 403

First criticizing the book as a conventional family romance that appeals psychologically to its fantasizing, adolescent audience, Byatt then criticizes Harry's adult readers, whom she sees as regressing. While she suggests that regression offers comfort and is common, she laments that adults are swept into the poorly constructed realm of Rowling's magic rather than into better, more exciting literary worlds.

At Issue: Sources for Developing an Evaluation Argument, p. 405

1. Her allusions to other thinkers and literary works suggest that Byatt presumes a highly literate audience and attempts to reinforce her own status as a qualified literary critic by touting her knowledge.
2. Byatt does criticize the books as derivative, conventional, and lacking in imagination, but she also seems to criticize both Harry Potter readers (particularly

adult readers) as well as cultural studies (which finds critical merit in the texts), and ultimately links both to a general dumbing down of culture that no longer appreciates true mystery but prefers, as she quotes Roland Barthes, "consumable" books (para. 15).

3. Byatt explains the appeal of Harry Potter books to children as a stage of psychological development, according to Freud, when adolescents romanticize the fantasy of having a heroic purpose. Similarly, she explains the books' appeal to adults in psychological terms, suggesting that adults find regression comforting.
4. In paragraphs 5, 7, 11, 12, and 14, Byatt speaks comparatively about the Harry Potter books and other works of literature. She sees the other works as superior because they are not derivative but original (5), have a greater sense of the numinous (7), construct authentic mystery (11, 12), and employ real wit and good writing (14).

Summary of "A. S. Byatt and the Goblet of Bile" by Charles Taylor, p. 406

Attacking A. S. Byatt's "Harry Potter and the Childish Adult" (p. 403), Taylor vehemently refutes Byatt's arguments about the text and applauds Rowling's work.

At Issue: Sources for Developing an Evaluation Argument, p. 410

1. Taylor refutes Byatt's idea that the work offers comfort (para. 2) and reassurance (4), is full of "ersatz" magic (6), lacks real mystery (7), and appeals to the uncultured. He argues, respectively, that the darkening plots and orphan theme deny comfort and reassurance, that her pronouncement about the series' lack of real magic is merely an opinion, that she herself is among the hordes of readers in the concrete jungle who do not know real mystery, and that judging society as uncultured and "stupid" (8) reveals her arrogance.
2. Taylor agrees that Byatt has a point—that many people embrace popular trash and shy away from the complexities of art; however, he denies that these acts are a typical reader's experience with the Harry Potter series. In other words, readers embrace the series as having the "troubling complexities of art" (3). Accordingly, for Taylor, reader experience and Rowling's narrative artistry seem the most important criteria for assessment. Student opinions about the validity of Taylor's criteria will vary; be sure to require students to offer reasons for their opinions.
3. Students will likely suggest that the informality and lack of scholarly allusion are a weakness in an essay evaluating works of popular literature. However, you may wish to point out that the essay is really a response to Byatt's work, which Taylor does quote and use as a source.

4. It is likely that students will view paragraph 9 as an *ad hominem* argument.

   Teaching tip: Consider having students search for other paragraphs where Taylor criticizes Byatt more than her essay (1, 2, 4, 7, 13). Ask students whether or not this tactic affects the author's credibility.

Summary of "Harry Potter's Girl Trouble" by Christine Schoefer, p. 411

Looking at female characters in the first three books of the Harry Potter series, Schoefer critiques what she reads as Rowling's inability to imagine a strong, female heroine who defies stereotype.

At Issue: Sources for Developing an Evaluation Argument, p. 413

1. Schoefer evaluates the Harry Potter books for sexism and establishes this criterion in her first paragraph.
2. Schoefer identifies Hermione and Minerva McGonagall as strong but stereotypical characters; she does praise the author for her imagination and ability to make passionate readers of children. Regarding features that Schoefer ignores, some students may suggest that she does not really discuss the shortcomings of the male characters or the oafish male characters—certainly Dumbledore is seen as a wise wizard by many, but Minister Fudge perpetually tries to discredit him. She does not mention Hagrid's clumsiness, Professor Lockhart's vanity, Professor Snape's cruelty, or Professor Quirrel's weak will. Likewise, some may argue that she does not see the flaws in Ron (temper, juvenile behavior, fear) or Harry (temper, secretiveness), or the strengths in Hermione (bravery, wit, knowledge) and Ginny (who by the fifth book proves to be a brave and formidable counterpart to Harry). Pointing to some of these omissions, students may be willing to suggest that Schoefer does unfairly slant her analysis.
3. Schoefer supports her argument that the Harry Potter books are sexist by pointing to the displacement of Hermione from real action; the strictness of McGonagall; the treatment of Ginny Weasley as a sniveling little girl in the second book; the dismissal of Trelawney's divination as a discredited and female art; fleeting, but more favorable, descriptions of male denizens in Diagon Alley; and generally stronger, more positive descriptions of male characters. As minor arguments against her position, Schoefer acknowledges that Hermione does earn the boys' respect (para. 5) and that girls can imagine themselves in male roles (12). However, as noted above, she does not acknowledge the weaknesses of male characters or offer a more holistic look at female characters' strengths.
4. Student responses will vary, but they should address the following questions:
   - Is our longing for a magical world so deep, our hunger to be surprised and amazed so intense, our gratitude for a well-told story so great that we are willing to abdicate our critical judgment? (12)

- Or are the stereotypes in the story integral to our fascination—do we feel comforted by a world in which conventional roles are firmly in place? (12)

Exercise 14.6, p. 414

For this exercise students fill in the blanks to create their own arguments. A sample response appears here with the given text in boldface.

Template for Writing an Evaluation Argument

The first Harry Potter book, published in 1997, was a publishing sensation that turned into a worldwide phenomenon. Many people saw the Harry Potter books as valuable for a variety of reasons. For example, many applauded the texts' imaginative plots that captivated readers of all ages. **Also,** supporters of the continuing series noted the growth of complexity in vocabulary, character, and theme to match the progress of texts' target simultaneously growing audience. **However, some people have criticized the series. They claim, for example, that** the story is poorly written and a poor derivative of older, better books. **Others believe that** the text is sexist or anti-Christian by virtue of its central theme. **Depending on the criteria used for evaluation, the Harry Potter books can be seen in positive or negative terms. If we judge on the basis of** reader reception and experience of the texts, **it seems clear that they are** successful children's books destined to become classics.

Exercise 14.7, p. 414

This exercise asks students to discuss in small groups their reactions to the Harry Potter books and to evaluate the texts based on their collective experiences; groups should write a paragraph summarizing their conclusions.

Teaching tip: If earlier in the chapter you did not ask students to freewrite about their first experiences with Harry Potter, you may want to have students write for a few minutes before joining a group. As with any class discussion of a popular subject, conversations can rapidly digress, so writing may help to focus conversations more clearly on substantive evaluation—rather than on unabashed praise or criticism.

Exercise 14.8, p. 414

For this exercise, students should write an evaluation argument that takes the At Issue question as its topic, arguing that the Harry Potter books either do or do not deserve their popularity; students should cite the readings within this chapter to support their position.

Exercise 14.9, p. 415

This exercise, like those concluding previous chapters, asks students to think foundationally about the arguments they formed for the previous exercise by reviewing the four pillars of argument discussed in Chapter 1. Students should look for these pillars in their own argument, add anything that is missing, and then label the essay by identifying these parts.

Writing Assignments: Evaluation Arguments, p. 415

The chapter ends by offering three writing assignments. The first asks students to write an evaluation argument about a course they feel strongly about, the second asks students to challenge a popular position on the quality of a product or service with which they are familiar, and the third asks students to write a comparative evaluation that argues one thing is superior to another.

Teaching tip: While each prompt offers several topic suggestions, a class brainstorming session to generate additional topics is always productive.

CHAPTER 15

Proposal Arguments

Another form of argumentative writing, the **proposal argument** suggests a solution to a particular problem. At first, students may think proposal arguments are rare or unusual, but you can easily give them examples, above and beyond those in the text, of this kind of argument showing up every day—from opinion pieces in the newspaper to print ads and television commercials.

The focus of this chapter's At Issue is whether or not college instructors should be required to make their lectures available as podcasts for students. The opening text box gives background, explains the main problem with traditional in-class lectures, and suggests a way that podcasts can help students stay up-to-date with their work. More information appears in the At Issue articles toward the end of the chapter.

Teaching tip: To prove to students that proposal arguments are, indeed, all around them, have them analyze the visual (p. 419) and discuss how this ad both illustrates a problem and proposes a possible solution to that problem. At some point in this chapter, you might consider bringing in other magazine ads or television commercials and leading a discussion on the ways proposal arguments appear in pop culture.

Stating the Problem, p. 420

The first thing a writer needs to do when composing a proposal argument is to establish that a problem needs attention. Remind students that for this part of their argument, they'll definitely need to think about how much information and background their readers need to understand a particular problem. In some cases, the writer will not need to explain much about the problem—especially, if readers will likely agree that it is a problem and are familiar with the debate surrounding the issue. But at other times, the writer *will* need to go further to explain in detail the situation he or she is addressing and to establish why it's a problem that needs a solution.

Proposing a Solution, p. 421

When proposing a solution, writers should consider how much evidence, support, and context are needed for readers to see the merit of the proposed action. Often, an anecdote or two—especially, if this solution has been used by others in similar situations—help. Students also need to consider the consequences of the proposed solution and be sure their solution is not overly idealistic or simplistic.

Teaching tip: Often, when students address a problem, they have difficulty proposing a detailed, specific, well-thought-out solution. In fact, they may avoid specificity altogether and say simply that "something needs to be done." Remind them that it's their job, as writers, to figure out what that "something" is and to be sure it can be implemented (see the section on feasibility).

Establishing Feasibility, p. 422

Along with considering the consequences of a proposed solution, students should consider what is feasible—that is, practical and doable. Determining feasibility—cost-effectiveness, legality, and logistics—may take some additional research. Questions of feasibility differ for each proposed solution.

Discussing Benefits, p. 423

One of the strongest parts of a proposal argument should be the way the writer explains the benefits of his or her proposed solution. To present these benefits effectively, students should discuss not only the immediate but also the long-term effects of their proposed solutions and categorize them as monetary benefits, quality-of-life benefits, health benefits, educational benefits, and so on.

Addressing Possible Objections, p. 423

Anticipating objections to their proposal argument and considering ways to address these objections amount to the process of refutation, mentioned earlier in this text. For all proposal arguments, writers should assume readers will have if not objections then at least questions about the proposed solution, so writers will want to explain the solution in detail.

Exercise 15.1, p. 423

This exercise asks students to consider proposal thesis statements and to give evidence they could present in support of each. Possible answers are provided.

1. *Evidence to support the placement of warning labels on all sugared cereals:* Sugary foods contribute to obesity and often lack important nutrients; Americans need to know the nutritional information of what they're eating; many Americans don't realize that a diet high in sugar can lead to various health problems; childhood obesity is also a problem, and a high percentage of people

who eat sugary cereals are children; illnesses and complications associated with obesity cost taxpayers a great deal of money every year.

2. *Evidence to support the banning of all gasoline-burning cars in ten years:* Climate change is a real problem; carbon pollution associated with gas-burning cars is one of the major causes of climate change; alternative fuels and sources of energy do exist and can be ready to go in ten years; phasing out gasoline-burning cars would likely drive down the cost of cars that rely on alternative fuels (and now are quite expensive); while people know they need to use cleaner-burning fuels, they won't do so until they absolutely have to.
3. *Evidence to support the mandate that candidates for president use only public funding for campaigns:* This requirement would level the playing field for candidates; it would cut back funding from special-interest groups and political action committees; the high costs associated with the election would come down greatly.
4. *Evidence to support a plan that teachers carry handguns to protect themselves and their students from violence:* School violence is a real problem, especially in inner-city schools; since students bring guns to school, teachers need a comparable means to defend themselves and their students; most schools do not have advanced systems in place to deal with gun violence.
5. *Evidence to support reducing prison overcrowding by releasing all nonviolent offenders:* Prisons in America already exceed capacity; in some cases, sentences are already reduced because there is not enough room to keep offenders behind bars; violent offenders should be the top priority of the prison system; nonviolent offenders can be monitored in other ways.

Exercise 15.2, p. 424

For each proposal in Exercise 15.1, this exercise has students state two problems that the solution would create. Possible answers are provided.

1. *Problem 1:* It is not the job of the government to regulate each American's eating habits or choices.

   Problem 2: If such labels are used on sugary cereals, the government would also have to consider labels on other sugary and fatty foods. Where would it end?

2. *Problem 1:* Some people could not afford cars that run on alternative forms of energy.

   Problem 2: Manufacturers have not agreed on a suitable replacement for gasoline energy. There needs to be an agreed-upon standard for the practical issues of getting fuel and maintaining the car.

3. *Problem 1:* If candidates had to use public funding, they would have to severely cut back on the number of campaign advertisements and appearances, reducing the information that goes to millions of Americans.

   Problem 2: With less funding, candidates would likely focus on urban centers, rather than more remote, small towns. They'd want to get the most for their dollar, and that would mean they would go only where the most voters would hear their messages.

4. *Problem 1:* Teachers may be forced to compromise their principles regarding gun control if they were made to carry guns with them to school.

   Problem 2: There would be an increase in gun-related accidents, as the guns may fall into the hands of students, or teachers may use their guns unnecessarily.

5. *Problem 1:* It is not safe to simply release nonviolent offenders, as they may repeat their crimes when released (and this group may include burglars, embezzlers, drug users, and so on).

   Problem 2: Releasing nonviolent offenders would send a message that laws forbidding nonviolent crimes are not enforced. There likely would be a rise in these crimes, as a result.

Exercise 15.3, p. 424

This exercise asks students to look at the ad (p. 424), which encourages recycling. Possible responses are provided.

- *Problem:* The advertisement identifies the problem as the disposal of paper waste in New York City, leading to climate change.
- *Solution:* The advertisement offers recycling of paper as a solution.
- *Support:* The ad announces the statistic that New York City throws out more than 400,000 tons of recyclable paper every year; the ad campaign is supported by the various organizations and companies identified in the black band.
- *Image:* The image memorably illustrates how the amount of paper New York City throws away each year could fill the Empire State Building. Ask students how the image provides support or if it's merely memorable.

Exercise 15.4, p. 425

As in Exercise 15.3, students should identify the problem, possible solutions, and the evidence that the writer, John Leo, introduces to support his argument. Students should also consider how the writer anticipates objections to his solution and what additional supporting evidence he might have used. Possible responses are provided.

- *Problem:* Leo addresses two main problems in his humorous poem. First, he confronts the fact that many underclassmen have only teaching assistants for teachers rather than tenured, full professors until later in their college careers. Leo thinks this is an injustice. Second, Leo takes on the issue of high tuition.
- *Solution:* Leo's solutions include assigning professors (not TAs) to undergrads; eliminating remedial classes; cutting the cost of tuition by canceling all courses that end in "studies" (such as, presumably, "American studies," "women's studies," "religious studies," and so on); cutting out certain courses that Leo thinks are worthless (the examples he gives mostly focus on pop culture).

- *Objections:* Leo anticipates that professors won't want to deal with underclassmen; that people will object to eliminating low-paying (that is, cost-efficient) TAs; that some will say remedial classes are "a must"; that the "fuddies" and "duddies" will be offended by eliminating certain courses.
- *Evidence:* Leo uses very little support—likely, because of the form of his argument, a humorous, rhyming poem. However, see if your students think he gives enough support or how they think he can creatively add more support for his solution.

Exercise 15.5, p. 426

This exercise has students consider John Leo's argument (in the form of a poem) that they read for Exercise 15.4. They should then write a one- or two-paragraph response in which they argue for or against his recommendations. Remind students to clearly identify the problem Leo is addressing, as well as the strengths or weaknesses of his proposal. You may have them share their paragraphs or thoughts aloud, to get them used to identifying problems, solutions, support, and objections.

Structuring a Proposal Argument, p. 426

There are several ways to structure a proposal argument, but this section provides one of the best and most logical outlines for this kind of writing: introduction, explanation of the problem, explanation of the solution, evidence in support of the solution, benefits of the solution, refutation of opposing arguments, and conclusion. These elements were outlined in detail earlier in the chapter.

Sample Student Essay: "Colleges Need Honor Codes," p. 427

To illustrate the suggested structure for proposal arguments, the text includes an essay by student Melissa Burrell. While there is no formal exercise directing students to interact with this essay, you might consider the following activity: have students go through the essay, paying particular attention to the labels for each element of the proposal argument as they go along; then have students get into small groups and consider whether the essay could be structured in a different way and if doing so would impact their reception of Burrell's argument.

Grammar in Context: *Will* versus *Would,* p. 430

Since *will* and *would* are frequently used in writing proposal arguments, this textbox provides examples of correct and incorrect usages likely to appear in student writing for this chapter.

Exercise 15.6, p. 430

This exercise instructs students to read the essay by T. Boone Pickens titled "My Plan to Escape the Grip of Foreign Oil." Students should then respond to the series of questions (p. 433) that looks at how Pickens's essay is a proposal argument. Possible answers are provided.

Summary of "My Plan to Escape the Grip of Foreign Oil" by T. Boone Pickens, p. 431

Pickens's proposal may at first seem surprising for an oil executive. In this essay, he argues that America's dependence on foreign oil is dangerous and that it is time to make use of the country's extensive wind and natural gas resources. Pickens outlines a plan that he says will reduce America's dependence on foreign oil by more than one third over the next five to ten years. Pickens wrote this essay just months before the 2008 presidential election.

Identifying the Elements of a Proposal Argument, p. 433

1. Pickens's thesis statement appears at the end of the introductory paragraph, when he states, "Now our country faces what I believe is the most serious situation since World War II." This statement is, of course, vague, and could be made stronger if he were to include or hint at his proposed solution. See what your students think and if they could clearly identify his thesis.
2. Pickens identifies the problem he wants to solve in paragraph 2, when he states, "The problem, of course, is our growing dependence on foreign oil—it's extreme, it's dangerous, and it threatens the future of our nation." Ask students why Pickens introduces the problem right away, without much background or discussion. (You might remind them that this essay was written just four months before the 2008 presidential election.)
3. The United States now imports 70% of its oil (para. 3), making us reliant on "[other countries'] good judgment, and most importantly, their good will toward us" (6). The United States spends a staggering amount of money on importing oil, with only 4% of the world's population (4, 5, and 6). Global demand now exceeds global output; as a result, oil prices will continue to rise and, eventually, the United States will find it difficult to obtain all the oil that it needs (7).
4. Pickens begins listing his solution—his "plan"—in paragraph 9 and spends paragraphs 9, 10, 11, and 12 outlining how it will work and what benefits it will produce.
5. *Benefits:*
   - Pickens discusses the solution and benefits simultaneously, beginning in paragraph 10. There he states that using natural gas for transportation would "displace more than one-third of foreign oil imports." He also adds that wind and natural gas are "cheap and clean."
   - In paragraph 11, he says his plan will afford us "time to develop new technologies and a new perspective on our energy use."
   - In paragraph 12, Pickens states that his plan not only reduces dependence on foreign oil but also "lowers the cost of transportation," "invests in the heartland," creates "thousands of new jobs," "reduces America's carbon footprint and uses existing, proven technology."
   - Ask students what other benefits Pickens's plan may produce.

6. *Counterarguments:*
   - Pickens could have addressed the issue of cost feasibility. Many of his opponents would cite this as an issue, as the wind turbines will need to be built, and more natural gas will have to be extracted from the earth. Should Pickens have explained the cost and his plan for paying for it in his essay?
   - Pickens states that the burden is on the government to act, but he also says his plan will be accomplished "solely through private investment with no consumer or corporate taxes or government regulation" (12). To some of his readers this statement may seem a contradiction. How could Pickens have explained his thinking better in his essay?
   - Pickens's readers, some of whom may live in the heartland, may object to having wind turbines and wind plants constructed in their communities. Pickens never addresses this dilemma. How could he have addressed it and refuted it?

Reading and Writing about the Issue: Should All College Instructors Be Required to Make Their Lectures Available as Podcasts? p. 434

As another example of an issue that affects our students, this collection of readings focuses on the use of technology in college classrooms, and, along the way, it gives students practice in identifying the elements and structure of proposal arguments. The sources—essays, articles, a blog, and an advertisement—identify various problems with current teaching styles and even problems with using technology to replace lectures. Each source then presents a solution. Equally important are the kinds of support the writers offer and the benefits they outline for readers, as both help determine the strength of their arguments.

Summary of "Lecture Is Dead: Take 3" by Murray Jensen, p. 435

As a college professor, Murray Jensen acknowledges the tumultuous relationship that higher education has had with technology over the years. In three different instances, Jensen says, technological advancements were predicted to replace the standard in-class lecture: first, the idea was videotaping the lectures; second, preparing the lectures via PowerPoint; and now, recording lectures as podcasts. But at least the first two times, technology did not improve student performance and, instead, caused a drop in student attendance. Still, Jensen acknowledges some of the benefits of podcasts and gives an example of how podcasts have benefited one particular student.

At Issue: Sources for Developing a Proposal Argument, p. 437

1. Jensen first recounts how videotaped lectures were the new technology in the 1970s, and then he describes the coming of PowerPoint in 2002. Finally, he

looks at how podcasts are being used academically and compares this development with the previous forms of technological advancements in the classroom.

2. Because of the way Jensen structures his essay, it seems that he fears the use of podcasts will cause a drop in student attendance, as did the use of videotaped lectures and PowerPoint presentations. Jensen thinks that podcasts may be effective only for motivated students and students who are able to teach themselves. For struggling students, podcasts will be an additional tool through which to learn biology, for instance, but these students will not have the personal interaction they need to do well (para. 9).
3. Jensen acknowledges that, for some students, lectures-as-podcasts are useful. In paragraphs 7 through 9, he describes one of his students, Melissa, and explains how podcasts allow her to still take classes while working and how they allow her to learn from home rather than making an hour-long commute to campus.
4. By book-ending his essay with quotations from a movie and a song, Jensen seems to indicate that pop culture is overtaking academia. Both quotations involve killing or death, which correlates with his title, "Lecture Is Dead: Take 3." See what your students think about these allusions. Did the quotations get their attention? How were the quotations supportive of Jensen's thesis?
5. Beginning with paragraph 7, Jensen acknowledges some benefits to making lectures available as podcasts. He states that for already-motivated and mature students podcasts are a way for them to teach themselves—much in the same way they might learn on their own from a book or by reading over lecture notes. But this example also allows Jensen to explain his reservations about the technology. If podcasts really help only motivated students, Jensen argues that the widespread use of podcasts could be detrimental to average or below-average students. See if your students understand the double-pronged nature of the Melissa example.
6. Jensen is really asking whether podcasts will be *the* technology that kills off in-class lecture. In the other cases he cites, the technology (videotapes and PowerPoint) did not win out, but this time, Jensen seems to think podcasts have staying power. See what your students think. Do they agree that podcasts will replace traditional in-class instruction? Why or why not?

Summary of "The Attack of the Pod People" by Robert Schneider, p. 438

In this forthright essay, Professor Robert Schneider describes how reading an article in his school's student paper led him to take up a cause against what he calls the "podcastification" of higher education (para. 19). He spends half his essay explaining why he is writing on this topic in the first place and then spends the latter half of the essay predicting what podcast lectures mean for education. Ultimately, he says that the use of podcasts to "teach" is an attractive option only for those who are either "lazy students" or "lazy professors" (18) and that while information can be transmitted "into a microphone for an hour and a quarter," he "would never call that teaching" (17).

At Issue: Sources for Developing a Proposal Argument, p. 440

1. The introduction runs from paragraphs 1 to 11 because Schneider has to set up his essay by explaining why he is writing about podcast teaching in the first place. In the long introduction, Schneider explains how he first encountered an article in his school's student paper that championed the use of podcasts as a replacement for traditional lectures. In frustration, Schneider drafts a response that is picked up by the paper and online but is distorted and "reduced to a silent sound bite in the ether, a floating phenomenon of technophobia" (9). Schneider goes on to compare this experience with the ways in which podcasts would distort his lectures. He states in paragraph 10, "What the electronic press had done to my arguments was exactly what I suspected podcasting would do to my lectures: shear them of all context and present them at the recipient's convenience, yes, but without style or conviction."
2. Schneider's disciplinary field is theater, and he compares its ephemeral and performative nature to teaching. One of Schneider's main points is that education is more than the transmission of facts—instead, his class meetings are events because they are a time of lively interaction and exchange (12); they require effort from both students and professors; class attendance indicates students' commitment to learning (13), and participation by students is necessary for him to know whether they're understanding his lecture or need more help (16). See if your students agree and if they consider your class an event. How would this "event" and interaction be lost via podcasts?
3. In addition to his argument that class time should be an event, Schneider says that making lectures into podcasts "dilutes the classroom experience" (18), that it rewards lazy students and lazy professors "whose principal goal is economy of effort, and whose principle product is boredom" (18), that it promotes "disengagement" (19) and is "an excuse for lack of commitment" (19). Ask students if they believe these arguments.
4. Have students go back through the essay and determine where Schneider uses slanted language or dismissive phrases. Do your students think Schneider's tone is productive or damaging to his argument (and his credibility)?
5. It's possible that because Schneider says he was criticized, unfairly, for not acknowledging how podcasts could benefit "handicapped students and students who couldn't come to class because of illness or religious holidays," his very mention of these cases may indicate that he's sympathetic toward using podcasts in these particular instances.

Summary of "Globalizing Education One Podcast at a Time" by Jeff Curto, p. 441

While Curto is also a college professor, he expresses a view opposite to the one Schneider articulates in his essay. He recounts how podcasts have opened his classroom to the world, allowing him and the students in his classroom to interact with a diverse group of students who attend virtually, from around the world. He also explains how easy it is for him to produce the material for his podcasts and then to upload the podcasts for delivery to his students. Curto argues that podcasts not only are more convenient for his students but also allow students to listen to lectures multiple times and learn the material more thoroughly.

At Issue: Sources for Developing a Proposal Argument, p. 443

1. Curto begins by saying that in the fall of 2005, he "opened the door of [his] 'History of Photography' classroom and found that there were hundreds of students on the other side" (para. 1). He goes on to describe the diverse group of students in his class, and says that "while the room only had 25 seats, hundreds of people were sitting in on my class session each week" (1). Only in the second paragraph does he acknowledge that many of these students were part of his *virtual* classroom, through podcasts. This strategy of letting information out slowly plays with readers' expectations and entices them to read more. Ask your students how they responded to this introduction.
2. Curto is clearly a supporter of podcasting in the classroom, and he states his position early on, in paragraph 2. Here, he quickly outlines the virtues of podcasting classes, allowing him to spend the rest of the essay giving details about how podcasting works and how it enhances both teaching and learning.
3. Ask students why Curto includes this definition of podcasting (3), and remind them that the answer might have something to do with audience consideration. What audience may he have in mind, and how much do they already know about podcasting? This article was published in *TheJournal.com*, which is a site focusing on education and technology. Curto considers his audience to be anyone interested in those issues. He doesn't, however, assume that his readership is familiar with all of the terms he uses, so he is careful to define those that might cause confusion.
4. *Arguments Curto presents to support his thesis:*
   - Podcasting allows for a diverse group of students to interact in the same virtual classroom (1, 2).
   - Class discussion is "not constrained by the classroom walls or by the cultural, educational, and personal backgrounds" of the students in a room (4).
   - Students see the world as a classroom (5).
   - Students have direct, immediate access to a variety of content, from audio files to visuals and other emailed content (5).
   - Students learn the material better because they can listen to it multiple times (5).
   - Podcasts are easy to create and allow the instructor to synchronize audio and visual files (6).
   - Podcasts are automatically delivered to students who subscribe (7).
   - Not many resources are needed to create podcasts, nor do they require much more of a time commitment on the part of the professor (8).
5. Curto's entire essay is a glowing look at how podcasts can revolutionize and improve nearly every aspect of the college class. Does this seem too slanted to

your students, and should he have acknowledged potential drawbacks of the technology? Ask them where they would add this material and how doing so might help to balance Curto's argument and make him seem more trustworthy.

Summary of "iPod Addiction Goes Academic," *Pitt News*, p. 444

This staff editorial gives a nod to the use of technology in the classroom but questions whether podcasting will help or hurt college education. The writer explains that making lectures available through podcasts follows a growing "trend of isolationism that is creeping up on Americans everywhere" (para. 6). Additionally, the writer questions the "cost" of turning to podcasting—both in the sense that virtual teaching can never equal the value of live lectures, presentations, and discussions, and in the sense that the literal cost of the iPods, laptops, and so on may not be feasible for all students.

At Issue: Sources for Developing a Proposal Argument, p. 445

1. One could argue that the whole essay—by explaining how podcasting is attempting to become the norm and how this is part of a trend toward isolationism in America, something else that has become the norm—is an answer to the opening question, "When does a fad become the norm?" Do students agree with the writer's assessment of what is the "norm"?

2. The writer seems to be sincere in praising educators, stating that they are trying to use the technology that so many students already have. Students should get the sense that, to the writer, the educators are making a good effort but that, in the end, the use of technology misses the mark. In this way, the congratulations in paragraph 5 are a bit sarcastic or at least tinged with doubt—because while educators are *trying* to use iPods as "academic tools," the writer believes that doing so lessens the quality of education that students receive (5, 10).

3. *The main disadvantages of using the iPod as an educational tool:*
   - Using iPods in lieu of live classes "reinforces the trend of isolationism that is creeping up on Americans everywhere" (6).
   - The cost of using iPods is not affordable for all students: one must consider the cost of an iPod itself, plus the cost of a computer (laptop or otherwise) that each student needs to download podcasts (8). As technology changes, students may have to buy new iPods (8). Students who can't afford the technology will be at a disadvantage (8).
   - Providing lectures on podcasts may make coming to class obsolete (9).
   - "There is no substitution for traditional teaching methods" (10).

4. The editorial comes out against lectures in the form of podcasts, categorizing them as a trend that cannot equal traditional lectures in quality. The writer acknowledges the good will of educators who are trying to use this technology as an "academic tool" (5) and explains why teachers would want to make content

available through podcasts (9). But the writer refutes those arguments by stating, in the last sentence of paragraph 9, that "making too much available to students is coming dangerously close to making in-class attendance obsolete." Further, the writer says that there is "no substitution for traditional teaching methods" (10).

5. Ask your students' for their opinions on this, and have them consider how the placement of the thesis affected their reception of the writer's argument. Students should discuss whether the delayed thesis made them more likely to hear the writer out or whether the delayed thesis made them too unsure of the essay's position.

Summary of "Teaching via iPod" by Fabienne Serriere (blog post), p. 446

The opening paragraph of this blog describes, briefly, the use of podcasts on college campuses and explains how some professors incorporate them as supplemental material, while other schools are introducing courses where "lecture casts" replace "actual human-led courses." The writer then invites input from readers, asking them what they think about classes that are "mp3/videocast only." Subsequent responses vary, but the most common thread among them is agreement that podcasts cannot replace "the real thing" (post 2) while admitting that podcasts are good to supplement the course, helpful for reviewing, and useful for distance learning.

At Issue: Sources for Developing a Proposal Argument, p. 448

1. It seems that most posters are in favor of *limited use* of podcasts. That is, they think that podcasts can be useful to supplement class lectures, that they help students review, and that they allow for distance learning. But all posters seem to agree that podcasts are not the equal of in-class experiences.

2. *Likes:*
   - More helpful than a PowerPoint and good for review/revision (post 1)
   - Useful for independent and "self-taught, self-motivated" types (post 3)
   - Helpful as a supplement to notes from the class and for catching up on notes students missed (post 4)
   - Valuable in allowing students to hear lectures by professors at other schools (post 5)

   Dislikes:
   - Useless without attached visual information and interaction (post 1)
   - Inadequate as a "substitute for the real thing" (post 2)
   - Missing commitment of going to class every day (post 3)

3. Posters 1, 2, and 3 all think that the podcasts cannot replace the value of being in class, with a real instructor in front of them.

4. Focus a discussion by asking students which classes are more suitable to being taught exclusively via podcast and which classes would not work well as only podcasts.

Summary of "iTunes U" (advertisement), p. 449

This is an advertisement for iTunes U, a site that distributes podcasts and course content. The various sections of the ad explain how iTunes U works and advocate for its place in higher education.

At Issue: Sources for Developing a Proposal Argument, p. 449

1. See if your students agree on who would be most likely to visit this site. Why would Apple advertise this service on its Web site? Have students consider the language used in the ad; phrases such as "what if you" and "teach you" mean that it is talking directly to students, not about them.
2. iTunes U is an interface that works through iTunes to deliver content and podcasts to students, directly from instructors. By going to the interface, students can sync their iPods and iPhones and take lectures, notes, and visuals with them wherever they go. Through this ad, Apple is hoping to underscore the ease of uploading, downloading, and utilizing on-the-go content, and the company is, therefore, advocating that colleges and universities use this technology in their courses.
3. The main point is that, in effect, podcasts are *better than* traditional learning methods. The world's leading thinkers are available *for free.*
4. Students should identify the two short paragraphs of the ad as its main support. Specifically, these state that podcasts are always available and are free. Some students may think that the short sections do not provide enough detail.
5. Students should see the elements of a proposal argument in this ad. Have students list the ad's specific problem, solution, benefits, and so on, reminding them that some elements might have to be inferred.

Exercise 15.7, p. 450

This exercise directs students to fill in the blanks of the provided paragraph to convince one of their instructors to make lectures available as podcasts. A possible example is provided below, with the given text in boldface.

Template for Writing a Proposal Argument

The traditional lecture method of education has a number of problems. For example, when some courses are conducted in large lecture halls, it can be difficult to hear the professor and follow along while writing notes. **In addition,** some students cannot make class every day, due to work, family, or commuting issues. **Making lectures available as podcasts, however,** alleviates these issues. **There are three reasons why this teaching method should be adopted. One reason is that** by providing lectures as podcasts, students can follow along at their own pace, reviewing and pausing as necessary to take notes and understand the information. **Another reason is that** podcasts allow for distance learning so that students can learn from home and still keep their job and family commitments. **Finally,** by communicating lecture material through podcasts, professors can free up time for discussion, study groups, office hours, additional help, and even lab time. **For these reasons, I believe that** certain courses should be offered as podcasts but only to replace in-class lecture time, not to replace discussion and student-professor interaction.

Exercise 15.8, p. 450

This exercise invites students to interview several of their instructors to see if the instructors would want to record their lectures as podcasts. On a separate sheet of paper, students should then edit the draft of the proposal argument they prepared for Exercise 15.7, adding comments from their instructors.

Exercise 15.9, p. 450

Now students write their own proposal argument, this time in an essay directed to one of their instructors, to argue that lectures be available as podcasts. They should present examples and support from their own experience as a student. In their essays, students should cite information and ideas from the readings in this chapter's At Issue selections and document each source.

Exercise 15.10, p. 451

This exercise, like those concluding the previous chapters, asks students to think foundationally about the essay they wrote for the previous exercise by reviewing the four pillars of argument discussed in Chapter 1. Students should review their own argument for these pillars, add anything that is missing, and then label the essay by identifying these parts.

Writing Assignments: Proposal Arguments, p. 451

This section allows you to take the concept of proposal analogy beyond the At Issue topic of college podcasting. In these three activities, students will look at how they can use proposals to reduce the amount of food that is wasted, improve school services, and decide on the best way to put a donation to use. The assignments give students freedom to consider how proposals can help them construct effective arguments about these and other current issues.

CHAPTER

16

Argument by Analogy

When discussing an unfamiliar or complex concept or idea, writers may construct arguments based on **analogy**. This chapter introduces students to the kinds of analogies they can make and helps them understand the various ways analogies create effective arguments. The text defines analogy, discusses favorable and unfavorable analogies, and advises students how to avoid constructing weak or faulty arguments by analogy. It also provides suggestions for how to structure an argument by analogy, useful information for students to have when they construct their own essays at the end of the chapter.

The readings in this chapter's At Issue address the question, Should Credit Card Companies Be Permitted to Target College Students? The opening text box explains the debate surrounding this issue: One side claims that while students are old enough to have credit cards, some are not responsible enough or, even if they are responsible, should not be subjected to the aggressive marketing of credit card companies on campus. On the other hand, some argue that because college students are considered adults, they should be able to make their own choices and have access to credit, which allows them to purchase necessary items such as textbooks. More information on this issue appears in the At Issue articles toward the end of the chapter.

What Is Analogy? p. 454

Some of your students may be familiar with the concept of analogy, but others may need more of a reminder of how analogies work. The text defines *analogy* as "an extended comparison between two items, situations, or concepts on the basis of a number of shared characteristics" (p. 454). Often, analogies are constructed to explain a difficult or unfamiliar concept in terms of something more familiar. You may remind your students of analogies that show up in movies or in books, or ask them how their professors have used analogies to explain, for instance, concepts about history or biology. In each case, the familiar is used to explain the unfamiliar.

What Is Argument by Analogy? p. 455

One of the most important uses of argument by analogy is to illustrate an idea, issue, or situation by comparing it with a similar idea, issue, or situation. The text provides a clear example: if someone argues that the government's job is to protect citizens from danger (for example, by making laws about speeding cars and guns), then a writer can argue that because certain dogs are dangerous, the government should protect citizens from dogs by passing laws that require licenses. Naturally, this kind of argument has its limitations, so you should caution your students that because no two situations are exactly alike, their analogies can go only so far. After that, writers need to support their idea with strong evidence. Often, arguments by analogy work well when paired with other types of argumentation, making the writer's thesis much stronger.

Avoiding Weak Analogies, p. 455

As stated in the previous section, arguments by analogy have their limitations. Students want to be sure that they don't compare two things that while similar in a few ways are drastically different in other ways. To do so would mean a loss of credibility, as readers will quickly see through the writer's argument and be less likely to agree with the writer's overall position. (For more about the logical fallacy of weak analogy, see Chapter 5.)

Exercise 16.1, p. 456

This exercise asks students to read over the provided list of topics (pp. 455–456) and explain how each one might be supported by an analogy. First, they should identify a possible analogy for each topic, consider how the topic is like and unlike the comparable one, and finally draft a thesis statement for each.

Teaching tip: There are many possibilities for this exercise, but keep in mind that your students may have some difficulty understanding analogy at first. If they are confused by some of the topics, just have them choose three to five of them (the ones they know something about). Alternatively, students can do this exercise in groups of two or three, as a kind of brainstorming session.

Favorable and Unfavorable Analogies, p. 456

It is important for students to realize that not all arguments by analogy have to argue *for,* or in favor of, something; in fact, many arguments by analogy argue *against* something by making an unfavorable analogy. The text provides a good example with the question of whether all U.S. citizens should be required to have government-issued identity cards. To create a positive analogy, one can argue that having an identity card of this type is similar to having, say, a driver's license. On the contrary, one can also argue against such identity cards by creating a negative analogy—for example, likening such cards to those issued in totalitarian governments (and in this way, the writer can explain that identity cards are an invasion of privacy, a method of government control, and so on).

Exercise 16.2, p. 456

This exercise gives students practice with favorable and unfavorable analogies. For each topic, students should write two thesis statements—one an example of positive analogy and the other an example of negative analogy. To help them with these analogies, remind them that they should begin by identifying ways in which the given item is like another item. Possible examples are provided here, with the given text in boldface.

- Bicycles should (or should not) have to be licensed.
  - *Positive analogy thesis:* Bicycles travel the same streets used by cars and follow the same traffic patterns and rules; therefore, just as drivers must be licensed, bicyclists should also be required to have licenses.
  - *Negative analogy thesis:* Like skateboarders or rollerbladers, bicyclists often travel on trails and paths, not on streets; therefore, bicyclists should not have to have licenses.
- Restaurants should (or should not) be required to post calorie counts for all their foods.
  - *Positive analogy thesis:* Restaurants are required to post warnings regarding undercooked meat because it can be hazardous to their customers' health; similarly, restaurants should be required to post calorie counts because high calorie foods are just as dangerous to their customers as food poisoning.
  - *Negative analogy thesis:* Restaurants are like any other kind of store, and stores do not post warnings about the hazards of spending too much or otherwise regulate their customers' behavior. For this reason, restaurants do not have a responsibility to be sure that their customers make wise buying decisions about food.
- Motorcyclists should (or should not) be required to wear helmets.
  - *Positive analogy thesis:* Helmet laws are very much like seatbelt laws, which not only protect citizens but also ensure that taxpayers do not have to cover health insurance costs of injured drivers. Therefore, motorcyclists should be required to wear helmets.
  - *Negative analogy thesis:* Motorcycles are like manual bikes, and bicyclists are not required to wear helmets, so neither should motorcyclists be so required.

Structuring an Argument by Analogy, p. 457

There are a variety of ways to structure an argument by analogy, but this section provides one of the best and most logical outlines for this kind of writing: introduction, evidence (first point in support of thesis), evidence (second point in support of thesis), opposing arguments, refutation, and conclusion.

Sample Student Essay: "Does Separate Housing for Minority Students Make Sense?" p. 457

To illustrate the suggested structure for an argument by analogy, the text includes a student essay by Anthony Luu. While there is no formal exercise directing students to interact with this essay, you might consider the following activity: have students read through the essay, paying particular attention to the labels for the elements of an argument by analogy; then have students get into small groups and consider whether the essay could be structured in a different way and if doing so would impact their reception of Luu's argument.

Grammar in Context: Using *Like* and *As*, p. 461

Since *like* and *as* are frequently used in writing arguments by analogy, this textbox provides examples of correct and incorrect usages likely to appear in student writing for this chapter.

Exercise 16.3, p. 461

This exercise instructs students to read the essay by Nat Hentoff "Civil Rights and Anti-Abortion Protests." Students should then respond to the series of questions that looks at how Hentoff's essay is an argument by analogy. A summary and possible answers are provided here.

Summary of "Civil Rights and Anti-Abortion Protests" by Nat Hentoff, p. 461

By drawing analogies between twentieth-century abortion protesters and nineteenth-century abolitionists, Hentoff argues that the pro-life stance is really a matter of upholding civil rights. He draws parallels between how the law viewed slaves and how the law regards the unborn, he criticizes civil rights leaders from the 1960s who have scorned the pro-life movement, and he justifies the protests and demonstrations by the group Operation Rescue by saying they are not unlike the methods used by Martin Luther King or even John Brown.

Identifying the Elements of an Argument by Analogy, p. 463

1. Hentoff argues that Operation Rescue's statements about the unborn are similar to the statements made by nineteenth-century abolitionists in regard to slavery. *Similarities between the two groups:* Pro-life advocates and the abolitionists both sought to uphold equal rights (para. 3); both believed social change comes through social upheaval (3); both opposed laws that legalized actions that they deemed immoral and unjust (4); both wanted the Constitution rewritten; and both fought against the notions, respectively, that slaves and fetuses were property, not people protected by the law (4). *Differences between the two groups:* Hentoff does not discuss how the groups were different, but students should be able to complete this section based on what they already know about the issues. For example, abolitionists sought to overcome laws based on racism (not the case for pro-life advocates); abolitionists advocated for the already-born, not the unborn; slaves were brought from other countries originally *as* property (no similar analogy exists for abortion); and

laws regarding slaves were not based on issues of health or safety (such as is often the case for abortion, when the mother's health is in danger). Hentoff's analogy is an interesting one. Depending on one's views of the status of a fetus, a reader will consider it strong or weak. Ask your students what other similarities they see between the two groups.

2. Hentoff says that slaves and fetuses are similar in the following ways: both were/are denied equal human rights (3); both were not/are not regarded as people before the law (slaves were regarded as property, fetuses are regarded as "property" of their mothers) (4, 5, 7). Hentoff argues that "some pro-lifers" are similar to John Brown because they "feel that nonviolence, however direct, is insufficient" (9). These examples strengthen Hentoff's main analogy between nineteenth-century abolitionism and twentieth-century pro-life arguments against abortion. The examples allow him to explain why social upheaval and protests should be allowed and why pro-life advocates are reasonable in protesting current laws.

3. Remind your students that language and word choice are very important to argumentative writing. For instance, it is more favorable to call someone a "pro-lifer" than "anti-abortion"; the former indicates being *for* something, and the latter indicates being *against* something, casting a person in a less kind light. In calling the other side "pro-abortion" rather than "pro-choice," Hentoff attacks most pro-choice advocates, who would never say that they are *for* abortions, only that they are for a women's right to choose. The phrase "abortion on demand" might be considered more neutral than the "pro" or "anti" terms. It has been used by those who oppose abortion as shorthand for abortions unrestricted by the state or the medical profession, leaving the decision solely to the pregnant woman. For the very same reason, many of those who favor the right to abortion see this term favorably.

4. Hentoff never comes out and directly states that he is pro-life or that he is in favor of Operation Rescue's agenda. However, his claim is evident through his analogy, which he states clearly in paragraph 3. This analogy helps him make the (unstated) argument that pro-life advocates are justified in their protests because their cause is really one of civil rights, not of religious persuasion or moral indignation. Hentoff's thesis could have been stated as follows: by comparing twentieth-century pro-life advocates to nineteenth-century abolitionists, it is evident that both causes are based on a belief in equality, civil rights, and the idea that the law should protect all people as citizens.

Reading and Writing about the Issue: Should Credit Card Companies Be Permitted to Target College Students? p. 464

Because arguments by analogy are often used to advocate that something *should* or *shouldn't* be done, this At Issue looks at how writers use analogies to answer the question of whether credit card companies should be able to market to college students on campus. In a growing trend, many colleges permit credit card companies to set up a display booth on campus during orientation week and then attempt to gain customers from the incoming first-year class (often winning students over by giving out free T-shirts, stress balls, and other merchandise). Some argue that access to marketing pitches is one freedom of adults—that targeting students should be allowed because they should be able to make their own responsible choices about credit cards and finances, in general. Still, some of the writers in this At Issue cite statistics that say today's college students are graduating with staggering debt, exacerbated by the availability of credit cards.

Summary of "The Young and the Indebted" by Erica L. Williams and Tim Westrich, p. 465

Writing on behalf of Campus Progress, the authors of this article explain how young people are targeted by credit card companies, led astray by unclear terms and agreements, and put into credit card debt during their college years that will affect them for five, ten, or even twenty years. According to Williams and Westrich, students need to be more informed if they are not to become the victims of predatory lending practices. Further, the authors argue that universities need to change their close relationships with credit card companies and the government needs to mandate restrictions for how credit card companies do business. Finally, the group Campus Progress, which the authors represent, is attempting to inform young people about the risks of incurring debt and believes that education is the key to successful financial decisions.

At Issue: Sources for Developing an Argument by Analogy, p. 468

1. The authors state that, like all Americans, college students fall victim to the "high fees, heavy interest rates, and complex terms" associated with credit cards (para. 5).
2. *Additional financial problems of college students:*
   - Students have lower income, so they have to devote a higher percentage of their income every month to paying down debt—22% according to a recent survey (6).
   - Students also have to borrow money to pay for their education, as well as costs associated with attending college (room and board, books, and so on) (7); students accrue an average of $20,000 in student debt (9).
   - Students are aggressively targeted by credit card companies that overwhelm them with advertisements and offers; many students can resist this "gamble" for only so long (8).
   - Students face a difficult economy and a tough job market, so there's no guarantee of when they'll be able to pay back the debt they incur during their college years (10).

- Students are often forced to return home to save money after college, or default on their debt because they are unable to pay the required amounts (11).

3. Have your students reread the opening of the article and discuss its effectiveness. Could they relate to Kali's story? Did they like the way the authors focus on one example to explain the problem? How else could the writers have begun their article? What other anecdotes could they have included to illustrate their points?
4. In this article, the blame is placed squarely on credit card companies for their "unfair" and unclear terms and conditions and for their predatory practice of targeting impressionable college students. The authors outline their solution in paragraphs 16–20. Have your students reread these paragraphs and list the various measures the authors advocate to make lending fairer and to ensure that college students are protected by law against credit card companies.
5. In paragraph 8, the writers state that "major borrowing from credit card companies is like visiting a Las Vegas casino," and they go on to state how predatory lending practices constantly lure students back to the "casino" of credit card lending. We think this is an appropriate analogy, one designed to draw attention to the issue by highlighting the drawbacks of credit card use by students.
6. Your students' paraphrases of the concluding statement should call for legislative action to protect vulnerable young Americans from predatory credit card companies and their unfair and unclear lending practices. You might note to your students that legislative action became effective in 2010 restricting the right of credit card companies to market on campus directly to students. However, such action falls short of the changes suggested in the conclusion of the article. The concluding statement could be changed to provide information on how readers could initiate or support further legislative action. We believe however that the concluding statement as it stands is consistent with the article's main argument.

Summary of "Non-Issue Needs No Law," *Contra Costa Times*, p. 469

Taking the point of view opposite Williams and Westrich's, the author of this editorial states that because lawmakers are busy enough with more serious legislation it is unreasonable to ask them to regulate credit card companies' interactions with college students. The writer states that, true, some college students will abuse their credit cards and incur debt; others, however, will do just fine and learn to be responsible with money. Either way, the writer believes that part of a college education is what happens outside the classroom and students will need to grow up and be financially smart, without the interference of new laws and government regulation.

At Issue: Sources for Developing an Argument by Analogy, p. 470

1. Have students go back over the short editorial and draw arrows between paragraphs that go together. You might also ask them whether the short paragraphs make the editorial easy to read or whether the editorial seems choppy.
2. Next to paragraphs 6 and 7, students may jot down examples of the skills and financial responsibility college-aged Americans must learn, or they may give additional analogies to prove the writer's point that students must learn many lessons of adulthood outside the college classroom, without help from the government.
3. You might have your students select two more paragraphs and brainstorm, in the margins, several examples of support that could be used in those paragraphs.
4. This article is written not to defend credit card companies but to argue college students must learn financial responsibility when they're first away from home. *A possible thesis statement:* College is a time when young people transition to adulthood, and at this time they need to learn to make smart financial decisions on their own, without the protection of special laws and regulations to keep credit card companies at a distance.
5. Editorials are written in response to a current debate or argument. This particular editorial is written to counter the outcry of some groups (like Campus Progress) and legislators who advocate the kinds of laws discussed in paragraph 1.
6. Your students' summaries should be something like the following: It is difficult for students to transition from the financial comforts of home to financial responsibility on their own; certainly, some will abuse this new freedom while others will handle it with care. Either way, the lessons they learn are part of growing up.

Summary of "Start Your Credit Today!" FindCollegeCards.com (online credit card application), p. 471

This Web site is a one-stop shop for college students looking to sign up for a credit card. The site says it provides information so that students can make informed choices.

At Issue: Sources for Developing an Argument by Analogy, p. 471

1. This Web page encourages students to apply for credit cards by providing resources for them to locate the card that best suits them. The language supports the message by providing specific information, such as the "regular APR" (annual percentage rate) and the "annual fee" for the cards. It is student friendly for the most part; see the sidebar at left explaining credit limits, though it might have explained the term "APR."

2. Other sites similar to this one often include an image of a smiling student so that the reader can project herself into the situation the page describes, a happy young person with credit. There are limited graphics on the site and information is chunked into small units. We find this to be a generally good design. It is not too flashy. Your students, however, might find it dull.
3. The site promises "facts you need to know about the misleading and complex world of student credit cards!" So while there may be linked information refuting those arguments, it isn't found on the opening page.
4. The bullet points highlight the benefits of one of the cards on the site: minimum income and "Thank You points" (whatever those may be). A credit card that doesn't require a minimum income is one that will attract college students, most of whom are not working full time (though of course many do).
5. The page does not include information on the rate of other credit cards on the site (and, further, includes only the introductory rate of the card, which is always lower than the interest rate after the introductory period expires), the length of time it would take to pay off a credit card while paying only the minimum payment each month, the impact of bankruptcy on credit card debt, the amount and terms of late fees, and so on. You might survey your students to see what kind of information that they would like to see on the site, based on their own experiences and on the information from the articles in this section.

Summary for "Majoring in Credit-Card Debt" by Jessica Silver-Greenberg, p. 472

Armed with real-life anecdotes, information on governmental intervention, and explanations of how credit cards can be harmful to students, Silver-Greenberg takes an in-depth look at the problems of college students with credit cards. The author divides her article into seven parts with subheads. The article is well balanced, and Silver-Greenberg explains what measures credit card companies are taking to educate students about financial responsibility.

At Issue: Sources for Developing an Argument by Analogy, p. 476

1. Silver-Greenberg provides insightful "rebuttals" from credit card companies, and these statements could easily be applied to Woodworth.
   - Credit card companies offer "extensive financial literacy materials for college students" so Woodworth should have made use of those resources (para. 6, 22).
   - Woodworth should have been responsible for his own actions, and it's not the job of banks to "act like responsible parents" (7).
   - Woodworth needed to read the fine print and take time to understand his card holder agreements (14).
   - Woodworth's spending was influenced by the "culture of debt" students live in, thinking little about what they charge or how they will pay for it (18).

- Woodworth procrastinated and should have asked for help (20).

2. The article is clearly in favor of more regulation over credit card company practices. Many times in the article, Silver-Greenberg comments on how difficult it is for students (and others as well) to understand their credit card agreement and terms. Silver-Greenberg never says students shouldn't have credit cards but argues that they should be more able to understand the agreements they're making when they sign up for credit cards. Some students may argue that the headings made the article seem organized; others may say the headings made it seem scattered.
3. As mentioned in Answer 1, the author does present various arguments that the credit card companies make to defend their practices in paragraphs 6, 7, 14, 18, 20, and 22. The writer counters these claims by saying that these practices "raise questions" (8), that their hidden fees and mysterious charges are "less well-known" (13), and that their contracts are dense, sometimes up to thirty pages long and written in language the average student cannot understand (14). Overall, Silver-Greenberg makes the point that credit card companies are taking advantage of a vulnerable group of people and exploiting them for monetary gain.
4. Once again, see what your students think of the conclusion, and ask them if the use of Woodworth's story, as an anecdote, was memorable. Silver-Greenberg chose to use Woodworth's story as bookends for her argument, usually an effective strategy. See if your students agree or if they can propose a stronger concluding statement.

Exercise 16.4, p. 477

Possible thesis statements are provided here, with the given text in boldface.

Teaching tip: Remind students that the main point of this exercise is to find suitable analogies—both a favorable and an unfavorable analogy—for the credit card debate.

1. Because credit cards are analogous to useful (and harmless) products such as car insurance offers that students receive in the mail or on campus, credit card companies should be permitted to target college students.
2. Because credit cards are analogous to potentially harmful (and even dangerous) products such as those advertised in email spam messages, sent directly to students, credit card companies should not be permitted to target college students.

Exercise 16.5, p. 477

This exercise directs students to fill in the blanks of the provided paragraph in order to take a position on the issue of whether credit card companies should be permitted to target college students. A possible example is provided below, with the given text in boldface. Note: The example provided uses an unfavorable analogy to make an argument.

Template for Writing an Argument by Analogy

Credit cards should not be marketed to college students. Credit cards can be very useful for students, but they can also lead to serious problems. For example, as in the spam email offers students find in their in-boxes every day, credit card offers present misleading information that takes advantage of a college student's financial vulnerability. **In addition,** like spam messages, credit card companies make dramatic claims in their promotional material, and the truth about the offer (and its risks) can be found only in the confusing fine print. **For these reasons, some people have suggested that colleges have a responsibility to regulate how credit cards are marketed to their students. For example, schools should not** allow credit card companies to set up tables at freshman orientation and to lure students in with free offers and flashy gifts. **Moreover, they should** consider providing information about financial responsibility, debt, and credit to all incoming students. **Some argue that because other items—for example,** personal care products—**are marketed on campus, it is acceptable to market credit cards as well. Others point out, however, that credit cards are potentially dangerous, as are** solicitations from cigarette and alcohol companies, **and so they should not be made available to students. On balance, it seems that,** at the very least, it would be wise to ensure that students are informed of the risk of credit cards and that some kind of financial management tips are incorporated into the first-year experience.

Exercise 16.6, p. 478

The text provides specific questions that groups of four should address in their discussions. Each group should, at the close of discussion, draft a paragraph that explains its opinions on the issue and why it holds those opinions.

Exercise 16.7, p. 478

In this exercise, students get the chance to draft their own argument that answers the question, Should Credit Card Companies Be Permitted to Target College Students? They should begin by selecting a suitable analogy (either positive or negative) between credit card companies and other products marketed to students. This analogy should help them create a thesis for their argument. Students should also cite information and ideas from the readings in this chapter's At Issue and document each source in their essay.

Exercise 16.8, p. 478

This exercise, like those concluding the previous chapters, asks students to think foundationally about the arguments they formed for the previous exercise by reviewing the four pillars of argument discussed in Chapter 1. Students should review their own argument for these pillars, add anything that is missing, and then label the essay by identifying these parts.

Writing Assignments: Argument by Analogy, p. 479

This section allows you to take the concept of argument by analogy beyond the At Issue topic of credit cards and college students. In these three activities, students will look at how they can use analogy to argue for or against laws forbidding smoking on campus, to determine to what degree their school's student newspaper should be subject to censorship by administration, and to discuss the issue of community service as a requirement for graduation. The assignments give students freedom to consider how analogy—whether favorable or unfavorable—can help them construct effective arguments about these and other current issues.

CHAPTER

17

Ethical Arguments

Like evaluation arguments, discussed in Chapter 14, ethical arguments make judgments; however, unlike evaluation arguments, ethical arguments focus exclusively on right or wrong, good or bad. The ethical arguments your students are likely to be most familiar with concern hot-button issues: abortion, gay marriage, euthanasia, the death penalty, and gun control. The At Issue section in this chapter focuses on a growing ethical debate within the issue of gun control: campus safety in the wake of so many campus shootings. Addressing the tragic shooting at Virginia Tech in 2007, the readings in this section offer a variety of perspectives, ranging from why reactionary security on some campuses adversely affects the learning environment to how campuses can best prevent these occurrences in the future to campus-wide profiling.

Teaching tip: Since profiling is a practice most students know about, comes up as part of this chapter's At Issue (see the pamphlet on p. 511), and lends itself to ethical argument, consider conducting a class debate. You might first encourage students to recall the lessons of Chapter 12 ("Argument by Definition") and to begin their debate by defining *profiling* and how it's been used. (Students will most likely gravitate toward *racial profiling,* which is certainly a topic for an ethical argument.) After constructing an operational definition, students may map out the rights and wrongs of the issue in order to understand its complexity. That is, looking at profiling in these terms as a class can help students to recognize the ambiguity of ethical issues and how a person's vantage point and position or privilege are central to how he or she forms ethical arguments.

What Is an Ethical Argument? p. 482

This chapter defines an **ethical argument** as an argument that makes a judgment based on a standard, such as a moral rule. A division of philosophy, ethics focuses on right or wrong, good or bad; within the field of ethics, applied ethics looks at real-life issues. Ethical arguments, then, focus on "whether something should be done because it is good or right" (p. 482). The text stresses that ethical arguments frequently begin with a clear statement of right or wrong that relies on a religious, philosophic, or ethical tradition for support. After offering this definition, the text reasons through several questions that lead to ethical arguments, including the question central to this chapter's grouped selections: How Far Should Colleges Go to Keep Campuses Safe?

Teaching tip: For each of the examples given in the text, ask students to construct an ethical argument that rests on a different tradition; this exercise will help students to differentiate among religious, philosophic, and ethics-based principles and will prepare them to discuss ethical principles, which are defined in the next section of their text.

Stating an Ethical Principle, p. 483

At the core of any ethical argument is an ethical principle, a principle that subscribes to a particular moral law and that can be used to argue in favor of doing something that will yield a particular benefit for society or against doing something that will be a detriment to society. The text suggests that, whenever possible, people should base their argument on a principle that is self-evident, a principle that is so basic and widely accepted that it needs no proof.

Teaching tip: Some students will not understand what qualifies as a self-evident ethical principle and may mention a religious belief; so it may be useful to list ethical principles that are self-evident, as such a list may also help students to understand the difference between *religious* and *ethical.* Since the line is quoted in the text, begin by identifying the self-evident ethical principles, or truths, that Thomas Jefferson identifies in the Declaration of Independence.

Ethics versus Law, p. 484

This section of the chapter differentiates between ethics (the study of how things are judged as good or bad, right or wrong) and law (the rules that govern a society). The text reminds readers that just because something is legal does not necessarily mean it's ethical; the text then offers examples of unethical laws—Nuremberg laws, for one—and concludes by offering examples of how the ethics of a person may cause him or her to reach beyond what is legally required.

Understanding Ethical Dilemmas, p. 487

As the text defines it, an **ethical dilemma** occurs when there is a conflict between two or more possible actions that will have the same consequence or outcome. The text offers the "lifeboat" dilemma as a primary example before mentioning real-world dilemmas such as selecting employees to lay off or surgically separating conjoined twins who share a heart. Here the text also cautions against setting up false dilemmas—that is, proposing only two possible choices when there are actually more—and of oversimplifying dilemmas.

Exercise 17.1, p. 488

This exercise lists topics for ethical argument and asks students to identify for each one an ethical principle as the basis of the argument. Here are two example principles for each of the stated topics.

- The United States should (or should not) prohibit the use of animals in scientific experiments. *Should:* all creatures deserve dignity and respect; *should not:* human life is more important than the life of animals.
- Students with special needs should (or should not) get preference in college admissions. *Should:* all persons are not created equal, and disadvantages must be taken into account; *should not:* all persons should be treated equally regardless, so we cannot privilege disadvantages.
- Homeless people should (or should not) be forcibly removed from city streets. *Should:* many homeless people have mental health issues, and taking them off the streets allows them to be treated; *should not:* all people deserve dignified treatment and the right to inhabit public streets.
- Gay and lesbian couples should (or should not) be allowed to marry. *Should:* all people deserve equal rights, including the right to marry; *should not:* the Bible declares marriage for heterosexuals only and decrees homosexuality immoral.
- Everyone should (or should not) be required to sign an organ-donor card. *Should:* human life should be preserved at all cost, and organ donation supports this idea; *should not:* In some religions, the human body is considered a temple, and the body/temple should not be desecrated by removal of an organ.

Exercise 17.2, p. 489

This exercise asks students to make a list of rules or laws that they find unjust and to identify the ethical principle they use to arrive at that conclusion. Students may look at laws regarding the drinking age, driving age, age of military service, and voting age. They are likely to argue that there should be no drinking age, recalling the causal argument of Chapter 13. Similarly, students are likely to argue that if one is responsible enough to drive at sixteen or die for his or her country at eighteen, he or she should be able to vote. You might encourage students to push a bit further by asking them to think about dormitory or campus rules; to stimulate a broader conversation, consider bringing in a list of obscure laws or laws frequently overlooked but still on the books—for example: sodomy laws, laws about prostitution, and rules about women in combat.

Exercise 17.3, p. 489

This exercise asks students to look at two ads and identify the ethical arguments of each and the ethical principles underlying each. The first advertisement is an environmental argument that asks those who drive through the great outdoors to keep areas clean by "treading lightly" on land. Students are likely to identify the ethical principle as respect for the land, the responsibility of each person to care for the land, or the respectful treatment of public property. The second, more graphic advertisement features a human positioned and labeled as meat for sale. Students will identify the ethical principle underlying the second ad as the prevention of cruelty to animals or valuing animal life as equal to human life.

Exercise 17.4, p. 490

This exercise asks students to read the poem "Ethics" by Linda Pastan, to identify the ethical dilemma, and to determine whether or not the poem resolves its dilemma. Students should identify the ethical dilemma as what has more value—an irreplaceable piece of art or an elderly woman's life? The poem does not neatly resolve its dilemma, as it deems the youths asked to decide unable to grasp the value of either. By its close, the poem compares the woman and the painting, suggesting that all are "beyond saving by children."

Teaching tip: Ask your students if they feel old enough to make such a decision and even why age matters in the first place. This question may lead to other discussions about the ethical treatment of the elderly and the ethics of what does and does not deserve historical preservation.

Exercise 17.5, p. 491

This exercise asks students to write one or two paragraphs in which they discuss the dilemma Pastan presents and the ethical principle they would use to resolve it; their writing will likely be enriched by a class conversation about the preceding exercise, as the Teaching Tip suggests.

Structuring an Ethical Argument, p. 491

As in previous chapters about forms of argumentation—such as Chapter 6, with its definitions of Rogerian, Toulmin, and oral forms of argument; Chapter 12 with its structure for an argument by definition; and Chapter 14 with its structure for evaluation arguments—this section offers a bulleted list for structuring an ethical argument.

Sample Student Essay: "The Promise to Educate," p. 491

This student essay argues that universities should not pay their athletes a salary. Despite the popularity and revenue generated by student athletics, the author maintains that universities have an ethical responsibility to prioritize education and not to divert focus and funds from this purpose by paying athletes.

Grammar in Context: Subordination and Coordination, p. 495

Coordinating and subordinating conjunctions are the words that join similar or contrasting ideas. Since students frequently struggle with how to express the relationship between ideas in their essays, this section includes examples of sentences for the two types of conjunctions and an explanation of how a given conjunction helps to express each idea.

Exercise 17.6, p. 496

This exercise asks students to read an essay titled "Animals in Scientific Research" and to answer questions about the essay; a brief summary of the essay and sample responses to the questions follow.

Summary of "Animals in Scientific Research," p. 496

From the Web site of the National Anti-Vivisection Society, this essay argues that it is morally and ethically wrong to experiment on one species for the "supposed benefit" of another.

Identifying the Elements of an Ethical Argument, p. 497

1. *Vivisection* is surgery conducted for scientific purposes on a living animal. The writers oppose the practice on the grounds that the harm to animals is not outweighed by the knowledge gained, even if that knowledge may help humans or even save human lives. The statement argues that animals have a "right to be alive, to be free from pain and suffering, and fulfill their biological potential" (para. 7).
2. The writers consider their readers to be neutral. They understand that readers may be visiting the site without being members of the society and may already be in favor of using animals for research. The site therefore provides an argument in favor of their position, grounding their beliefs in a coherent ethical stance and anticipating readers' objections.
3. The writer introduces and addresses several opposing viewpoints—namely, that animals are seen as resources (2), that it is merely sentimental to view animals as anything more (2), and that animals have no feelings (5).
4. In support of their thesis, the writers list animals' status as fellow creatures (3), animals' susceptibility to pain (4, 5), and animals' inability to make a choice, thereby creating a moral obligation for humans (7).
5. The conclusion emphasizes the idea that society moves in a trend toward greater morality, and it argues that ethical treatment of animals furthers that goal. It is an effective conclusion, because it broadens the topic from the specific area of the treatment of animals to encompass a larger question of what makes for a good society, therefore giving a greater sense of importance to the question of the treatment of animals.

Reading and Writing about the Issue: How Far Should Colleges Go to Keep Campuses Safe? p. 498

In the wake of several tragic campus shootings in recent years, this group of selections asks students to consider the lengths to which campuses should go to keep students safe.

Summary of "Openness vs. Security on Campus" by M. Perry Chapman, p. 499

Author M. Perry Chapman is a consultant who helped to create the open campus plan for Virginia Tech, a land-grant university. Sensitive to the tragedy at the college, Chapman still supports the open design of the campus as an expression of its egalitarian roots and cautions against losing sight of that emblematic openness.

At Issue: Sources for Developing an Ethical Argument, p. 500

1. In paragraph 3, Chapman lists the institution of call boxes, security lighting, key card systems, and surveillance cameras. While the author understands that in some cases these are appropriate measures, he cautions against more invasive security measures, such as gated campuses, that emblematically reinforce the notion of a campus as restrictive and elitist and counter to the notion that campuses are part of and in service to their surrounding community.
2. In paragraph 2, Chapman suggests that the tragedy is especially unsettling to those who have championed the open campus plan as an extension of the ideals of a university. Since these campus layouts reinforce the "central ideas of openness and engagement on American college campuses," Chapman seems to suggest that the tragedy also threatens the possibility of open campuses.
3. Because Virginia Tech is a land-grant university, created by the passing of the Morrill Act (1862), which granted land to create sixty-nine public institutions and to make higher education more accessible, it has a "special responsibility" to remain an accessible campus. It's likely that Chapman mentions Virginia Tech's responsibility to support, both figuratively and literally, his argument for an open campus.
4. At the core of Chapman's argument is an ethical argument about socioeconomic class, access to education, and the university's responsibility to the surrounding community.
5. Chapman might have refuted an argument against the risks of an open campus design by citing research that shows no or minimal difference in crime rates based on design.

Summary of "How Not to Respond to Virginia Tech—II" by Brett A. Sokolow, p. 501

Sokolow, president of the National Center for Higher Education Risk Management, offers a point-by-point counterargument in response to reactionary suggestions, immediately following the shootings at Virginia Tech, to tighten security on campuses nationwide. Instead, Sokolow repeatedly points to the problems of these inflammatory suggestions and encourages university officials to focus efforts and funding on better mental-health services.

At Issue: Sources for Developing an Ethical Argument, p. 504

1. The terms *pundits* and *talking heads* refer to the representatives of the media, most of whom have no understanding of campus security and only exacerbate the problems by entertaining inflammatory solutions.

2. Without knowing Sokolow's credentials, students may suggest that these statements undermine his credibility. However, knowing his credentials, students are likely to consider his statements credible and may suggest that he includes these *qualifiers* (***Teaching tip:*** consider asking students to recall Toulmin logic here) to lend himself more credibility and to differentiate himself from the pundits and talking heads whom, he notes in the same paragraph, offer him "inaccurate and incomplete" coverage.

3. Sokolow advocates mental-health screening and improved mental-health services to improve campus safety; he also agrees that a loudspeaker system and evacuation plan are necessary for safety. In focusing on mental health, Sokolow places the burden on students, professors, administrators, and, most particularly, on mental-health prescreenings and mental-health professionals for recognizing changes in patterns of behavior or self-destructive tendencies. While he mentions that he does not advocate discriminative profiling (para. 10, 11), he seems to suggest a system of mental-health profiling to identify and watch at-risk students. Students' opinions about how convincing his suggestions are will vary.

4. Students should suggest that each paragraph of Sokolow's argument really begins with a counterargument—a tactic for increasing security—that he refutes. He introduces and refutes the following arguments:
   - Emergency texting system—too costly, hard to regulate, helpful to perpetrator
   - Criminal background checks—probably unreliable because most incoming students will have only a juvenile record likely to have been expunged
   - Student control of locks on dormitory rooms—hindering to campus security in emergency situation or suicide attempt
   - Allowing guns on campus—dangerous
   - Excluding students with mental-health issues—illegal

5. Sokolow suggests that in most school shootings shooters suffer silently from a mental-health issue, and he suggests that a combination of prescreening, campuswide awareness, and treatment is the best way to prevent school shootings in the future. Student opinions about Sokolow's argument will vary.

Summary of "Guns Don't Belong in the Hands of Administrators, Professors, or Students" by Jesus M. Villahermosa Jr., p. 505

A deputy sheriff, SWAT responder, and the defense-tactics instructor for the state of Washington, Villahermosa argues against arming administrators, professors, or students. He suggests that the time, practice, and dedication needed to use a weapon well, effectively, and accurately in a crisis situation is greatly beyond what most people can actually invest.

At Issue: Sources for Developing an Ethical Argument, p. 507

1. At the end of the first paragraph, Villahermosa offers his thesis, when he writes: "allowing guns on campus will create problems, not solve them."
2. The author tries to establish credibility in this paragraph by offering the reader a substantive reason for trusting his opinion. Student opinions about the paragraph's necessity will vary.
3. Villahermosa poses a series of rhetorical questions that raise important points about the logistics, liability, training, expense, and responsibility of using firearms; the questions are meant to deter readers from supporting pro-weapons policies on campus.

   Teaching tip: Ask students to recall the discussion of rhetorical questions from Chapter 4 of this text and to discuss the effectiveness of this tactic for Villahermosa's argument. Does he leave readers too many questions to answer on their own to make an effective argument?
4. Villahermosa argues that many will not be a good shot in stressful situations, that accidental shootings are likely liabilities, that these accidental shootings can land professors or students in jail, and that weapons skills will likely be subpar because faculty and students will not have the time to study weapons handling. Students' responses about which argument is the most convincing will vary.
5. Villahermosa is making an ethical argument. His principle is that we should take the course of action that causes less harm than the possible alternative. He argues that allowing guns on campuses would cause more harm than good and so it is wrong to allow guns in the hands of students and faculty.
6. In his conclusion, Villahermosa emphasizes the training of law-enforcement officers and the inability of the general public to mimic that type of training and dedication. Opinions about whether or not Villahermosa should emphasize other points will vary.

Summary of "There's a Reason They Choose Schools" by Timothy Wheeler, p. 508

Wheeler, a doctor and the director of Doctors for Responsible Gun Ownership, advocates arming students and points to instances of successful intervention in shootings by armed students and faculty as support for this position.

At Issue: Sources for Developing an Ethical Argument, p. 510

1. What Wheeler finds "depressingly similar" is that the mass murders were committed in gun-free zones—school campuses. A school, he argues, is a "soft target."

2. Wheeler disagrees with those who say guns are the root cause of violence and responds with a degree of animosity, as he notes Sheldon Greenberg's "audacity" and the "arrogance" of his zero-tolerance policies on guns (para. 4, 5).
3. According to Wheeler, administrators and bureaucrats ignore the fact that no-guns policies on campus have not prevented school shootings and advocates pro-gun policies because students have been and can be, he argues, first responders. He refutes objections by pointing to successfully thwarted attacks due to the presence of guns on campus.
4. Wheeler believes that people who are on the campus every day should be allowed to carry guns. Student agreement or disagreement with Wheeler will probably not be universal; ask students to assess the quality and amount of Wheeler's evidence.

   Teaching tip: Ask students to recall the tips for evaluating arguments covered in Chapter 8.
5. Wheeler's use of "gem" is mildly sarcastic; his use of "politically correct," a term of scorn used by those who do not agree with its principles, indicates that he does not favor the position and does not think highly of those who do. Students may also suggest "audacity" and "arrogance" (5), which are mentioned in the response to question 2, above.
6. Wheeler is in favor of responsible gun use and believes that students and instructors can and should act as first responders. This opinion contrasts with that of Villahermosa, who does not believe that students or faculty should be armed or can combat shooters.

Summary of "Warning Signs: How You Can Help Prevent Campus Violence," Isothermal Community College (pamphlet), p. 511

This pamphlet, made available online to all students on campus, provides a list of warning signs for identifying potentially violent students.

At Issue: Sources for Developing an Ethical Argument, p. 514

1. The pamphlet emphasizes watching for violent or aggressive behavior, changes in mood or behavior, and threats or risk-taking behavior. Some students may also suggest that this pamphlet seems to target men.
2. Students may suggest that a cautionary note about the pamphlet's limitations might have been included; for instance, there may be other warning signs not mentioned here or no warning signs.
3. The brochure does position students to watch other students and encourages students to report these behaviors. Students familiar with George Orwell's *1984* may suggest that the proposition of watching one another is a bit reminiscent of Big Brother.

4. Students may suggest carrying mace or pepper spray, programming emergency numbers into their cell phones, and even setting up student patrols or outreach groups.

Description of "Gone but Not Forgotten" by Amy Dion (antiviolence poster), p. 515

A hand print on a red and gray background that repeats "gone but not forgotten" commemorates those killed in the shootings at Virginia Tech University, Louisiana Technical College, and Northern Illinois University.

At Issue: Sources for Developing an Ethical Argument, p. 516

1. The poster records the deaths of forty people, reinforcing the idea that these tragically and publicly lost lives cannot be forgotten.
2. The image also includes the dates of the crimes, the number of lives lost in each crime, a crackling and fading background to symbolize destruction, the use of red to symbolize blood or violence, and the repetition of "gone but not forgotten" to reinforce the central point that these violent crimes will not be forgotten.
3. Student opinions will vary; it's likely that students will consider the poster ineffective in combating campus violence. However, students might suggest that such a poster may lead to campus dialogue, which can help psychologically.

   Teaching tip: Since this poster resembles a public service announcement (PSA), another frequent purveyor of ethical arguments, consider showing students a few PSAs and asking them to assess their underlying ethical principles and to evaluate their effectiveness.

Exercise 17.7, p. 517

For this exercise, students follow the template and fill in the blanks to create their own arguments. A sample response appears here with the given text in boldface.

Template for Writing an Ethical Argument

Recently, a number of colleges have experienced violence on their campuses. For example, in April 2007, thirty-two people were murdered in a school shooting at Virginia Tech. **Many colleges have gone too far [or not far enough] in trying to prevent violence because** they have reactively instituted extreme security procedures that hinder access to campus and compromise the learning environment. **One reason** is that administrators want students to be hypervigilant in their recognition of possible threats on campus. **Another reason** is that officials want to ensure the safety of all students and faculty. **Finally,** some campuses have even permitted students to carry weapons. **If colleges really want to remain safe,** they will maintain their no-tolerance policies, keep weapons out of the hands of students, and focus on recognizing when students are at-risk and in need of faculty and student support in order to prevent violence.

Exercise 17.8, p. 517

This exercise asks students to interview friends and teachers about whether they think campus violence-prevention programs are excessive or ineffective and to incorporate those voices in a revision of the paragraph written for Exercise 17.7.

Exercise 17.9, p. 517

For this exercise, students should form an argument about the question central to this chapter's At Issue section: How Far Should Colleges Go to Keep Campuses Safe?

Exercise 17.10, p. 518

This exercise, like those concluding the previous chapters, asks students to think foundationally about the arguments they formed for the previous exercise by reviewing the four pillars of argument discussed in Chapter 1. Students should review their own argument for these pillars, add anything that is missing, and then label the essay by identifying these parts.

Writing Assignments: Ethical Arguments, p. 518

This chapter ends by offering three potential writing assignments. The first asks students to consider the ethics of allowing hate groups to distribute literature on campus, the second asks whether English should be the official language of the United States, and the third wants students to consider whether or not celebrities have an ethical duty to set a good example for young people.

PART

6

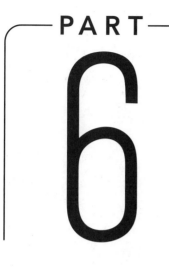

Debates, Casebooks, and Classic Arguments

CHAPTER 18

Debate: Should We Eat Meat?

Summary of "Let Them Eat Dog" by Jonathan Safran Foer, p. 523

Foer models his argument after Jonathan Swift's famous satire, "A Modest Proposal" (p. 672)—even to the point of including a recipe for stewed dog. Rather than making a straightforward case for vegetarianism, Foer uses irony and indirection to illuminate the ethical and logical inconsistencies of those who eat meat yet maintain a taboo against eating domesticated animals such as dogs and cats.

Reading Arguments, p. 525

1. A taboo is a prohibition on behaviors, objects, and people that are forbidden by a particular society or culture. Ostensibly, taboos are put in place to protect individuals and the society as a whole from harm; such rules carry the connotation of a sacred prohibition—as well as strict penalties (from shaming to death) for disobedience. We often have visceral reactions to those who break taboos. By using this term, Foer suggests how our culture's unquestioned and seemingly natural prohibitions against eating dogs and cats conflict—logically and ethically—with common attitudes about eating other animals. As taboos are often culturally specific, he also points out that people in other countries do eat dogs and cats, demonstrating that such rules and attitudes are not universal or natural, even though they may seem that way to us.
2. Foer's argument relies on an extended analogy between domesticated pets and animals raised for consumption; the comparison highlights both the similarities between these two (ultimately) arbitrary categories of animals *and* our disparate, ethically inconsistent attitudes toward the two categories: "While it's widely believed that adrenaline makes dog meat taste better—hence the traditional methods of slaughter: hanging, boiling alive, beating to death—we can all agree that if we're going to eat them, we should kill them quickly and painlessly, right?" (para. 14) At such moments, Foer counts on omnivores to recoil from the thought of using dogs in this way; but implicitly, he hopes that meat-eaters will realize that they passively accept such treatment of other animals.

3. Foer makes several proposals in the course of the essay. As we already render dead dogs into food for livestock and other pets, he proposes that we eat the dogs ourselves and "eliminate this inefficient and bizarre middle step" (13). He also argues that the "colossal task" of feeding the world's omnivores means that we need to "use dogs" more efficiently: "If we let dogs be dogs, and breed without interference, we would create a sustainable, local meat supply with low energy inputs that would put even the most efficient grass-based farming to shame. For the ecologically-minded it's time to admit that dog is realistic food for realistic environmentalists" (15). The writer is being ironic in that he knows that meat-eating readers will find these schemes grotesque; yet, the proposals are logically consistent and seem to partake of environmental and ethical good sense.

4. The most direct statement of Foer's overall argument comes in paragraphs 17 and 18, after he provides the recipe for "Stewed Dog, Wedding Style." He states that there is "an overabundance of rational reasons to say no to factory-farmed meat" (17), including the indefensible suffering of animals, the industry's complicity in global warming, and the role such farming plays in the development of deadly diseases. But in addition to these reasons, we are viscerally repulsed by the prospect of killing and eating dogs: "The instinct comes before our reason, and is more important" (18). So essentially, Foer argues that the wholesale killing of animals for food is irrational but also wrong on a level that we "know" instinctively and emotionally. Some students will agree with Foer; some will not.

Summary of "Why I Stopped Being a Vegetarian" by Laura Fraser, p. 526

Laura Fraser offers an idiosyncratic account of how she became a vegetarian—and then returned to omnivorous eating after fifteen years. In the process, she addresses many of the common reasons for giving up meat, from the presumed healthfulness to the utilitarian social benefits. She also considers the ethics of vegetarianism in the context of social customs and manners: "If eating is a socially conscious act, you have to be conscious of the society of your fellow homo sapiens along with the animals" (para. 21).

Reading Arguments, p. 528

1. Fraser emphasizes her mixed motives for becoming a vegetarian—and how she often gave people "vague" reasons for her choice (health, the environment, politics) that belied her real motivations. The choice to be a vegetarian was "emotional"; it made her "special" and "slightly morally superior"; eating meat was expensive; not eating meat allowed her to "prove her political mettle" as a "privileged white girl" (3–5). With time, she came to believe more substantive arguments for vegetarianism, but the acknowledgment of her own less-than-noble reasons undercuts the presumed "moral superiority" of her decision not to eat meat.

2. The writer concedes that there is "a lot of evidence that vegetarians live longer, have lower cholesterol levels and are thinner than meat-eaters" (7). In her case, the diet lowered her cholesterol. But Fraser points out that it is possible to eat a relatively high-fat and unhealthful diet and remain a vegetarian. As she writes: "I was basically a cheesetarian" (7).
3. Dating back to the first half of the nineteenth century, utilitarianism is a philosophy that ties goodness and virtue to usefulness, says actions should be judged by their consequences, and argues human behavior should be directed toward promoting the greatest happiness—and the smallest amount of suffering—for the greatest number. Many animal rights proponents include animals in this ethical framework. Fraser also uses the term *utilitarian* for comic effect in her argument, as when she writes that she ate fish because doing so made it "a lot easier to be a vegetarian when you go out to restaurants. Now that's utilitarian" (13).
4. Part of Fraser's argument is that human beings are omnivorous and naturally crave meat in their diets. After consuming chicken for the first time in years, she writes that for the "first time in a long time, [she] felt satisfied" (20). Indeed, Fraser emphasizes her animal nature, describing how she ripped into her friend's chicken "like a starving hyena" (18). In doing so, she suggests that craving—and eating—meat is instinctive, natural, and necessary human behavior. Fraser's piece is a polemical, personal essay; the title is "Why *I* Stopped Being a Vegetarian" (emphasis added). She could have used less opinionated language, but that would have made for a different kind of essay.

At Issue: Should We Eat Meat? p. 529

1. Students could answer this question in a number of ways. For example, they could disagree with the premises of Foer's question, giving specific reasons for doing so. They might concur with Fraser that humans naturally crave meat, regardless of any "reasonable" considerations. You may ask students which part of Foer's argument they find most persuasive in this context: the "rational" case for being a vegetarian or the instinctive responses he provokes throughout most of the essay.
2. Fraser suggests that applying utilitarian standards to all the relationships between humans and other animals is extremely difficult. How should we measure the "happiness" or "satisfaction" of animals? What kind of moral rights can we ascribe to them? How do we calculate all the consequences of human actions toward animals? For example, what if increasing crop cultivation and harvesting to feed more vegetarians encroached on animal habitats or indirectly killed more animals? As a practical matter, living as a vegan—one who avoids the use and consumption of *any* animal products—is difficult in a contemporary industrialized society.
3. Fraser's essay touches on all the complex and interrelated aspects of personal dietary choices mentioned by Foer. For example, she explicitly connects her decision to become a vegetarian with her desire to identify with an "oppressed minority group" (5). Similarly, she discusses diet in the context of both primal cravings and societal standards.

Writing Arguments: Should We Eat Meat? p. 529

1. Students may wish to get started on this essay by responding to a specific aspect of either Foer's or Fraser's argument. The assignment should give them an opportunity to reflect on the wider implications—nutritional, cultural, moral, religious, personal—of food choices.
2. Students should consider what set of standards is best for their argument: nutritional, moral, social, natural, etc. They may also want to investigate sources beyond these two essays.

CHAPTER 19

Debate: Do We Still Need Newspapers?

Summary of "Requiem for Real News" by Chris Hedges, p. 533

Hedges's article is, indeed, a **requiem**: a composition written for the deceased. But where most such works are traditionally written in honor of people who have died, the writer here is eulogizing and lamenting the death of "real news." For Hedges, true reporting is about "transmitting information that doesn't care what you think" (para. 9). Such journalism "challenges, countermands or destabilizes established beliefs" (9). It is also a public trust—one essential to informed citizens in a democracy. According to Hedges, that trust has been superseded by news-hating corporations, a distracting fusion of news and entertainment, and unaccountable Internet screeds: "pandering, packaging and partisanship" (10).

Reading Arguments, p. 535

1. Hedges's thesis is that the decline of newspapers is not simply a matter of technological progress or new media forms; rather, it signals the end of disinterested journalism as a whole and the rise of the corporate state, a development that threatens our democracy and will leave citizens "deaf, dumb and blind" (18). Although Hedges makes this argument and others throughout his essay, your students should locate the primary thesis statement as the second paragraph. They should also note that the introductory paragraph anticipates those who argue that the Internet simply provides the same news in a new format or that it is an "inevitable" technological development and should be accepted or lauded as "progress."
2. Hedges blames "the rise of the corporate state, the loss of civic and public responsibility on the part of much of our entrepreneurial class and the intellectual poverty of our post-literate world" for the declining influence of newspapers (2). Another explanation, one that Hedges explicitly disagrees with, is that when news on the Internet is free, subscribers to newspapers find it hard to justify their cost. News, they feel, is news.

3. By "public trust," Hedges means that newspapers are supposed to provide impartial information that allows citizens to hold powerful people and institutions—public or private—accountable; to give voice to people who otherwise would have no voice; to keep track of local, state, and federal government in ways that a private citizen cannot. In democratic societies, Hedges sees newspapers as accountable; they admit and retract errors of fact.

4. Propaganda is the spreading of ideas, images, rumors, or information for the deliberate purpose of helping or hurting a cause, person, or institution. By "competing propaganda," Hedges is saying that an outfit dispensing propaganda will not encourage a response by a legitimate authority but only by another outfit with the same questionable goals and values.

5. The writer suggests that we are falling victim to "bread and circuses" in the same way the ancient Romans did. If students indeed see historical parallels between the decline of Rome and conditions in twenty-first-century America—at least in regard to distribution of news—they will find Hedges's reference effective both as support for his argument and as a conclusion.

Summary of "Yes, Newspapers Are Doomed" by Gary S. Becker, p. 536

According to Becker, the Internet is supplanting newspapers—and will inevitably replace them—because it "provides information, opinion, and entertainment more frequently and effectively than newspapers do" (para. 4). He sees attempts by newspapers to present themselves online as futile because their traditional ways of bundling content are outdated. Web sites tend to be highly specialized and appeal to readers looking for specific topics or services; in contrast, newspapers are too broad and general in their scope. But in Becker's view, only older people who are accustomed to reading traditional newspapers will regret or lament the end of daily print journalism.

Reading Arguments, p. 537

1. To support his case that newspapers are doomed, Becker offers anecdotal evidence: "It is now rare to see anyone under age 30" reading a major newspaper (2). But Becker also notes that a broader consumer trend, not just his personal observation, confirms the end of daily print journalism. For example, he cites the declining number of newspapers, their decreasing profits, and cuts in staff. In contrast, consumers are "voting with how they use their time" and prefer to spend time online (8).

2. According to the writer, the Internet is such a threat to hard-copy newspapers because it can offer "information, opinion, and entertainment more frequently and effectively than newspapers do" (4). In addition, Web sites can provide content in "real time," while newspapers cannot (4). Internet sites are also taking advertising revenue that used to go to print media (3).

3. In discussing Becker's claim that the demand is down for verifying facts and separating fact from opinion, you may want to ask students about their own choices and views—particularly, in the context of Becker's and Hedges's arguments. *Possible follow-up questions:* Should the gathering and presentation of news be entirely driven by consumer demand? Is there a significant difference between being a "consumer" and being a "citizen" in the context of news and information?

4. Newspapers are attempting to adapt and present their content online. But the "general-purpose hard copy newspaper that combines opinions, sports, advertisements, comics, and information" (1) does not work in the highly specialized and segmented world of the Internet, according to Becker.

At Issue: Do We Still Need Newspapers? p. 538

1. Jefferson's statement that he would opt for "newspapers without a government" fits with Hedges's assertion that democracy depends on its citizens having "access to trustworthy and impartial sources of information" (para. 17). It presumes that reasonable people can make decisions about themselves and their country if they have the right knowledge. Students should consider where they get their information about important issues and how that information and those sources affect their view of government, politics, and business.

2. You may want to ask students about their own preferences for getting news and information. Do they choose sources that reinforce their own beliefs or challenge them? When, if ever, have they been made "uncomfortable" by a piece of reporting? This question raises the issues of impartiality and objectivity. Is such disinterestedness possible? Many people, particularly on the political right, complain of "media bias." What kinds of biases do students see? Even professional editorial judgment of what is "newsworthy" and what is not might constitute a bias. Is that a problem?

3. Hedges points out that a few corporations "control nearly everything we read, watch, hear and ultimately think" (13). He also claims that corporations "hate real news" (16). Do his observations make legitimate concerns? What is the connection between corporate-owned news outlets, celebrity journalists, and sensationalism? Becker seems willing to leave the future of news to the will of consumers. Yet consumer choice may lead to more sensationalism and ideological bias, as people self-segment and choose sources that support their own views. A sales cliché holds that "the customer is always right." Does the statement apply to news as well?

Writing Arguments: Do We Still Need Newspapers? p. 538

In writing an essay in response to Becker's observation about the "rapid and continuing decline" of major print newspapers, students should incorporate—and address—the views of both Hedges and Becker in their essays. The process of writing this essay should give students a chance to reflect on their own media choices as well as on how those choices affect them as citizens.

CHAPTER

20 Debate: What Should Be Done about Our Nation's Homeless?

Summary of "Throw the Bums Out: But Do So with Compassion—Coolidge-Style Compassion" by John Derbyshire, p. 543

In this essay, John Derbyshire looks at the growing homeless problem in San Francisco and finds the city's response illogical, self-defeating, and cruel. He begins with graphic and unflattering depictions of "vagrants" and their effects on San Francisco's public spaces. Then he argues that specific welfare policies, including "cash payments" to "indigent adults," are making the situation worse. According to Derbyshire, the city (and the United States, generally) should return to Calvin Coolidge's maxim that "self-government means self support" (para. 10).

Reading Arguments, p. 545

1. A euphemism is usually an inoffensive, agreeable word or phrase that is used to replace an offensive or unpleasant expression. *Homeless* is a euphemism in that it evokes a more abstract, less culpable, and less visceral image than *bum* or *vagrant.* It also carries the sense of a larger social problem, a sense that *vagrant* does not carry. Students should see that word choice is significant in debates such as this one.

2. The writer seems nostalgic for the "sound system" (10) of the past, but his primary evidence of its effectiveness is a fictional character. Moreover, it is hard to see just how Huckleberry Finn's father in the Twain novel relates to "humane and sensible" (9) community problem solving. Ask students what other evidence might have provided stronger support. For example, they may suggest the poorhouse or almshouse system that existed previously in the United States. Derbyshire seems to suggest that private individuals and charities would do a better job helping the indigent. Do students agree with this opinion?

3. *A restatement of Derbyshire's thesis:* San Francisco's approach to homelessness, which includes cash payments to "able-bodied" (6) indigents, makes the problem worse and goes against the American ideal of self-support and respect for the individual.

4. To support his opinion that the current approach to homelessness, which devalues the agency and responsibility of individuals, is "much crueler" than the approaches of the past, Derbyshire cites the values of self-sufficiency espoused by Calvin Coolidge. He also thinks that the city's initiatives only encourage people to remain indigent and dependent on the government. By "humanitarian cant," Derbyshire means ways of speaking and thinking that excuse or encourage vagrancy and offensive public behavior "in the name of 'compassion' and 'rights'" (12). (The word *cant* itself suggests expressions that are trite and sentimental.)

Summary of "The Meanest Cities," *America* (a national Catholic weekly magazine), p. 546

The magazine focuses on the trend toward criminalizing homelessness, whether in the form of ordinances that make panhandling illegal or laws that prohibit sleeping in public spaces. According to the essay, such restrictions can be unnecessarily cruel for an already vulnerable population; they make homeless people less likely to get jobs or find housing; they may also restrict the charitable work of religious groups hoping to help the indigent and needy. The article seeks a broad range of reforms and initiatives from both the public and private sectors.

Reading Arguments, p. 547

1. The thesis is located in the final paragraph: "Instead of criminalizing homelessness, greater efforts should be made nationwide to help people move out of this condition, or—better yet—to help them avoid falling into it in the first place." Students may think that placing the thesis statement earlier—before the evidence of "mean" policies—would have less impact.

2. The "dark phenomenon" is the prevalence of policies, such as those that restrict the charitable feeding of poor people, which essentially make homelessness a crime. One unfortunate outcome of these laws and ordinances is that homeless people who get arrested and charged for sitting, eating, or sleeping in public places acquire criminal records that make finding employment or housing even more difficult. In addition, the financial cost of arresting and housing these people and keeping them in jail is higher than providing "supportive housing" (2).

3. The editorial's specific language with regard to charitable works seems to be an appeal to a broad religious audience. For example, the editorial refers to church groups who "view their work as a concrete response to the biblical call to feed the hungry" (3). Still, the emphasis is subtle; the editorial does not proselytize in a heavy-handed way.

At Issue: What Should Be Done about Our Nation's Homeless? p. 548

1. Regarding the attitudes of the writers, the more practical Derbyshire shows an overt disgust toward homeless people; the writer perceives many of the homeless as having shirked their responsibilities, even as they are supported by the city government. They are, he feels, a public nuisance to be reduced, not encouraged or enabled. He wants all able-bodied people to support themselves; he longs for a time when local communities maintained public standards and "private citizens . . . could exercise the virtue of private charity to any degree they wished" (9). He writes in the first person and bases his view on personal observation. Ask students if they find Derbyshire's tone refreshingly honest or merely cruel. The editorial in the Catholic publication sees homelessness in a broader context than Derbyshire does; its solutions are more systemic and involve government actions—for example, changing laws, increasing the supply of transitional housing, and raising minimum wage levels (7). Compared with Derbyshire, the editorial is impersonal and detached, but at the same time, some students may see it as more ethical. It may be helpful to have students role-play the differing approaches in these two essays. For example, how might Derbyshire respond to the editorial? Does the editorial display "humanitarian cant"? How might the editorial board of *America* view Derbyshire's disgust at the homeless?
2. This question about governments' obligation to help the homeless is likely to provoke a range of responses from students, depending on their political views, religious beliefs, and perhaps backgrounds. You may want to note that both essays leave room for some public intervention and both praise the role of private charities. For example, the *America* editorial praises the work of the Task Force for Ending Homelessness (6).
3. This question about the legality of begging will also produce a variety of responses as well as a lively discussion. How do students weigh individual freedoms (say, the freedom to ask for money in a public place) against the need for social order or the rights of people to move in public without being harassed (Derbyshire's word choice) by panhandlers? Do students distinguish between certain public behaviors (eating, panhandling, even sleeping) as acceptable and others (lewdness, urination, verbal harassment) as criminal?

Writing Arguments: What Should Be Done about Our Nation's Homeless? p. 548

As students prepare to write their arguments about the homeless, encourage them to think about both their point of view and their tone. Specifically, they should consider the advantages and disadvantages of writing in the first person and basing an argument on observation as opposed to a more detached, less personal approach. This assignment should get students to consider the effects of language—especially, particular words and phrases—on debates.

CHAPTER 21

Debate: Should the U.S. Government Drop Its Sanctions against Cuba?

Summary of "Opposition to Rep. Rangel's Amendment to Lift Embargo on Cuban Regime" by Lincoln Diaz-Balart, p. 553

In this speech on the House floor, U.S. Representative Lincoln Diaz-Balart (R-Florida) adamantly opposes the lifting of the Cuban embargo and the "normalization" of relations between the United States and Cuba. He argues that doing so violates the charter of the Organization of American States and rewards an oppressive, undemocratic, and dangerous regime.

Reading Arguments, p. 554

1. The speech by Diaz-Balart is an ethical argument in that he believes rewarding a government like the one in Cuba is morally wrong. His emphasis on Cuba's executions, repression, torture, and other immoral activities underscores this point. In contrast, he places little or no emphasis on whether or not the sanctions have been effective as a practical matter: effectiveness is not his standard. Rather, the embargo policy should remain in place because to lift it would be an immoral choice.
2. Diaz-Balart's thesis can be restated as follows: U.S. sanctions on Cuba demonstrate America's commitment to the O.A.S. charter, human rights, freedom, democracy, and the Cuban people; lifting the sanctions would reward tyranny and oppression.
3. Diaz-Balart quotes Rangel to show that Rangel had previously had no interest in communicating with the Castro dictatorship and that Rangel was being hypocritical by sponsoring an amendment to lift the embargo on Cuba. This

argument is a refutation because it uses Rangel's own reasons for opposing lifting the embargo, that the Castro dictatorship put three men to death for trying to leave the country.

4. Diaz-Balart's statement that he wishes "to stand with the Cuban people today" connects with the representative's overall argument because it bypasses questions of the policy's effectiveness or its unintended consequences. His main point is that the sanctions must continue because they represent the Americas' support of freedom, democracy, human rights, the rule of law, and the Cuban people, who live under an unjust government.

Summary of "Thanks for the Sanctions" by Jacob Weisberg, p. 555

For Jacob Weisberg, the malevolence of tyrannical governments is secondary in the sanctions debate. He takes it for granted. The more important issue is whether such measures are effective—or whether they ultimately help tyrants and dictators consolidate their power. He acknowledges the "admirable" aims and sacrifices of U.S. sanctions over the years (para. 3). But after a brief historical survey, Weisberg concludes that sanctions rarely succeed, even as the leaders and governments we seek to punish "thrive on the political loneliness we inflict and in some cases appear to seek more of it" (5).

Reading Arguments, p. 557

1. Weisberg uses inductive reasoning by working from a variety of particular cases—Cuba, North Korea, Iran, and others—to achieve a general principle that "sanctions don't work" (3). While he concedes that there may be a limited number of "debatable exceptions" (3), Weisberg seeks to demonstrate that his argument is, in all likelihood, true—given the preponderance of specific historical evidence.

2. Weisberg's essay is an argument by evaluation in that it offers a critique of U.S. sanctions policy over the years. While he acknowledges the good intentions of these measures, he evaluates their effects and concludes that they have mostly failed. He also infers from his evidence that sanctions will do further harm in the future, as in the case of Iran (7). Weisberg's essay moves on to become a proposal argument when it proposes a policy of "constructive engagement" (6), including trade, tourism, cultural exchange, and "participation in international institutions" (6). According to Weisberg, such contact helps "erode the legitimacy of repressive regimes" and has proven effective in the Philippines, South Korea, Argentina, and other countries (6). Does this proposal seem persuasive to students, even if it might mean "engagement" with tyrants such as Kim Jong-Il? What are its benefits and drawbacks?

3. By capitalizing "on the law of unintended consequences," Weisberg means that sanctions are a blunt instrument that can have "collateral damage . . . on the civilian populations . . . we target" (3). Such damage tends to turn the

population against the "proximate cause of its devastation, not the underlying causes" (4). That is, civilians tend to blame the United States rather than their own leaders. Weisberg supports this view by pointing to various "unintended consequences" and the benefits tyrants derive from them: Global isolation strengthens the power of state propaganda; "pariah" leaders can blame their country's suffering on "external enemies"; the material devastation from sanctions makes it "less likely that the oppressed will throw off their chains" (4). His specific historical examples include Bashar Assad, Kim Jong-Il, Robert Mugabe, Fidel Castro, and others.

4. Weisberg implicitly addresses opposing arguments when he acknowledges the "admirable" and reasonable aims of sanctions (3). He concedes that they are a "palatable alternative to military action" (9). He allows that his "constructive engagement" proposal can often sound "like lame cover for business interests" (6). In paragraph 8, he addresses the example of South Africa, which is "always cited" to prove that sanctions can be effective. He agrees that sanctions did contribute to the fall of the regime and help the country's transition to democracy. But he also notes that South Africa had distinctive characteristics that made it "amenable" to sanctions in ways that places such as North Korea are not. Moreover, even in the case off South Africa, where the policy was effective, it took nearly three decades for the sanctions to have much impact.

At Issue: Should the U.S. Government Drop Its Sanctions against Cuba? p. 557

1. Students will most likely find Weisberg's essay more persuasive than Diaz-Balart's speech. The former is pragmatic and results oriented. But it also takes into account the presumably good intentions of people like Diaz-Balart as well as the moral issues at stake when sanctions have unintended consequences. You may want to consider the relative effectiveness of the two arguments in terms of their form and their audience. Diaz-Balart is an elected legislator speaking on the floor of the House of Representatives against a particular policy proposal. Weisberg is writing a thoughtful essay on foreign policy for a general-interest online publication aimed at affluent and educated readers. How might their goals be different? What restrictions on content and expression might apply to a legislator but not to a magazine journalist? For example, ask students if a politician who is beholden to his constituents or party affiliation might be limited by such loyalties. Similarly, you might also have them consider whether the moral or ethical obligations of an elected representative would be different from those of a magazine writer.

2. In considering this question of whether the United States has the right (or even obligation) to change other governments in the Western hemisphere and outside it, you may ask students which foreign policy arguments tend to be more persuasive: those that claim the United States should act solely for its own self-interest or those that propose a moral, philosophical, or political obligation to "spread democracy" or stand with "oppressed" people throughout the world. Some may argue that the two premises are related rather than

opposed. How does a person make the argument that the United States has the right to change the governments of other countries? Diaz-Balart cites the O.A.S. charter, for example. Is that charter sufficient to the continuation of U.S. sanctions on Cuba? Would it ever justify military intervention on the part of the United States?

3. "Collateral damage" is often used as a euphemism for the unintended consequences of military attacks or sanctions policies that cause harm to civilian populations. The term suggests an accident, or a mistake made with good intentions. In considering the question of whether the United States bears moral responsibility for such damage and weighing the choices, students might want to research the actual damage that occurs due to sanctions. For example, the United States imposed sanctions on Iraq after the first Gulf War, causing significant material hardships for the civilian population. Is the United States still culpable if its overall goal was the displacement of a dictator? Why or why not?

Writing Arguments: Should the U.S. Government Drop Its Sanctions against Cuba? p. 557

Students may want to fashion their essays as direct responses to Diaz-Balart, Weisberg, or both. For example, they could begin by examining what it means, exactly, to "stand with the Cuban people" or any other civilian population in another country. They may also want to look for examples that Weisberg may have overlooked or misread.

CHAPTER

22

Debate: Should Undocumented Immigrants Be Entitled to Driver's Licenses?

Summary of "Fact Sheet: Why Denying Driver's Licenses to Undocumented Immigrants Harms Public Safety and Makes Our Communities Less Secure," National Immigration Law Center, p. 561

This document asserts that the debate over driver's licenses for undocumented immigrants is a distraction from real immigration issues and important questions of public safety. The law center argues that such a restriction is bad policy, which jeopardizes public safety, drives up automobile insurance rates, harms national security, and undermines law-enforcement efforts. Instead, policymakers should focus on "Practical Driver's License Reforms that Improve the Integrity of the License" (above para. 20), as well as on realistic solutions to the country's immigration problem.

Reading Arguments, p. 566

1. The thesis of this document appears in the first paragraph and can be summarized as follows: denying driver's licenses to undocumented immigrants is bad public policy because it increases uninsurance rates and the number of unlicensed drivers while also undermining effective law enforcement.
2. Controversial and highly charged discussions related to immigration lend themselves to demagoguery, pandering, and sloganeering. The writers argue

that such simplistic rhetoric and thinking may be effective in the media, but they will not fix real problems. Ask students if they agree that this distinction exists or whether it seems like an either/or fallacy. The writers cite Democrat Bill Richardson as well as Republicans Jeb Bush and David Ure to demonstrate that people can agree on "realistic solutions," regardless of their political party. Do students agree that partisanship can cause officials to "ignore reality" (5)?

3. The fact sheet deploys a range of evidence—especially, traffic safety data, insurance statistics, and financial figures. The writers also refer to several authorities, such as a professor at the U.S. Military Academy at West Point, Los Angeles Police Chief William Bratton, and others. Ask students about the total effect of this evidence. Does it all cohere and further an overall argument? What are the fact sheet's strengths and weaknesses? For example, how persuasive and compelling is the 1999 quotation from Utah state legislator David Ure?
4. According to authorities cited in the fact sheet, denying these licenses "increases the size of the suspect pool for law enforcement" (14). It also keeps illegal immigrants "out of the largest law enforcement database in the country" (15). In 2005, the Government Accountability Office reported that driver's license databases were more current and more reliable than the database of the Department of Homeland Security.
5. The documentation bolsters the authority of the fact sheet. Readers can examine the sources to see for themselves how reliable they are and see that they have been used in proper context.

Summary of "States Should Not Issue Driver's Licenses to Illegal Immigrants" by Michael W. Cutler, p. 567

A long-time veteran of the Immigration and Naturalization Service, Michael Cutler takes issue especially with those who claim that immigration laws are not enforceable. According to Cutler, granting the licenses would aid and abet illegal aliens in living and working illegally in the United States. He considers driver's licenses flawed as identity documents and concludes that the "only thing worse than no security is false security" (para. 10).

Reading Arguments, p. 570

1. Cutler makes the point that the shift from *illegal alien* to *undocumented worker* blurs the distinction between "what is legal and what is illegal" (5). According to him, the blurring encourages the "rampant entry of illegal aliens into the United States" as well as other criminal activities (5). He sees this shift as part of a larger trend toward "political correctness"; he makes the comparison to George Orwell's novel *1984,* which examined the link between words, perceptions, and thoughts. Students should explain why they agree or disagree that language is an important part of the driver's license and immigration debates.

2. The thesis is in the eighth paragraph, where Cutler explains that the issuance of driver's licenses to illegal aliens is wrong because it "aids and abets illegal aliens in living and working illegally in the United States." Cutler chose to announce his thesis only after he established his authority, defined his terms and his larger point of view, and even addressed a counterargument.
3. Cutler uses inductive reasoning to address the opposing argument that "immigration laws are not enforceable." He points out that since motor vehicle laws, drug laws, firearms laws, and others are enforceable, it would follow as a general rule that immigration laws are enforceable as well (6). He asserts that no human law can have a 100% compliance rate. You may want to have students look more closely at the logic here. Cutler's rebuttal would seem to head off *any* criticism or questioning of the validity of immigration laws as they are. A reader, however, might respond that some laws are more effectively enforced than others and that the failure of immigration policy should provoke a closer examination of why it fails and a reevaluation of specific laws and enforcement strategies.
4. Cutler evaluates when he describes political correctness as permeating our society and leading to lawlessness (5). He also evaluates when he questions the conventional wisdom that immigration laws are unenforceable (6) and when he concludes that our current system of issuing driver's licenses gives us a "false sense of security" (10). Cutler argues by analogy when he compares our society with that of Orwell's *1984* and our discussion of *undocumented workers* with Newspeak (5). He compares a "country without borders" to a "house without walls" (5). He also makes an argument through analogy when he compares immigration laws with "enforceable" laws (6).
5. Cutler proposes a number of cause-and-effect relationships in structuring his argument. For example, as noted above, he sees the move from the term *illegal alien* to *undocumented worker* as part of a "blurring" of what is legal and illegal; he implies that the act of using such language helps "encourage the rampant entry of illegal aliens into the United States" (5). But perhaps the most important cause-and-effect argument in this speech is the one that underlies his main point: "The issuance of driver's licenses will make it easier for aliens who are living and working illegally in the United States to circumvent our laws"; the policy will also "aid criminal aliens and terrorists" (16). Ask students to look closely at the cause-and-effect relationship here. Does Cutler effectively and conclusively establish probability, or is he, rather, arguing by assertion?

At Issue: Should Undocumented Immigrants Be Entitled to Driver's Licenses? p. 571

1. In this context, *ideology* means the theories, assertions, and aims of an individual, a culture, or a political group. To be "ideologically senseless" means to be so invested in abstract ideals or unrealistic goals as to lose sight of practical realities and probabilities. For example, a nationalistic person devoted to law, order, and perfect immigration policy might insist that every single one

of the 8 to 14 million estimated illegal immigrants in the United States be deported to their countries of origin. Such a goal would be "ideologically senseless" because it is impossible as a practical matter. While Cutler does not propose an impossible plan, do students find his argument ideological in any way, or is he more focused on a practical solution?

2. Students will probably define *political correctness* as an attempt to eliminate language and practices that can offend political sensibilities. They may associate political correctness with liberals and indicate that the term is disparaging and connotes excessive sensibility. Regarding the use by the National Immigration Law Center of the term *undocumented immigrant* instead of *illegal alien,* students may differ on whether the word choice undermines the organization's argument. You may also ask how Cutler would respond to the fact sheet.
3. While both sides make reasonable arguments about licenses and criminality and security, students may say that the center's fact sheet seems more comprehensive. For example, the center points out that driver's license restrictions cause immigrants to "avoid contact with state and local law enforcement" (17) and make them "unwilling to report crimes" (17). On the other hand, Cutler speculates that access to driver's licenses help those who are in the United States illegally in "their quest to create new identities for themselves" (11). However, in both of these specific examples, neither the center nor the testimony provides statistical or empirical evidence to back assertions.

Writing Arguments: Should Undocumented Immigrants Be Entitled to Driver's Licenses? p. 571

Students may want to write a straightforward argument for or against granting driver's licenses to undocumented immigrants. Or they may prefer to write an argument about a particular aspect of the licensing and immigration debates that you or they suggest—for example, the language we use regarding immigration, the oft-cited failures of American immigration policy, the problem of sound bites in political discourse, and so on.

CHAPTER

23

Debate: Should the United States Permit Drilling for Oil in Environmentally Sensitive Areas?

Summary of "Drill, Baby, Drill" by Pete Du Pont, p. 575

Du Pont argues that America must access more of its own natural energy resources, which he claims will be plentiful if the government will loosen restrictions on exploration and drilling. For example, he cites Interior Department estimates that restricted offshore areas contain "the equivalent of perhaps 30 years of oil we will import from Saudi Arabia" (para. 5). He also suggests that the American people are becoming increasingly receptive to more domestic oil and gas drilling.

Reading Arguments, p. 577

1. Du Pont begins with broad statistics regarding America's oil and gas production, importation, and consumption to demonstrate that "we need to discover and access more of our own energy resources" (1). His argument presumes that oil and gas consumption will remain constant and implies that reducing imports is necessary, among other premises. If his premises are true, his conclusion will likely be true as well. Similarly, his second paragraph proposes premises that, if true, should lead to his conclusion—although he qualifies his conclusion with the word *could*: "If full access to these resources were permitted, together they could replace America's imported oil for some 25 years, and no doubt reduce the price of oil, gas and gasoline" (2).
2. Du Pont sees several benefits to allowing more domestic drilling, including lower domestic fuel prices, reduced dependence on imports, and access to drilling areas that will not be threatened by hurricanes in the Gulf of Mexico.

3. The writer addresses the environmental argument against offshore drilling in paragraph 6. According to Du Point, less than 0.001% of oil from the Outer Continental Shelf was spilled between 1993 and 2007. Students probably will not all agree that this point adequately covers the various objections to more domestic drilling or assuages more general concerns about pollution in the oceans, coasts, or coastal areas.
4. Du Pont may be correct, and no doubt *some* people began to call for more domestic drilling. Yet, he offers no polling data, empirical research, or any other evidence to back this generalization about Americans. Moreover, he does not demonstrate that offshore drilling at the time of the 2008 gas price spikes would have significantly lowered gas prices in the United States, although he implies that effect.
5. To some, the quotation by Pelosi in paragraph 9 portrays her as self-important and out of touch with people struggling with high gasoline prices. It supports Du Pont's argument because it suggests his opponents and their arguments are bombastic. Indeed, the Speaker of the House did make this statement in the context of her opposition to domestic oil exploration and other issues, but students may debate the validity of using the Pelosi quotation in this way, given that Du Pont is making a serious argument. Ask students if they think Pelosi's remark accurately encapsulates or represents those who oppose drilling, generally.

Summary of "To Drill or . . ." by Senator Lamar Alexander, p. 578

Although he initially opposed opening the Arctic National Wildlife Refuge (ANWR), Lamar Alexander went on to support "responsible drilling" (para. 4). He argues that by using a small portion of ANWR, we could stave off fuel gas prices, job losses, and cold homes, but he also claims we need to seek to balance energy exploration with conservation.

Reading Arguments, p. 579

1. Alexander tries to portray himself as someone with a connection to the land and a genuine commitment to conservation and the environment. The autobiographical information underscores his thesis that one can support domestic drilling and still behave responsibly with regard to the "Great American Outdoors."
2. Alexander argues that fuel prices cannot go "to a level our citizens cannot afford." If they do, the country will experience higher unemployment, cold homes in winter, and other problems.
3. In Rogerian style, Alexander carefully and deliberately finds common ground with those who oppose his argument: he acknowledges that he once agreed with them. He notes his youth in "the foothills of the Great Smoky Mountains" and his commitment to balancing risks to the environment with benefits to the environment. He also explains how he changed his mind on the issue, after he "gathered all possible facts" (2) he could find. His tone is con-

ciliatory, trustworthy, and optimistic rather than polarizing, scathing, or dismissive. How do students react to this approach? What are its advantages—and disadvantages?

Summary of ". . . Not to Drill" by Representative Ed Markey, p. 580

According to Ed Markey, those who want to open the Arctic National Wildlife Refuge to drilling demonstrate a "lack of vision that will prolong our dependence on dangerous foreign oil, not solve it" (para. 6). He argues that ANWR is a national treasure and that its limited oil reserves would have little effect on fuel prices or overall U.S. energy dependence. Instead, he proposes that the country look to technological innovation and more fuel-efficient automobiles.

Reading Arguments, p. 581

1. Markey supports his statement about America's "ravenous appetite for oil" by pointing out the United States consumes 25% of the world's oil, even though the country contains less than 5% of the world's population. "Ravenous" implies that the United States should focus on curbing consumption, rather than just looking for more oil. As he writes, "With only 3 percent of the world's oil reserves, the United States cannot drill its way to independence" (3). The emphasis on fuel conservation and finite resources ties in with his proposals near the end of the argument.

2. Markey argues that drilling in ANWR would reduce U.S. dependence on foreign oil from 70% to 66% in twenty years and would lower gas prices by less than one cent per gallon. He states that oil from the refuge would not reach the market until a decade into production. In the opening paragraph, Markey notes in passing that British Petroleum (BP) has no interest in drilling in ANWR, suggesting the refuge's oil supply is limited.

3. Markey's argument has an explicitly partisan tone, as he targets the Bush administration as well as the Congressional Republican leadership who seek to end drilling restrictions in ANWR. By citing a Bush administration department's own numbers and estimates, he can counter accusations that he is using biased or partisan sources. You may want to point out to students that Markey's argument is more partisan and less Rogerian than Alexander's. Ask students which approach is more effective and why.

4. Markey claims that if scientists of the 1960s could "respond to President Kennedy's Cold War challenge" and put a man on the moon, then today's "technological geniuses" can build more fuel-efficient cars. The analogy has its strengths. First, it implies that the quest for energy dependence is as urgent as the need to win the Cold War. Second, it conjures up images of America's greatness—as well as inspiring political leadership. Third, the comparison calls on the country's sense of itself as a technological leader. At the same time, some students may argue that the analogy is trite or even that Markey uses the comparison to score a political jab at a president from the opposing party.

Summary of "Arctic National Wildlife Refuge: Why Trash an American Treasure for a Tiny Percentage of Our Oil Needs?" National Resources Defense Council, p. 582

The National Resources Defense Council makes an argument similar to Ed Markey's: The pristine ANWR needs to be protected; oil from the refuge will not significantly alleviate America's energy problems; the country needs to seek solutions in new technologies. But the NRDC emphasizes the significance of public opinion, noting that the "American people have consistently made clear their desire to protect this treasure and rejected claims that drilling . . . is any sort of answer to the nation's dependence on foreign oil" (para. 2). In part, its argument is that ANWR should not be open to drilling because most Americans disapprove. The organization claims that opening the Arctic Refuge will lead to a slippery slope as "oil interests" and other industries get their way: "Next up: Greater Yellowstone? Our Western canyonlands?" (6).

Reading Arguments, p. 584

1. To substantiate the generalization that Americans have consistently rejected drilling in ANWR, the writers cite persistent congressional opposition (2), "hundreds of thousands of emails, faxes and phone calls from citizens" (5), and a June 2008 poll that found 55% of the American public supports continued protection for ANWR (5). Students may be skeptical of any broad claims about public opinion; some may be suspicious of polling itself (the wording of polls can have a significant effect on responses, for example).

2. The thesis might be restated as follows: "ANWR should remain off-limits to drilling because its limited oil supply will not solve America's energy problems and its pristine wilderness needs to be protected from big business. Americans understand this situation and, therefore, consistently oppose drilling."

3. An unqualified claim that Yellowstone will be opened for mining or drilling if ANWR is opened would be a slippery-slope fallacy. But in paragraph 6, the writers phrase their concern using questions, not statements. Students should recognize the function of such rhetorical questions—to allow writers to raise objections or suggest arguments without necessarily having to support them thoroughly. Still, the NRDC's point could be valid if the push to drill in ANWR were shown to be part of a verifiable, larger, concerted effort on the part of industries or political officials to open these other wildlife areas. As for the consequences of drilling on the environment, the NRDC report notes the deleterious effects in Prudhoe Bay, which is near ANWR (12).

4. The NRDC addresses drilling proponents who claim that there are 16 billion barrels under ANWR's coastal plain by pointing out that "the U.S. Geological Survey's estimate of the amount that could be recovered economically . . . represents less than a year's U.S. supply" (9). In addition, the writers of this report accuse their opponents of distracting from real issues and acting in bad faith:

"The drive to drill in the Arctic Refuge . . . has nothing to do with energy independence. Opening the Arctic Refuge to energy development is about transferring our public estate into corporate hands so that it can be liquidated for a quick buck" (7). How do students react to this aspect of the NRDC argument? Is it effective? Would the report be improved if it employed Rogerian elements, or would it be weakened? You might also view these questions in the context of audience: who is likely to read this report?

At Issue: Should the United States Permit Drilling for Oil in Environmentally Sensitive Areas? p. 585

1. Students may have a wide variety of responses to the oft-cited statistic that the United States is home to less than 5% of the world's population but consumes 25% of its oil. For example, some will see it as evidence of an excessive consumer culture and an unsustainable way of life; others might see it as one of the benefits of the country's global status, productivity, and high standard of living. Students may want to look more deeply into the meaning and context of the disparity: Where does the oil go, specifically? How does this consumption compare with that of other industrialized or developing nations? Does the statistic, on its own, suggest that Americans should make changes in their habits as citizens and consumers? Why or why not?

2. While ANWR is "among the world's last true wildernesses," it is also a region that few people will experience firsthand. Students might consider how to place value on such places—balanced against, say, the need for less expensive fuel. The NRDC points out the variety of wildlife in the area. Is that argument persuasive?

3. Energy dependence is often discussed in the context of national security. For example, Markey refers to "dangerous foreign oil." Ask students about the implications of our dependence on these imports. Which countries actually provide us with oil? Although the United States does import most of its oil now, the majority comes from Canada, Mexico, and South America, not the Middle East (as is widely presumed). Would being energy independent make the United States safer? How?

Writing Arguments: Should the United States Permit Drilling for Oil in Environmentally Sensitive Areas? p. 585

1. You might advise students to conduct some research outside these essays—perhaps to challenge the arguments made or research cited by the authors in this chapter.

2. This assignment should allow students to connect their own experiences and observations with larger energy issues facing the country. They might want to consider how high fuel prices or fuel shortages might affect their lives—especially, in ways that are not immediately obvious. For instance, Lamar Alexander claims that higher fuel prices might mean higher unemployment. Do students think about that wider context?

CHAPTER

24 Casebook: Should Felons Permanently Forfeit Their Right to Vote?

Summary of "Felons Don't Merit Automatic Rights" by Bill McCollum, p. 589

For McCollum, criminals lose civil rights under the principle that "a person who breaks the law should not make the law" (para. 1). He opposes the automatic restoration of these rights to felons upon release from prison as "a matter of justice, respect for crime victims, and public safety" (2). He argues that high recidivism is a central issue in this debate: the "revolving door effect" of restoring rights only to revoke them for repeat offenders diminishes "the integrity of our democratic government and the rule of law" (5). McCollum believes in waiting periods and reviews by clemency boards, instead of automatic restoration, "to determine if felons are truly rehabilitated or still leading a life of crime" (6).

Reading Arguments, p. 590

1. Some students might agree that while in prison felons should lose voting rights. Discuss with students whether this loss of voting rights is primarily an ethical consideration or a practical one? A small number of states actually allow prisoners to vote during incarceration; in other states, felons lose voting rights for life, even after release.
2. The central issue in the debate about whether to restore voting rights to convicted felons, according to McCollum, is his state's "high repeat offender rate" (5). According to the Florida Department of Corrections, nearly 40% of offenders commit another crime within three years of release. He believes the "revolving door effect" of granting and then revoking voting rights harms "the integrity of our democratic government and the rule of law" (5).
3. In paragraph 8 McCollum suggests that we take steps to "ensure fairness in the clemency process" as an alternative to automatically restoring voting rights.

In so doing, the cases would be examined on an individual basis. Your students may note, however, that such increased attention would come at an increased cost.

4. In the second, third, and fourth paragraphs, McCollum evaluates current practices in Florida and finds them "safety-conscious" and "responsible." He also notes that most felons receive restoration of civil rights once their sentences are complete. He opposes an initiative that would change these procedures and eliminate "critical" waiting periods. Instead of wholesale change, McCollum proposes improvements in the system, such as "increasing the number of Clemency Board meetings from a quarterly to a monthly basis" (8).

Summary of "Should Felons Vote?" by Edward Feser, p. 591

Feser sees politics and partisanship as animating motivations for the movement to grant wider voting rights to felons, who tend to vote Democratic. As he writes, "Democrats need to enlarge their base. If that means reaching out to lock in the pedophile and home-invader vote, so be it" (para. 2). He argues that those who support the restoration of rights engage in fallacious thinking and "pure sentimentality" (14). Additionally, Feser claims that some advocates of voting by felons "have trouble with the basic concept of criminal justice" because their "hearts bleed more for perpetrators than for victims" (16).

Reading Arguments, p. 594

1. Feser argues that Democratic supporters of voting rights for felons claim that their interest in the issue is "moral," but he maintains that their motives are either self-interested or misguided. In his sixth paragraph, Feser accuses his opponents of committing the "genetic fallacy," which judges the merits of an argument or a policy on the basis of its origins: "even if felon disenfranchisement *did* have a disreputable origin, it wouldn't follow that the policy is bad" (6). Does Feser himself commit this fallacy by focusing on the motivations of those who support the restoration of voting rights? Moreover, the fact that one political party or another may benefit from a policy does not, by itself, make the policy flawed or wrong.
2. Feser argues that voting rights supporters have their facts wrong when they say disenfranchisement is racist: such laws existed well before the Reconstruction-era in America and elsewhere (5). He also states that a *New York Times* editorial misinterprets "the (alleged) causal connection between voting and keeping out of trouble," which is a version of the *post hoc, ergo propter hoc* fallacy ("after this, therefore because of this") (13). In discussing fallacies, you might also note and discuss Feser's use of the phrase "begs the question" in the seventh paragraph.
3. Feser cites Locke, in part, because the English philosopher is "generally regarded as having the greatest influence on the American founding" (8). In a

discussion of rights and laws in America, calling on Locke is not a fallacious appeal to authority; Feser is establishing foundational principles and an intellectual pedigree for his arguments. At the same time, the seventeenth-century thinker is not the final arbiter of this specific, contemporary issue. That Locke did not view voting rights as "basic and inalienable" does not conclusively demonstrate that felons and ex-felons should forfeit the right to vote. Furthermore, Feser does not specifically identify those who make this "claim" about the inalienability of the vote (8).

4. According to the writer, the *New York Times*'s argument that voting rights should be restored to ex-felons because former offenders who vote are less likely to return to jail is analogous to arguing that nonrecidivist ex-convicts should be rewarded with free rental privileges at Blockbuster because they probably turn videos in on time (13). The comparison seems strained and unclear: how are "free rental privileges," which would be a special benefit, comparable to general voting rights? The analogy also gets confounded with Feser's subsequent accusation of *post hoc, ergo propter hoc* (13). Ask students if they can come up with a more precise and convincing analogy.

5. Feser is alternately dismissive, contemptuous, and even deliberately condescending to his opponents, although the conservative *City Journal* readership would likely be in agreement with his argument. He charges his opponents with selfishness, vanity, and hypocrisy: Democrats "need to enlarge their base," even if "murderers, rapists, and thieves" are an "odd constituency for a party that prides itself on its touchy-feely concern for women and victims" (2). He finds opponents' arguments fallacious or historically inaccurate. At other times, he suggests that those who support voting rights for felons are mush-headed, delusional, and motivated by "pure sentimentality": they assume that "deep inside the typical burglar or car jacker lurks a Morgan Freeman–type character" (14). Feser's word choice when discussing the *New York Times* is particularly revealing. Like much of his audience, apparently, he finds the *New York Times*'s advocacy of felon voting "no surprise" (noted in an aside); he writes that the editorial "coos" over countries abroad that allow felons to vote in prison. The word *coos* evokes an action that is childish, sentimental, or trivial; the rest of the sentence implies the paper's supposedly misguided internationalist and liberal biases (16). Ask students how they react to Feser's style and attitude. Do they find it witty, iconoclastic, and bracing? Too snarky? Would Feser's piece be likely to persuade people who support voting rights for felons to change their mind? Why or why not? Alternately, how might this essay affect those who already oppose felon and ex-felon voting?

Summary of "The Last Disenfranchised Class" by Rebecca Perl, p. 595

Perl believes that the franchise will ultimately be expanded for felons and ex-felons, as the cause becomes the "next U.S. suffrage movement" (para. 7). But she acknowledges that "if history offers any lessons, it won't be an easy fight or a quick one" (8).

Indeed, although Perl supports loosening or eliminating these voting restrictions, especially in the context of their disproportionate effect on African American men, she takes a hard look at the political implications and practical problems with achieving that goal. Perl also considers the circumstances of specific people in an ever-increasing population of prisoners, former prisoners, and parolees.

Reading Arguments, p. 599

1. Perl's personal histories, at the beginning of her essay and elsewhere in the article, help humanize the issue. It is easier to dismiss an abstract felon or a general prison population than it is to consider the circumstances of a specific person such as Jan Warren.
2. According to this article, only Maine and Vermont allow prisoners to vote (5). This information is important because it provides a context for the issue. Readers might react differently if they knew that a much greater number of states than only two allow prisoners to vote.
3. In the context of U.S. law, the large percentage of Americans favoring restoration of the vote to ex-felons (at least according to Perl's unspecified poll) would be more relevant to changing federal and state legislation than the practices of other countries. But ask students how they view the practices of other countries in Europe and Africa as compared with practices in the United States. Is it ever valid to use international laws and customs as a general standard? Is it valid to use them in this case?
4. Most notably, Perl considers the view of a woman (Janice Grieshaber) whose daughter was murdered and who "[doesn't] want these people having access to making changes in my life; they have already done that" (15). But the writer uses this story to make a point in her argument: "Yet even Grieshaber makes a distinction between the rights of violent and nonviolent criminals" (16). Perl suggests that seeking an expansion of rights for nonviolent offenders may be a more politically effective strategy, in the short term, although this approach is unsatisfactory to an NAACP Legal Defense Fund attorney (16).

Summary of "Felons and the Right to Vote," *New York Times* editorial, p. 600

The *New York Times* editorial says that the "whole idea of permanently depriving felons of their right to vote" needs to be "wiped away" (para. 9). According to the editorial, such a policy is "antidemocratic" and "undermines the nation's commitment to rehabilitating people who have paid their debt to society" (1). Restrictions on felon voting rights disproportionately affect the black community; moreover, they are carried out in a "chaotic and partisan way" (1).

Reading Arguments, p. 602

1. The statistics effectively support the main argument—particularly, with regard to the racial impact of felon disenfranchisement laws (1). You might ask your students what other effective openings might be. You could suggest a

brief narrative or anecdote focusing on the writer or on a particular person affected by the law. Such an opening might help to make a more interesting story and create a more personal connection with the reader than the dry recitation of statistics. Other options for effective openings include a quotation from an expert or influential figure or a series of questions.

2. As evidence of the chaos and partisanship surrounding voting privileges for felons, the editorial mentions the inconsistent way these policies are carried out in different states as well as within the state of New York. The editorial claims that this issue is too often perceived through the lens of partisanship: "In state legislatures, it is usually Democrats who try to restore voting rights, and Republicans who resist" (6). In particular, the editorial points to purges and irregularities in Florida that may have changed the outcome during the 2000 election; in 2004, the *Miami Herald* reported that 2,100 eligible voters may have been removed from the rolls (3). The editorial also includes claims by some activists that Republican governor Jeb Bush "moved slowly" on reinstating rights for ex-felons in Florida to help President Bush's reelection prospects in 2004 (6).
3. By saying that "ex-convicts do not have much of a political lobby," the writers of the editorial mean that ex-convicts lack a group of people or organization that advocates the ex-cons' positions to political leaders.
4. Ultimately, the writers want an end to disenfranchisement of felons. But in the shorter term, they propose that current rules be applied more fairly, that mechanisms for restoring voting rights be improved, and that the entire process of reinstating rights be streamlined. They also call for an end to partisanship on the issue.

At Issue: Should Felons Permanently Forfeit Their Right to Vote? p. 602

1. Perl humanizes felons by focusing on the stories of specific people. Her approach evokes both empathy and sympathy for those who have lost their voting rights. Jan Warren was "desperate" and made a mistake (para. 1); her circumstances were enormously difficult; although Perl does not explicitly absolve Warren of guilt, she most certainly minimizes it. The image of Warren, contemplating her limited citizenship on Memorial Day, is powerful (2). As a registered Republican, Warren goes against the common stereotype of felons as Democratic voters. Similarly, Jazz Hayden is clearly a thoughtful, literate, perhaps even sympathetic character, although he was convicted of murder (12). Perl also respectfully addresses the objections of Jan Grieshaber (14). In contrast, Feser's style is ironic, unsentimental, and acerbic; he generalizes about felons as "murderers, rapists, and thieves" (2). Although he criticizes the "sentimentality" of liberals and their views of the "typical burglar or car jacker," Feser offers no specific examples of his own. Ask students if Feser's point is well served by this detachment from particular cases of those seeking voting rights. Is he simply more interested in principles than in individual people? Is commitment to principles the best way to approach such an issue?

2. This question about the role race should play in felon voting will lead to a lively discussion. Students' views may break down along the lines of those who agree with Feser that race is "irrelevant" and those who find the larger impact on the black community unacceptable. Some may notice that the *New York Times* editorial complicates Feser's assertions: clearly, the purging of legally eligible voters is wrong—an injustice that is exacerbated if it singles out African Americans.

3. Selections in this chapter provide a range of views on the question of whether restoration of voting rights should be a significant part of helping prisoners reenter society. For example, Feser focuses on "traditional notions of desert, punishment, and retribution" rather than rehabilitation (16). He is cynical about the power of voting and citizenship as part of reformation: "an ex-con hell-bent on new rapes and muggings isn't going to turn over a new leaf just because he gets to vote" (14). Where do students stand on the question of punishment versus rehabilitation? Should voting rights even be tied to personal virtue or good citizenship in the first place? NAACP attorney Janai Nelson, quoted by Perl, says no: "the right to vote does not vary based on our different ideas about what we would ideally like you to be as a person in this country" (15).

Writing Arguments: Should Felons Permanently Forfeit Their Right to Vote? p. 602

1. For this assignment asking students to take a stance on the issue of whether felons should be permitted to vote, you should encourage students to investigate and test some of the statistics and research in the selections they have read.

2. This assignment asks students to work with the idea that punishment is often easier to administer and can be more satisfying than rehabilitation. Both, however, are important. For a revision of this essay, you might ask students to consider further the relative importance of *deterrence* (how the threat of punishment prevents criminal behavior), *prevention* (since an imprisoned convict cannot break laws if he is not in society), and *retribution* (the fitness of a punishment for a particular crime).

CHAPTER

25 Casebook: Should Openly Gay Men and Women Be Permitted to Serve in the Military?

Summary of "Second Thoughts on Gays in the Military" by John M. Shalikashvili, p. 607

A retired army general and chair of the Joint Chiefs of Staff during the Clinton administration, John M. Shalikashvili originally supported "don't ask, don't tell." The policy, which forbids openly gay men and women from serving in the military, has been controversial since its inception in 1993. Shalikashvili now believes that gay men and lesbians should be allowed to serve openly. In supporting his argument, he cites shifting cultural circumstances in both the military and the country as a whole.

Reading Arguments, p. 608

1. In 1993, Shalikashvili thought changing military rules to allow gays to serve openly "would have been too burdensome for our troops and commanders" (para. 3). At the time, many in the military thought that homosexuality was incompatible with service and feared that permitting it would undermine morale, recruitment, and cohesion. After fourteen years, Shalikashvili thought that both the military and American culture had evolved enough to accept gay men and women in the armed forces.
2. Shalikashvili bases his argument (in part) on meetings with gay members of the military; these conversations demonstrated to him "just how much the military has changed, and that gays and lesbians can be accepted by their peers" (6). He cites a Zogby poll that showed that three quarters of the service members polled "were comfortable interacting with gay people" (7). Accord-

ing to Shalikashvili, twenty-four foreign countries allow gays to serve openly without "reporting morale or recruitment problems" (7). He also sees a new policy as a necessity: "Our military has been stretched thin . . . we must welcome the service of any American who is willing and able to do the job" (8).

3. Shalikashvili thinks that the policy served a legitimate purpose: it was "a useful speed bump that allowed temperatures to cool for a period of time while the culture continued to evolve" (4).
4. He is careful to acknowledge that this issue can be divisive, even as he aims to support his side of the argument: "the issue will give rise to passionate feelings on both sides. The debate must be conducted with sensitivity." (2). He does not impute malicious motives or goals to those he disagrees with; he does not advocate sudden, radical action. Rather, "the timing of the change should be carefully considered" (9). He warns against fighting a legislative battle in an intemperate way that is not likely to add to the healing of divisions. Rogerian argument is an especially effective way to create common ground with those on the other side of a contentious issue such as this one.

Summary of "Statement to the Subcommittee on Military Personnel, House Armed Services Committee, U.S. House of Representatives" by Vance Coleman, p. 609

In his written statement, Coleman makes his case by drawing parallels between his own experience as a black soldier in a still-segregated army and issues facing gay service people today. He argues that, far from being resistant to change or relying on homogeneity, the military "excels at blending people together from different backgrounds and beliefs" (para. 8). Additionally, Coleman points out that excluding openly gay men and women from the armed forces comes at too high a cost and "hurts our military readiness" (17).

Reading Arguments, p. 611

1. Coleman sees the issue of gays as analogous to his experience as a black man in the army when segregation was the law of the land: "I know what it is like to have your hard work dismissed because of who you are or what you look like. I also know what a difference it made when we placed qualification ahead of discrimination and tore down the walls of racial prejudice in our fighting forces" (6). In his view, the military "excels" at integration, whether in terms of race or sexual orientation, when it focuses on performance (8). Some of the same arguments that are made about gays in the military now were made about African Americans in the military back then (integration would hurt morale, etc.). This extended analogy supports Coleman's point of view well: if the military survived and thrived after integration, the same will be true if homosexuals are allowed to serve openly.

2. Coleman supports his statement about how the army "excels at blending people together from different backgrounds and beliefs" with personal experience in Korea; his unit "consisted of individuals from all walks of life who were white, black and brown" (9). In combat situations, these differences proved to be irrelevant. Coleman's support is relevant to his argument in this piece because it is an example of difference making no difference.
3. Coleman addresses the argument that the exclusion of gay troops "won't make a difference" (13). He writes that the armed forces has always promoted the "very true idea that one person can make a real difference in our country and our military" (13). More specifically, he points out that the loss of Arabic translators, nurses, and other skilled personnel who happen to be gay can have real costs to "military readiness" (17).
4. According to Coleman, the policy not only "hurts our military readiness" but also "undermines our commitment to being a nation where we are all equal in the eyes of the law" (17). In practical terms, he notes that nearly 800 people with "mission-critical" skills have been dismissed, as have five dozen Arabic translators; he cites an estimate that another 41,000 gay and lesbian Americans want to serve but are reluctant to do so (16).
5. The phrase *first-class patriots* groups together all the troops and focuses on similarities rather than differences; Coleman wants to depict all service members as first-class patriots, regardless of their color, background, or sexual orientation.

Summary of "Don't Ask, Don't Translate" by Stephen Benjamin, p. 612

Benjamin makes an argument based on his own experience as a gay soldier, ousted from the military after the army discovered his sexual orientation. His personal loss seems unnecessary and unjust, given the circumstances; but Benjamin's larger point is the loss to the military—of his skills as a translator and of the valuable service of other gay men and women whose military careers have been terminated.

Reading Arguments, p. 613

1. Benjamin's introductory paragraphs bring a sense of immediacy and urgency —particularly, by the use of the present tense in paragraph 1. The paragraphs also show what is at stake in the loss of qualified translators: the lives of servicemen and women, perhaps even the civilian casualties on September 11, 2001.
2. Benjamin's noting that he was an Arabic translator establishes him as a credible authority on the issue because he was personally involved with the issue. It is also important that his role was a key one that is understaffed because of the current policy.
3. The military discovered that Benjamin was gay when an inspection of his base included the perusal of the government computer chat system. Benjamin had

been corresponding with another gay friend on the system. Does this seem like a true violation of "Don't Ask, Don't Tell"? Are his comparisons with the others who violated the rules, but remained in the army persuasive? Your students are likely to have differing opinions on this issue. You might ask them to discuss what rights a soldier gives up when he or she joins the military.

4. *Evidence of causal argument:* Benjamin argues that purging the army of gay men and women results in the loss of valuable personnel—Arabic translators as well as people holding "critical jobs in intelligence, medicine and counterterrorism" (13). "Don't ask, don't tell" also causes an "untold number of closeted . . . members" to not reenlist (13). He suggests that the continuation of this policy may cause the loss of lives: "How much valuable intelligence could those [gay] men and women be providing today to troops in harm's way?" (12). *Evidence of argument by evaluation:* Benjamin's argument evaluates the military's current policy and finds it profoundly flawed: "'Don't ask, don't tell' does nothing but deprive the military of talent it needs and invade the privacy of gay service members just trying to do their jobs and live their lives" (11).

Summary of "Homosexuals in the Military: Combat Readiness or Social Engineering?" by Daniel L. Davis, p. 614

Former cavalry officer Major Daniel L. Davis seems as concerned with the tenor and quality of the public discussion over gays in the military as he is with the actual issue. According to Davis, nearly every news story and media sound bite is supportive of gays serving openly; he argues that the important issue "ought not be decided based on such an out-of-balance ratio" (para. 1). He asserts that many of these supporters are misusing a Zogby poll to make their claims. In his view, lifting the ban will cause tensions and "likely undermine" attempts to form "harmonious, well-trained" military units (7).

Reading Arguments, p. 615

1. The phrase social engineering generally refers to efforts to influence or change popular behavior on a large scale, whether by the government or other groups. Such efforts can include a range of initiatives from antismoking legislation to rules that influence the relationships between men and women or people of different races and ethnicities. The term often has a negative connotation, suggesting a sinister and often subtle agenda on the part of an organization to control the behavior or limit the freedom of individuals. Does social engineering seem inherently bad? Do students agree that allowing gay men and women to serve openly in the military amounts to social engineering?

2. Davis thinks that the debate is one-sided and that opponents of gays in the military are left out of the discussion. As he writes, the debate has "not been a dialogue so much as a monologue" (1). He also argues that the supporters

of gays in the military misuse a commonly cited Zogby poll that, they claim, shows members of the military wanting to overturn the ban. "But," according to Davis, "when the details of the report are examined, a more complicated picture emerges" (4). Indeed, he uses the poll to support his own side of the argument.

3. Davis's main thesis is essentially a causal argument: lifting the ban on gays in the military will cause tension in fighting units, undermine military commanders, and force religious people in the armed forces to "compromise their convictions" (8).
4. Davis says that the only factor worthy of consideration when making policies for the armed forces is determining what will "create the most effective combat unit possible" (9). Do students agree with this view? Why or why not?

Summary of "Statement to the Subcommittee on Military Personnel, House Armed Services Committee, U.S. House of Representatives" by Brian Jones, p. 616

Retired Army Ranger Brian Jones emphasizes the "selfless service" required for good morale in the military. He argues that the presence of openly gay men and women would "elevate tensions and disrupt unit cohesion" (para. 9). He also dismisses the argument that because other countries allow homosexuals to serve, the United States should, as well: "As an American soldier, I can't imagine comparing our military to that of a foreign nation to justify a change in policy" (11).

Reading Arguments, p. 618

1. Jones emphasizes selflessness as the most important virtue in the military. In the context of his argument in paragraph 8, he seems to be implying that gay men and women—"a minority faction"—are putting their own interests and "concerns" over other more important priorities.
2. Jones argues that in the "corporate world" people act in their own interest and are rewarded for it with "bonuses and job security" (6). He contrasts the military world, where teamwork and self-sacrifice are more valuable. This difference is important to Jones, who suggests that civilians cannot—and should not—impose their values on the military. Although he is not explicit, he appears to believe that requests to repeal the 1993 "don't ask, don't tell" policy would be an example of this interference.
3. Jones discusses foreign militaries because those who wish to repeal "don't ask, don't tell" often cite them in support of their arguments. For example, John M. Shalikashvili points to Israel and Britain, countries that allow gays to serve openly, as evidence that such forces can be effective. Jones argues that the comparisons are invalid because the "discipline, training, and core values" of foreign militaries are "quite different" (10). To substantiate this assertion, he

recounts his own experiences with the Polish and Italian armies—two narratives that disparage those forces. Are the two experiences relevant to the issue of gays in the military? How do students weigh Jones's analysis of foreign military forces against those of Shalikashvili?

Summary of "Allow Gays to Serve in Non-Combat Roles" by David Benkof, p. 619

In the controversial "don't ask, don't tell" debate, David Benkof argues for a gradualist approach that acknowledges the vital role gays and lesbians play in the armed forces: he proposes that they be allowed to serve openly in noncombat roles. After five years, the armed forces can then evaluate whether the policy should be extended to combat positions.

Reading Arguments, p. 620

1. Benkof's argument has Rogerian elements. Benkof claims that the armed forces should move—or consider moving—toward allowing gays and lesbians to serve openly; he believes these people play important roles and can display "heroic service in uniform" (para. 2). However, he acknowledges that the military has "legitimate concerns about unit cohesion, morale, good order, and discipline" (2). His gradualist approach seeks to mediate—find common ground—between those who do not want gays and lesbians to serve at all and those who believe that "nothing is more important than complete and total equality" (8). He finds both of these positions too extreme while conceding the limited merits of both.

2. Benkof uses analogy when he cites the precedent of World War I: African Americans "served in mostly non-combat positions" (6). According to Benkof, the gradual racial integration of the military between World War I and the Korean War ultimately made segregation "unnecessary and counterproductive" (6). Implicitly, the same process will follow his proposal for gays and lesbians in the military. He also suggests that people who want an immediate end to "don't ask, don't tell" are analogous to those who "think women should have been equal combatants in the American Revolution" (7). His examples in paragraph 5 may demonstrate subtle sexism in their assumptions about gender roles: "Would it hurt the military mission if a uniformed secretary used the Xerox machine even though she's a lesbian? Who would it harm for a gay man to be a drill sergeant at a Marine base in California?"

3. Benkof intends to demonstrate the ideological extremism of those who value the abstract principle of equality over all other considerations—over the "welfare of our children," religious freedom, and national security. But his anecdotal account leaves unclear just how many gays and lesbians take this extreme position. As a result, the statement may be an unfair representation of the majority of those who wish to repeal "don't ask, don't tell." The reference to Hitler is, we think, a red herring. Once an arguer invokes the Nazi Party or Adolph Hitler, that is a sign that he is on unstable rhetorical ground.

4. Certainly, most people value national security and a "strong military." Yet, Benkof does not define or qualify what constitutes strength. Those who opposed the racial integration of the military could make the same argument. Taken to its extreme, the principle that there is "literally nothing more important than a strong military" could be used to make absurd policies in the interest of undefined military "strength"—for example, peacetime conscription of every healthy male between the ages of eighteen and twenty-five. You might also ask students if they accept Benkof's implication that values such as tolerance and equality can be antithetical to a strong military or national security.
5. We don't see Benkof sidestepping the larger issue of whether the policy of "don't ask, don't tell" should be repealed. Rather, he is taking a nuanced approach, proposing a response that isn't an either/or solution.
6. Your students will likely have varying responses to the question of whether Benkof's suggestion that gay men and women serve only in noncombat roles is reasonable. While some will see it as insulting or demeaning, others will note that the current policy totally excludes gays and lesbians from openly serving at all.

At Issue: Should Openly Gay Men and Women Be Permitted to Serve in the Military? p. 620

1. Clearly, there are limits and restraints on this "single imperative"—especially, since determining "the most effective combat unit possible" is a subjective and vague standard. Moreover, similar arguments were made against racially integrating the army. But do Davis and Jones imply that military leaders should make decisions about military policy on their own, without civilian or political interference? Would this be a problem? The question raises fundamental issues about the connections between the civilian and military spheres in the United States. Ask students how they view this relationship.
2. Discussions of homosexuality can be provocative or controversial, although Shalikashvili thinks that our culture has evolved in the last fifteen to twenty years. The debate over gays in the military still seems to expose various fault lines: between the military and civilian societies; between those who disapprove of homosexuality, generally, and those who do not; between conservatives and liberals. The controversy also lends itself to competing claims about who has the country's best interests in mind and who (in Jones's words) "is demanding that their concerns be given priority over more important issues."
3. Comparing the current debate about gays in the armed forces with desegregation of the military is perhaps the most common analogy used in this discussion. You may have students go back and examine the arguments that were made against desegregating the military. Is the rhetoric similar? If so, is that similarity relevant to the merits and substance of the contemporary issue?

Writing Arguments: Should Openly Gay Men and Women Be Permitted to Serve in the Military? p. 621

1. Given the number and scope of readings in this chapter, students will have more than enough source material for their own arguments.
2. The second assignment allows students to explore the issues raised in the first At Issue question.

CHAPTER

26 Casebook: Should Every American Go to College?

Summary of "On 'Real Education'" by Robert T. Perry, p. 625

Perry responds to those who believe that sending a larger percentage of Americans to college is wasteful "educational romanticism" (para. 7). According to Perry, the country needs more, not fewer, college graduates: "It simply makes sense—both economically and socially" (7). He points out that 90% of the fastest-growing job categories will require postsecondary training (2). He also notes that his own state (South Dakota) is facing shortages in professions that require a college education; to keep pace with countries such as Canada, Japan, and South Korea, the United States will have to produce 63.1 million degrees. Perry's essay—like all the selections in this casebook—should get students thinking about the meaning and value of their own college work.

Reading Arguments, p. 627

1. Perry refutes, convincingly, we think, Murray's idea that "we are wasting our time trying to educate too many people" (1). Murray's arguments flow from this thesis.
2. Perry states that "low-skill careers are disappearing rapidly, as manufacturing jobs head overseas" (4). In contrast, the "knowledge-based" economy, according to Perry's preceding paragraphs, includes teaching, accounting, physical therapy, software engineering, and so forth; these professions require cognitive, writing, and critical thinking skills, as well as adaptability (7). In other words, they usually require some postsecondary credentials.
3. Perry uses cause-and-effect relationships in several places. For example, he shows that the shift to a "knowledge-based" economy was partially caused by the loss of manufacturing jobs; this unskilled work has gone overseas, where companies are "willing and able to use unskilled work at a lower cost" (5). He

also argues that reducing the number of college graduates in our workforce "would result in a lower standard of living for most Americans" (5).

4. Perry sees the general benefits of a higher education in three ways. First, he argues that it "allows people of all backgrounds to hone their writing, reading, cognitive and critical thinking skills that enable them to actively participate as citizens" (7). Second, college work itself is "valuable and marketable" in a knowledge economy; employers need people "who can craft memos, reports and strategic plans" (7). Third, Perry notes that those with secondary degrees tend to be healthier, more productive, more community minded, and "less likely to be involved in crime" (7). You may want to ask students how they see Perry's assessment of a college education. For example, do they think of a college degree as related to their role as citizens? Do they see the thinking, reading, and writing they do as "valuable and marketable"?

Summary of "The Privileges of the Parents" by Margaret A. Miller, p. 628

Miller prefaces her essay with the old folk saying, "The apple doesn't fall far from the tree." Not surprisingly, then, she focuses on how higher education levels of parents correlate to higher academic achievement of children: "In short, a college education has benefits that ripple down through the generations" (para. 8). She also argues that a degree is more important now than ever, just to "help people navigate contemporary life" (1). But she writes that college-going rates are now "stagnating" and completion rates are a "disgrace" as income gaps widen (8). According to Miller, educators can help solve these problems by finding promising first-generation students and making college affordable to them, instead of simply pursuing the "best and the brightest" (11).

Reading Arguments, p. 630

1. Miller acknowledges the economic benefits of a college degree—higher wages, for example. But she argues that higher education, which cultivates "advanced intellectual abilities," is important just to "navigate contemporary life" (1). People need "to do so many things that other people used to do for us" (2): organizing travel plans, making choices about health-care benefits, planning for old age. Workers in the new economy must "hop from job to job" and acquire skills and knowledge continually; they must also deal with a wider variety of people than in the past.

2. Miller refers to a study showing the correlation between parental education and children's grades, but she does more than present it as evidence. Instead, Miller ties the correlation to her own anecdotal evidence (3) and shows the ways the "differential" between highly- and less-educated parents functions in "innumerable small, intangible ways" besides good grades (5). She also connects it to other studies done by the Education Testing Service (5) and the National Survey of Student Engagement (7). Students should notice how Miller builds her case progressively, using this mixture of research and personal observation.

3. By saying that the United States is "becoming as caste-bound a society as any in the Old World" (9), Miller means that the advantages of educated parents are passed down to children in a continual cycle; those who do not inherit these benefits are disadvantaged not because of their talents or personal merits but because of their backgrounds. The effect is to limit merit-based success and hinder social mobility among, say, first-generation students. Another result: an informal, hereditary quasi-class system rather than a true meritocracy. To support her position, Miller cites widening income gaps, stagnating college attendance rates, and the statistic that "the richest one percent of Americans hold a third of the nation's wealth" (9).
4. Miller worries that educators focus too much on the children of the privileged. She quotes another writer's description of the American education ideal, which is to "mediate opportunity [and] expand merit-based success without surrendering individual responsibility" (9). She wants the system to do a better job of reaching toward this goal. In her last paragraph, she proposes that schools focus on the "most promising first-generation students" (11); doing so means both attracting them and retaining them in colleges.

Summary of "What's Wrong with Vocational School?" by Charles Murray, p. 631

In Murray's view, too many people go to college. A traditional, four-year degree program should teach "advanced analytic skills and information at a level that exceeds the intellectual capacity of most people" (para. 4). More than 45% of recent high school graduates now enroll in four-year degree programs, mainly because of the "false premium that our culture has put on a college degree" (9). Murray argues that this enrollment should be reduced to around 15% of the population (5). Because of market demands and cultural shifts, he expects to see a rise in the relevance of online education, vocational schools, and skilled craftspeople; he also hopes that the traditional four-year college experience becomes the province of a smaller, more qualified group of elite students.

Reading Arguments, p. 634

1. A syllogism of the opening of Murray's argument might look like this:

   Major Premise: College requires a high level of intelligence.

   Minor Premise: Those with IQs around 100 will have difficulty at four-year colleges.

   Conclusion: Those with insufficiently high IQs should not go to college.

   Of course, one might note that IQ tests are notoriously elastic and are unreliable as indicators of much of anything (except perhaps one's competence in taking IQ tests), and so basing life decisions on a few point's difference in the results of such a test may strike some as absurd.

2. Murray claims that in engineering and the natural sciences, "the demarcation between high-school material and college-level material is brutally obvious" (4). The intellectually unqualified fail these courses. In contrast, subpar students may pass classes in the humanities and social sciences because the demarcations between precollege material and college material are "fuzzier" (4). As a result, degrees in engineering certify qualification, while a degree in sociology, psychology, economics, or literature "certifies nothing" in the context of finding a job (10). This disconnect between college work and employment is significant in the context of Murray's larger argument: it suggests (among other things) that too many unqualified students are sitting through unnecessary and meaningless courses when they could be attending other kinds of schools and learning valuable, practical skills in a much more efficient way.
3. Murray uses several cause-and-effect relationships in this essay. For example, he claims that large numbers of both the intellectually unqualified and the intellectually-qualified-but-uninterested attend college because "their parents are paying for it and college is what children of their social class are supposed to do after they finish high school" (7). The market also creates too large a demand for college degrees because American culture places a "false premium" on them (9).
4. Murray's dispassionate, authoritative deductions and assertions imply that the "intellectually unqualified" be weeded out of higher education. Whatever its merits, his argument is profoundly undemocratic and elitist in its view of higher education. It also raises some other, potentially troubling questions: who will make the judgments about who gets to go college? Given his admission that there is "no magic [IQ] point at which a genuine college-level education becomes an option," what standards will be used to decide? Murray blunts the impact of these issues by emphasizing that many unqualified or uninterested students would, *on their own,* choose not to pursue a college degree. In his analogy, why would they want to—"any more than someone who is athletically unqualified for a college varsity wants to have his shortcomings exposed at practice every day"? (6). Ask students if they think this is a good analogy. You may also want to discuss, more generally, the implications of Murray's point as it applies to education and social class. For example, might some students view themselves as "not college material" because of, say, their family background or income, even if they were interested in attending college or had high-level intellectual abilities?
5. Murray writes that finding a good doctor or lawyer is easy, while finding good craftspeople—carpenters, plumbers, electricians, etc.—is difficult (13). His point is that the job market for these trades is showing an "explosive increase"; moreover, these workers make "incomes in the top half of the income distribution" (13). Such jobs are recession-proof; they cannot be outsourced to another country. He also states that these trades provide "wonderful intrinsic rewards" for those who practice them (13).

Summary of "Is College for Everyone?" by Pharinet, p. 635

For Pharinet, the answer to the question in her essay's title is no. Too many students attend four-year degree programs to get a job, please their parents, or conform to societal expectations. These unprepared undergraduates have "no real desire for learning" and embrace an ethos of "C's get degrees" (para. 5). She acknowledges the importance of education but concludes that Americans should "embrace the reality that college is not for everyone" (7).

Reading Arguments, p. 637

1. Although Pharinet is not specific, in stating "there is no doubt that every person has the right to an education" but "not every person should attend college," she seems to mean that Americans have a right to a basic education as provided by public schools. You might use her point to begin a discussion of exactly what "rights" people have, in this context. For example, is a college education a right in the same way that an elementary school education is a right? What makes one level a "right" and the other a privilege? The distinction is important to her discussion because, in her view, too many people are attending college without being ready, intellectually and financially.
2. "Political correctness" used derisively can be seen as shorthand for distorting the idea that everyone *should* be treated equally regardless of race, creed, sexual orientation, and other such factors and claiming instead that the "politically correct" believe that everyone *is* equal, with respect to intelligence and ability—an uncharitable rhetorical sleight-of-hand.
3. According to Pharinet, the biggest challenge educators face is "motivating students to learn" (5).

At Issue: Should Every American Go to College? p. 637

1. This question should raise important issues of education, meritocracy, and social mobility. Ask students if they view their education as a means of changing their socioeconomic status. You may also wish to compare and contrast Miller and Murray in this context. For example, Miller focuses on how the education levels of parents influence the academic achievement of their children. How does this view complicate Murray's emphasis on "objective" IQ levels and intellectual qualifications? Would Murray's approach help expand "merit-based success" or make it contract? How might it reinforce a caste system?
2. Murray's use of IQ distribution allows him to generalize broadly; he works from premises about the intellectual abilities of different segments of the population and the "proper" standards for universities; then, he moves to more specific arguments about who should (and should not) attend college. His approach does not lead to many considerations beyond "objective" measurements of intelligence, the demands of the free market, and a vague if traditional notion of the university as a place for a small, highly privileged elite—although he is

careful to claim that such people are "not better or worse than anyone else" (15). How would students compare Murray's argument with that of Perry, who calls for an *increase* in college enrollment? Perry begins with statistics from the Department of Labor and moves to more general conclusions; he does not mention IQ in his argument, but he does discuss the demands of the job market, as well as the realities of globalism. Which of these writers do students find more persuasive, and why?

3. Ask how the meaning and value of a college degree has changed. Were students more motivated by a pure desire to learn in the past? You may want to discuss this question in the context of the democratization of higher education. How have the increased access to college and higher enrollments over the past several decades affected the worth of a four-year degree? In a way, it would appear that the bachelor's degree has become simultaneously essential yet also devalued. Addressing Pharinet's contention that people today go to college for different reasons than people in the past, you might point out the term *Gentlemen's C,* which goes back to the nineteenth century and referred to grades given to idling, academically undistinguished (but socially privileged) students at Ivy League colleges. How are these two versions of "going through the motions" similar? How are they different?

Writing Arguments: Should Every American Go to College? p. 637

1. Students are—or should be—considering questions about who should go to college as they apply to their own college careers. They may use the assignment to respond to one of the readings—especially, given that Perry's essay is itself written as a response to Murray.

2. This assignment, asking students to identify challenges students face as they make their way through postsecondary education, should give students a chance to move from their own experiences and observations to more general assertions about higher education.

CHAPTER

27

Casebook: Do We Still Need Unions?

Summary of "Union Label" by Paula Green and Malcolm Dodds, p. 641

Written in 1975, the song "Union Label" was part of a media campaign to raise awareness of unions, generally, and the International Ladies' Garment Worker's Union, specifically.

Reading Arguments, p. 641

1. The lyrics of "Union Label" develop the argument that one should buy union-made products because doing so benefits working families in the United States.
2. The claim in the song is that one should purchase goods made with union labor. The grounds are that doing so benefits the United States and its individual workers. The warrant is that it is important to help the United States and one's fellow citizens.
3. This song is addressed to all consumers. Audiences at the time the song was written are likely to have been more receptive to it than audiences today, who might consider it corny. Given the widespread influence of Wal-Mart and the ready availability of cheap, imported consumer goods such as clothing, it is likely much more difficult for contemporary consumers who have come to expect low prices to convert to the idea of purchasing American-made products at a higher cost, even with an implied social benefit.

Summary of "How Wal-Mart Keeps Unions at Bay: Organizing the Nation's No. 1 Employer Would Give Labor a Lift" by Wendy Zellner, p. 642

Since its founding in 1962, Wal-Mart has avoided the unionization of its workers. Wendy Zellner examines more recent attempts of its employees to unionize—as well as the company's efforts to stop them. According to Zellner, "A win at Wal-Mart, the country's No. 1 employer, with more than 1 million workers, also could give the entire labor movement a lift" (para. 4). She notes that interest in unionization has increased since the 1990s, even as "Corporate America has perfected its ability to fend off labor groups" (6).

Reading Arguments, p. 644

1. According to Zellner, the company's early strategy of opening stores in small towns and rural areas kept it free from exposure to organized labor. More recently, though, Wal-Mart has expanded into the "heavily unionized supermarket industry, as well as into big cities where workers are more familiar with organized labor" (3). She implies that "corporate scandals and the troubled economy" have also contributed to union activity (5).
2. The possibility of unionization at Wal-Mart is significant because the company is such a large retailer and employer. Zellner claims that the labor battle at the Sam's Club in Las Vegas could be "a proxy for many unionization attempts around the country" (5).
3. Zellner does not make an explicit pro-union or anti-union argument in this article. At the same time, readers might infer a generally sympathetic view of employees and organizers. Wal-Mart is described as a "retailing behemoth" (1). Zellner writes about the company's intimidation and "hardball tactics," which are "company policy" (11). According to some accounts, store managers have "scared workers away" from joining unions or harassed them (8, 9); Wal-Mart "parachuted in" (1) labor experts to run anti-union campaigns at specific stores. Discuss this aspect of the story with students. For example, how do the quotations from employees and former employees at Wal-Mart compare with the writer's sentence at the end of the first paragraph: "Wal-Mart denies it did anything illegal"? Are there really two sides to every story? Would conscious attempts by Zellner to make Wal-Mart more sympathetic be propagandistic or a matter of false-balancing?

Summary of "Labor and the Nation" by John L. Lewis, p. 645

In "Labor and the Nation," this towering figure of the labor movement not only defends the purposes and goals of the Committee for Industrial Organization but also gives an emotionally charged history of organized labor and solicits moral support for his cause. Delivered in the midst of the Great Depression, the 1937 speech is a tour de force. But Lewis writes and speaks with a depth of commitment and passion that may strike students as overly dramatic and even archaic. If so, use their responses to discuss Lewis's word choices and the effects of his style.

Reading Arguments, p. 649

1. Lewis frames his organization—and the labor movement, as a whole—in moral terms. The Committee for Industrial Organization became a powerful

"instrumentality" (para. 1) only because of its "economic, social, political and moral justification in the hearts" of its members and supporters (2). The workers needed organized labor to "right their economic wrongs, to alleviate them of their social agony" (3). Indeed, Lewis paints the entire struggle of the labor movement in broad, almost cartoonish images of aggrieved-but-unbowed victims and dastardly villains. Workers, who stand "for the right guaranteed them by the Congress and written in law" (8), are slaughtered or have their "brains clubbed out by police, or armed thugs in the pay of the steel companies" (8). At nearly every moment in "Labor and the Nation," the reader has a vivid idea of who is in the right and who is in the wrong.

2. Lewis evokes the Bill of Rights to place the struggle of workers within the larger American tradition of achieving and securing rights, going back to the founding of the country. In the process, Lewis links economic rights to political rights and democracy: labor is dedicated to the "proposition that the workers are free to assemble . . . voice their own grievances . . . and contract on even terms with modern industry for the sale of their only material possession—their labor" (3). Consequently, the labor movement is not radical or dangerous but merely part of an established American tradition. This rhetorical move is significant because Lewis must defend unionization against "those who have hatched this foolish cry of communism in the C.I.O." (23). You may point out that Lewis ultimately turns this charge of communism and subversion back on his opponents: "The real breeders of discontent and alien doctrines of government and philosophies subversive of good citizenship are such as these who take the law into their own hands" (19).

3. The tone and diction of "Labor and the Nation" should be striking to students: How do they respond to the speech? How would they characterize its style? Lewis delivered the speech in 1937, during the Great Depression. Why might a phrase like "the agony and travail of economic America" (1) resonate at the time? Would it now? Indeed, the language is often melodramatic, even in its use of archetypes: "Labor, like Israel, has many sorrows. Its women weep for their fallen and they lament for the future of the children of the race" (36). What is Lewis referring to, here? What does it suggest about his audience? Lewis's characterization of the C.I.O.'s opponents is similarly charged; they are violent, murderous "snoops, finks, [and] hatchet gangs" (18), a "bibble-babbling mob of blackguarding and corporation paid scoundrels" (20). Would rhetoric like this—in the service of labor or other causes—still be effective today? Why or why not? Could this speech be rewritten in a different way—say, using cool, ironic detachment?

4. Relentlessly, pointedly, and dramatically, "Labor and the Nation" promotes its point of view in stark images and highly charged rhetoric. The speech is designed to persuade and galvanize rather than offer disinterested information or an "objective" point of view. Lewis even provides a historical narrative for organized labor that places the movement in the American political tradition and in an ongoing struggle for "social justice" (24). His rhetoric leaves no room for middle ground, as labor "feels that its cause is just and that its

friends should not view its struggle with neutral detachment or intone constant criticism of its activities" (34). You should, of course, discuss the term *propaganda* with students—its meaning and connotations. You may also want to ask students to investigate some of Lewis's claims and test their historical accuracy.

5. Lewis often dispatches opponents of the C.I.O. with labels and epithets, as in the case of the "steel puppet Davey" (Martin Davey, governor of Ohio in the 1930s) or "goose-stepping vigilantes." But at other times, he does make substantive rebuttals of counterarguments and criticisms. For example, he spends several paragraphs explaining the differences between "unionization" and "communism" in order to distance the labor movement from accusations that it was communist (21–25).

Summary of "Watch Out for Stereotypes of Labor Unions" by Fielding Poe, p. 650

Self-described "union man" Fielding Poe takes issue with those who disparage unions or stereotype union workers. He argues that people who tout their own individualism and "disdain unions for harboring the lazy and dishonest" are misguided (para. 5). Many of them enjoy benefits that were purchased with the "toil of union workers" (4); moreover, almost every "breathing" person has banded together with others at some point to "accomplish some common purpose" (6).

Reading Arguments, p. 651

1. Poe opens his piece as he does because it is a good-faith gesture to establish his orientation to the issue. (He might have easily concealed his position, leaving him open to charges of bias should it be discovered.) It is also effective because it establishes a personal connection with the reader by providing important information about the writer.

2. Stereotypes are conventional or formulaic understandings of people, places, and things. They are often reductive, simplistic, or inaccurate. Poe says that union workers are often stereotyped as "lazy and dishonest" (5). He also evokes the stereotypical organized labor supporter as a "soft-headed social liberal" (8), while he describes himself as "about as conservative as they come" (1). Ask students about stereotypes they may hold of labor unions, both positive and negative. Do they agree with Poe?

3. Poe argues that "self-described individualists" have actually participated in a "corporate act"; they have signed petitions, joined professional organizations, donated to causes and campaigns (6). He writes, "It's our nature to have a certain social dependence on one another" (6). In essence, Poe is breaking down the false dichotomy between individual action and group action, a dichotomy that some use to disparage unions. Additionally, he notes that nonunion workers, managers, and entrepreneurs have derived benefits from organized labor (7).

4. Poe uses a form of deduction in paragraph 7, where he argues that "if every laboring person only made minimum wages," our "present economy" could not exist as it is. His most significant argument-by-analogy is that labor unions are comparable to professional organizations, churches, and other associations that illustrate our "social dependence on one another" (6).

5. Poe's argument is Rogerian in that he seeks common ground between opposing points of view. To do so, he claims that unions are just a variety of social organization devoted to a common cause—just like the associations joined by "self-described individualists" (6). He emphasizes the common benefits of organized labor. His concluding sentences highlight this point nicely: "I'm a union man. And in some way, I bet you are too." By emphasizing his own political conservatism, Poe demonstrates that debates about unions do not have to be divided along partisan or ideological lines; instead, liberals and conservatives can find common ground on the issue.

Summary of "Do Americans Today Still Need Labor Unions?" by James Sherk, p. 652

According to Sherk, organized labor once had a useful place in the manufacturing economy. But in a "knowledge economy," which places more value on "individual insights and abilities" (para. 5), the "one-size-fits-all" (6) union approach stifles initiative, productivity, and economic growth. The writer claims that organized labor could become relevant again. However, modern economic realities are only aggravating long-standing union problems: "corruption, unaccountable leadership, and members' dues funding union bosses' lavish salaries . . . [and] excessive political activism" (13).

Reading Arguments, p. 654

1. In his introduction, Sherk proposes an abstract scenario that readers will find obviously and completely unappealing or even unjust. Then, he states that labor unions actually create this situation for workers. You may ask students to look more closely at his generalizations. For example, is it true that people working in unionized jobs are never promoted or rewarded for individual merit? Is organized labor's traditional emphasis on seniority ultimately detrimental to both workers and companies? Are there benefits to collective bargaining that Sherk does not acknowledge?

2. Several changes have occurred to make unions less relevant and useful. According to Sherk, unions worked well in the manufacturing economy of the 1930s because "an employee's unique talents and skills made little difference on the assembly line" (4). But in "today's knowledge economy," employers want workers for their "individual insights and abilities" (5); he then lists presumably fast-growing occupations to support his point (5). Because of economic changes, unions can "no longer deliver large gains to their members" (7). Additionally, deregulation and free trade "have increased competition and benefit both con-

sumers and the economy" (9). But the competition means that unions cannot win higher earnings through collective bargaining, as companies no longer have the profits to pay "those inflated wages" (9).

3. In charting the decline of organized labor, Sherk proposes a number of cause-and-effect relationships to make his argument. His main point, for example, is that changes in the economy—the end of manufacturing, a new emphasis on the individual, free trade, etc.—have caused unions to become irrelevant or even harmful to employees.

4. Sherk sets up the opposition between individualism and the need for collective action in the first paragraph and uses it throughout his essay. Individualism generally has positive connotations; he uses these connotations and associations to further his argument. For example, Sherk focuses on the "knowledge economy," which values "individual insights and abilities," as well as "creativity" (5, 6). These qualities suggest freedom, personal merit, and Sherk's own point of view. In contrast, he associates organized labor with undistinguished assembly-line jobs of the past; a "one-size-fits-all" approach to workers; corrupt, unaccountable leadership; and heavy-handed tactics that force employees to join and conform. He also links unions with the "public sector," where "government employees are used to bureaucracy that does little to reward individual initiative" (15). All of these comparisons reflect poorly upon collective action, as Sherk presents it here. Sherk's appeal to the value of individualism is a logical appeal because it is developed through a series of facts. Sherk includes statistics such as the types of "fastest growing occupations" (5), amount of costs savings due to NAFTA (9), and poll results from nonunion workers (17), and so on. An emotional appeal might have included personal stories of workers who did not benefit or who were harmed by unions. Such stories could be moving but would likely be anecdotal and would not necessarily illuminate the larger issues concerning the benefits and drawbacks of unions.

At Issue: Do We Still Need Unions? p. 654

1. No doubt, the power and prestige of organized labor have declined significantly in the last several decades. But Zellner's article implies that unions can still be vital. You may ask students whether her stories about Wal-Mart seem in accord with Sherk's view of unions as irrelevant or detrimental. Does Sherk engage in the stereotyping that Poe describes? Is it generally true to say, as Sherk does, that "employers now want employees with individual insights and abilities?" (para. 5). On the other hand, to what degree are unions responsible for their own decline? Have they adversely affected the American economy? Could they "reform to become relevant" (in Sherk's phrase) without losing sight of the goals originally espoused by John L. Lewis? Such questions might require looking beyond the essays in this unit.

2. Poe and Sherk make useful antagonists. Poe is not a stereotypical "union man"; he also rejects Sherk's fundamental dichotomy. You might have students role-play a dialogue between the two.

3. Sherk writes that labor unions planned to spend $300 million to defeat John McCain in 2008. Do students view organized labor as significantly different from any other political interest group? Does the term *union* have connotations that are better or worse than the term *corporation*? As Poe's article implies, support for labor unions is associated with "soft-headed social liberal" politics (8). What does that mean, exactly? How do political labels and associations like *liberal* and *conservative* connect to views of organized labor? Do students agree with Lewis's premise that economic rights are connected to political rights?

Writing Arguments: Do We Still Need Unions? p. 655

1. As the debate over unions touches on economics, politics, history, and other issues, you might want to encourage students to conduct research beyond these selections.
2. Students may want to think about this question in the context of their own career plans and prospects. They may also choose to respond to specific essays in the chapter.

CHAPTER

28

Classic Arguments

Summary of "The Allegory of the Cave" by Plato, p. 657

Probably the most famous section of Plato's *Republic,* "The Allegory of the Cave" proposes that we are imprisoned in a world of shadows, images, and falsehoods. Through a difficult process of enlightenment, we can ascend into the "intellectual world" and see the "universal author of all things beautiful and right . . . and the immediate source of reason and truth" (para. 35). But Plato's vision is not merely personal. Rather, he uses the allegory as the basis for larger conceptions of society, political leadership, and the well-run state.

Reading Arguments, p. 662

1. In Plato's analogy, the cave or "prison house" represents the everyday, material world of people, things, and ideas; the chained prisoners are common people, who live in darkness and have no direct contact with reality or truth; they see only shadows, which they believe are real. The "liberated" (or properly educated) person struggles out of the cave and sees reality directly; he or she also sees the sun itself, which Plato associates with god. Plato's allegory is a foundational analogy in Western thinking; it has long evoked the sense of coming to knowledge and wisdom as coming out of darkness. That includes the difficulty of the process, as a person acclimating to bright light would be "pained and irritated" as well as enlightened (19). At the same time, all allegories are simplifications. Students may find Plato counterintuitive: for the philosopher, reality exists in an abstract, transcendental, disembodied realm. In contrast, we often locate "reality" in material things and empirical data.
2. The benefits of becoming educated about the true nature of reality would be an unmediated experience and knowledge of truth and reality. For example, a person who escaped the cave would understand "absolute justice" rather than the "images or the shadows of images of justice" (39). But the costs would be high. If the person returned to the cave, he would not be able to see well in the darkness; the other inhabitants would think him blind and execute anyone else who tried to escape (33). Enlightened people would want to live only in the "upper world," but Socrates argues that they would be obligated to return to the cave. He means that the educated and enlightened members of a society must be "instruments in binding up the State" (59).

3. Plato proposes that this educated and enlightened class participate in (and govern) the life of the "cave"—the world of everyday people and politics. That such people would prefer not to lead is a big reason that they should: "Whereas the truth is that the State in which the rulers are most reluctant to govern is always the best and most quietly governed, and the State in which they are most eager, the worst" (61). Ask students how they respond to this idea. Does Plato mean merely "intellectuals," or would these leaders have other qualities, as well? One need only to scan news headlines to see that Plato's proposal applies to contemporary politics. Examples of short-term thinking for personal gain abound in the political realm, from questionable lobbying practices to pork-barrel politics to outright corruption.
4. Glaucon plays a role similar to that of the reader of Plato's allegory. At times he asks for clarifications ("What do you mean?"); mostly, he responds by agreeing with Socrates, which suggests the correctness and validity of Socrates' arguments.

Writing Arguments, p. 662

This assignment should bring out the contrasts between Plato's conception of unselfish philosopher-leaders ("just men," as he describes them), devoted to true and beautiful ideals, and Machiavelli's view of good governance, which focuses on the "real truth of the matter" rather than on "what people have imagined" (1). At the same time, there may be similarities between the two writers. Machiavelli claims, for example, that people are "simple of mind and so much dominated by their immediate needs" (15). Plato would likely agree, but how might he interpret the implications of that statement differently from Machiavelli? Is the state that Plato envisions one of Machiavelli's imagined "states and princedoms such as nobody ever saw or knew in the real world" (1)?

Summary of Excerpt from *The Prince,* by Niccolò Machiavelli, p. 663

In the last several years, bookstores have swelled with popular volumes on leadership, whether written by entrepreneurs, athletic coaches, or political figures. None, however, is as amoral and unsentimental as Niccolò Machiavelli's *The Prince* (written 1513, published 1532), a guide for those seeking to maintain political power. In this excerpt, the author shows how generosity will lead to ruin, why it is better to be feared than loved, when princes should break their promises, and several other guiding principles.

Reading Arguments, p. 669

1. Machiavelli writes that his subject "has been treated frequently before, and . . . people will think [him] rash for trying to do so again" (para. 1). He distinguishes his treatment from the many that have preceded it and implies both the deficiencies of his predecessors and the value of his own argument: "But since I intend to write something useful to an understanding reader, it seemed

better to go after the real truth of the matter than to repeat what people have imagined" (1).

2. From his first sentence, Machiavelli is proposing "what style and principles a prince ought to adopt in dealing with his subjects and his friends" (1). *The Prince* is a manual for conduct: it proposes how one should act—and which actions or attitudes to avoid. To support these principles and recommendations, he often makes causal arguments. For example, he claims that princes should not exhibit generosity; he then shows, by cause and effect, how generosity will result in the leader becoming "contemptible" and "hateful" (5).
3. To support his generalizations, Machiavelli often draws on the case histories of specific historical figures: Pope Julius, Caesar, Alexander the Great, Scipio. He justifies the need for princes to break their promises by stating, "history will furnish innumerable examples" of leaders who did this to their advantage (15). He also cites classical literature such as Virgil's *Aeneid.* This inductive method is effective, although it is open to challenge by those who use different examples or even by those who might interpret Machiavelli's choices differently to make different points. You should note that the writer uses deductive reasoning, too, and occasionally begins with broad principles: "For it is a good, general rule about men . . ." (7).
4. Machiavelli's evaluation of human beings is uniformly dim and negative. They are "ungrateful, fickle, liars and deceivers, fearful of danger and greedy for gain" (7). Machiavelli's most famous formulation is the direct, logical result of this view of humanity: "People are less concerned with offending a man who makes himself loved than one who makes himself feared: the reason is that love is a link of obligation which men, because they are rotten, will break any time they think doing so serves their advantage; but fear involves dread of punishment, from which they can never escape" (7). The essential rottenness of people has other implications as well—for example, the justification for leaders to manipulate or deceive them.
5. The writer considers counterarguments throughout *The Prince.* In his discussion of generosity, Machiavelli writes, "Someone may object that Caesar used a reputation for generosity to become emperor" (5). He acknowledges that Caesar used this perception of himself to become the ruler of Rome but argues that maintaining power requires different principles: "after [Caesar] had reached his goal, if he had lived, and had not cut down on his expenses, he would have ruined the empire itself" (5). Ask students to propose their own counterexamples and counterarguments to Machiavelli's argument.

Writing Arguments, p. 669

1. Machiavelli's focus on superficiality and manipulation is always timely. He counsels that leaders must keep up appearances at all times—particularly, with regard to religion: "Nothing is more necessary than to seem to have this last virtue" (17). He generalizes, "Everyone sees what you seem to be, few know what you really are" (17). Do students see today's political leaders as too preoccupied with appearances or maintaining power? Is there another,

viable vision of politics and leadership, or do more idealistic approaches "neglect the real" at their own peril? Finally, in response to whether Machiavelli's argument seems relevant and applicable, reiterate that the term *Machiavellian* is still widely used. Be sure students understand its connotations.

2. It is difficult to imagine two figures more antithetical than Machiavelli, whose thought is often distilled (however reductively) into *the ends justify the means,* and Martin Luther King Jr., an apostle of peaceful nonviolence. Machiavelli would not recognize or understand King's rhetoric of rights, equality, and democracy; he would probably reject King's discussion of "moral law" (15–16). For Machiavelli, the highest virtue of a state is order and stability, not justice, equality, or securing individual rights. But he might understand the civil rights movement (generally) and King (particularly) in the context of a political power struggle. How might King respond to Machiavelli's statement "there's such a difference between the way we really live and the way we ought to live that the [leader] who neglects the real to study the ideal will learn how to accomplish his ruin, not his salvation" (1)?
3. Students should consider how they balance the "real" and the "ideal" in formulating their own "styles and principles." They may also want to use Machiavelli's inductive method, building their argument on specific cases.

Summary of "To His Coy Mistress" by Andrew Marvell, p. 670

"To His Coy Mistress" is an ingenious attempt at seduction and part of a long tradition of carpe diem poems. It is a meditation on human mortality and on the transience of physical and romantic love as well. But students should also recognize that Marvell's poem uses the techniques of formal argument.

Reading Arguments, p. 671

1. *The major premise (lines 1–20):* if the couple were not limited by time, the speaker could extend his poetic, Platonic adoration until the end of the world and her reluctance to have sex with him would not be unreasonable or a "crime." *The minor premise (lines 21–32):* they, however, are mortal, and time is fleeting; if they do not consummate their love now, both will grow old and die unfulfilled. *The conclusion (lines 33–46):* therefore, they must seize the day and consummate their relationship.
2. *Coyness* suggests shyness, reserve, and reluctance, but it also carries connotations of disingenuousness and even flirtatiousness. The poem's language is that of a private occasion and seduction; it implies that the woman is susceptible to sophisticated, ingenious flattery but also to logic, argumentation, and emotional appeals. The mistress, of course, does not speak, although the reader can infer that the poem is part of a longer conversation: clearly, she has expressed reluctance or even denied the speaker. Ask students how people today might respond to a plea like the one in this poem. Does the speaker seem sincere and logical? Does he appear genuinely in love? Self-interested?

Manipulative? Ultimately, "To His Coy Mistress" is a poem, not philosophy or an exercise in formal logic. On the question of the mistress's response, students may suggest that the mistress could deny the validity of the speaker's argument: even in the relatively short lifespan of human beings, there are valid reasons to defer or delay pleasures.

3. The speaker shifts from praise of his mistress's beauty—as well as the prospect of praising her through eternity—to darker themes: the passing of time, human mortality, even the decomposition of the body. He reminds her that she will inevitably die; if their love remains unconsummated, "then worms shall try / That long preserved virginity" (lines 27–28). Although lines 21–32 continue the logic of the poem's argument, they are also designed to elicit an emotional response: fear.
4. Deduction works from general premises and principles to specific cases. The speaker of the poem has established his general premises in the first two stanzas. In the third, his words "Now therefore" suggest the validity and irrefutability of his conclusion: since time is implacable and death is inevitable, he and his beloved should "sport [themselves] while [they] may" (line 37). Again, "To His Coy Mistress" is a poem rather than an example of formal logic. Scholars have long pointed out that, among other problems, the speaker commits the formal fallacy of "denying the antecedent." But students do not need a background in formal logic to read the poem: most will recognize that its argument is refutable in a number of ways.

Writing Arguments, p. 671

1. Marvell's speaker is preoccupied with earthly, material, and sexual desires—whether in the physical beauty of his beloved or his proposal that they "tear" their "pleasures with rough strife" (line 43). If she took a Platonic point of view, the mistress might respond that the speaker is looking only at shadows, illusions, and untruths in an unreal material world rather than the true and beautiful realm of the "upper world." The mistress would likely see him as a "prisoner"; she might even compare him with the "clever rogue" with a "paltry soul," who (in Plato's words) is "mischievous in proportion to his cleverness" (para. 49).
2. Students are likely to identify with this theme, as it is associated—often in a clichéd way—with youth. They might also consider it in the context of their own lives, which are likely filled with both inducements to "live for the moment" (consumerism, the desire for a social life, a world of instant media, etc.) and demands that they defer gratification (pressure to succeed as a student, the need for financial stability, career goals, etc.).

Summary of "A Modest Proposal" by Jonathan Swift, p. 672

In this famous satire, Swift's narrator proposes that the plight of the poor in Ireland could be alleviated if the impoverished Irish would sell their children as food to the rich. Along the way, Swift skewers not only the indifference of the

English but also the ostensibly rational, benevolent schemes of utilitarian social reformers.

Reading Arguments, p. 678

1. Explicitly, the persona of "A Modest Proposal" proposes subjecting poor Irish babies to infanticide and cannibalism as a rational method for dealing with Ireland's high poverty rates. The practice will bring a number of other benefits, including reducing the number of Catholics, giving poor tenant farmers something of value to sell (their babies), relieving the poor of the financial burden of children, encouraging marriage, and giving "some pleasure to the rich" (para. 33). But the real point—implicit, as an attentive reader should notice—is that the wealthy are already eating their poor tenants *figuratively,* so they may as well do so literally. Near the end of the essay, he proposes (and dismisses) a host of reforms, from taxing the landlords and encouraging them to be more merciful, to "curing the expensiveness of pride, vanity, idleness, and gaming in our women" (29). The entire paragraph is an indictment of English society and England's exploitation of (or indifference to) the Irish poor. Even the persona urges his reader not to consider the merits of this critique or its implications: "Therefore, I repeat, let no man talk to me of these and the like expedients, till he has at least some glimpse of hope that there will be ever some hearty and sincere attempt to put them in practice" (30).
2. "A Modest Proposal" uses inductive reasoning by recounting a set of specific facts—such as the monetary value of a baby (2), the number of poor children born in Ireland annually (6), the weight of a newborn child and its weight after a year (11)—and making a general conclusion, that these children will make "a most delicious, nourishing, and wholesome food" (9).
3. "A Modest Proposal" is an ethical argument in that it implies that English treatment of the Irish is already cruel and unconscionable. By using irony—taking a position that it is obviously wrong, even if it's "reasonable"—he relies on his readers to see past the detached, reasonable voice of the persona and to recognize the immorality or even madness of (for example) using the skin of babies to make "admirable gloves for ladies, and summer boots for fine gentlemen" (15). He also counts on his readers to infer a more general critique of the English (29) and make a similar moral judgment.
4. The limitations of irony are that a reader may miss it and dismiss the larger point Swift tries to make, or that a reader may find the essay disgusting or simply amusing and not take it seriously. A satiric writer must negotiate between those extremes.
5. "A Modest Proposal" includes all the elements of a proposal argument. Swift states the problem in paragraph 1, proposes his solution in paragraph 9, demonstrates it will work in paragraphs 10 through 16, establishes feasibility in paragraph 28 (the weakest part of his proposal), discusses its benefits in paragraphs 20 through 27, and addresses objections in paragraph 29 (another weak section).

Writing Arguments, p. 678

1. Students might already be familiar—or fluent—with Swift's kind of verbal irony, even if they do not realize it. You might want to point to examples in popular culture, such as Stephen Colbert and others who use ironic masks or exaggerated personas.
2. Swift's satire cuts more than one way. He is criticizing the English, of course. But he is also mocking rationalistic and "progressive" programs for social reform—schemes that rely on economics, demographic research, empirical data, etc. Students may see this mockery in light of contemporary so-called reform efforts or large-scale social programs, put in place either by private or public institutions. Do they share Swift's cynicism? What are the larger political or social implications of his attitude?
3. Students may want to contrast Swift's ironic or satirical approach with Sanger's more earnest, urgent, and straightforward proposal. Which would be more effective at swaying readers or promoting real, practical change?

Summary of the Declaration of Independence by Thomas Jefferson, p. 679

The Declaration of Independence is an explanation and justification of why the thirteen American colonies claimed to be independent and no longer part of the British Empire. In part, it is a list of grievances against Great Britain. But the document is also a statement about natural rights, the foundations of legitimate governments, and the right of people to revolt against unjust authority.

Reading Arguments, p. 682

1. The opening paragraphs of the declaration are deductive. Jefferson uses them to establish his general premises and principles: that when political bands are dissolved, justification is required; that certain rights are self-evident and inalienable; that governments derive their powers from the consent of the governed, etc. He moves from these general premises, once they are in place, to the specific grievances and arguments of the colonists.
2. Jefferson anticipates those who would claim the colonists are acting rashly; that is, opponents might argue that the colonists' desire to dissolve their government might set a bad precedent or lead to anarchy. He agrees that long-established governments should not be changed on a whim or because of superficial problems; rather, only fundamental abuses, evils, and usurpations require radical, systemic change.
3. Governments exist to secure the inalienable rights of life, liberty, and the pursuit of happiness. They derive their legitimacy from the "consent of the governed": the will of citizens, expressed through the institutions of a constitutional republic.

4. Jefferson explains in the opening paragraph that such a declaration requires an explanation: the "causes which impel" this "separation." The document is, in part, a catalog of grievances against the king; these are the causes of the action by the colonists.
5. Jefferson supplies a long list of specific "injuries and usurpations" to support his case. Some of these accusations and statements are offered dispassionately; others are more provocative and passionate in their wording: "[The king] is at this time transporting large Armies of foreign Mercenaries to complete the works of death, desolation and tyranny, already begun with circumstances of Cruelty & Perfidy scarcely paralleled in the most barbarous ages, and totally unworthy the Head of a civilized nation" (18). The tone of the declaration is sometimes one of quiet exasperation, the voice of a person who has exhausted every other option: "We have appealed to [the British government's] native justice and magnanimity, and we have conjured them by the ties of our common kindred" (22). You may point out that the declaration was written to be read aloud in public, and reading aloud would have heightened the effects of repetition in the list of "injuries and usurpations."

Writing Arguments, p. 682

1. The claim would be that the people of the United States must dissolve their political relationship with Great Britain and set up a new government; the grounds would be the list of grievances; the warrant would include the general principles that Jefferson presents and explains in his opening two paragraphs. Students might notice that the declaration also includes a rebuttal, as when Jefferson acknowledges that governments should not be dissolved for "light and transient causes."
2. Students should bring a range of responses to this question, which asks, What conditions or actions on the part of an established government justify its overthrow? They may wish to refer to contemporary controversies and political issues when completing this assignment. Are there any current problems that require revolutionary or radical action?
3. Machiavelli would likely disagree with Jefferson's assumptions about government. But he might also seize upon the errors of the king that lead to the revolution. For example, Machiavelli warns about the consequences of leaders who "confiscate people's property."

Summary of Declaration of Sentiments and Resolutions by Elizabeth Cady Stanton, p. 683

Using the style, form, and even some of the content of the Declaration of Independence, Elizabeth Cady Stanton declares that women must throw off the tyranny of male abuses and usurpations and seize their full rights and privileges as American citizens.

Reading Arguments, p. 685

1. The title and the form of Stanton's document illustrate the analogy. For Stanton, American women have been oppressed and denied their rights by American men in the same way that the colonists were oppressed and denied their rights by King George III and the English government.
2. There are significant differences in aims and methods between Stanton and Jefferson. For example, the Declaration of Independence essentially ended the authority of a king and dissolved a government. Stanton, on the other hand, wishes to work within existing institutions to achieve the goals of women, not dissolve those institutions altogether (para. 20).
3. Men have circumscribed and assigned roles to women, excluding them from social, political, and economic life—the public sphere of action. Men have also forced women to submit to their wills and their laws. According to Stanton, God has the right to act in this way, but men do not. Moreover, women have the right to act in accordance with their own conscience without the interference of male prerogatives.
4. Stanton asserts, "The history of mankind is a history of repeated injuries and usurpations on the part of man toward woman, having in direct object the establishment of an absolute tyranny over her." She supports this assertion with a litany of unjust laws and restrictions, including the following: women cannot vote; they must submit to laws that they have no role in creating; they have limited or no rights to property or wages; men have closed off career opportunities that might lead to "wealth and distinction" for women; men have made women dependent and abject.
5. Stanton states, "We shall employ agents, circulate tracts, petition the State and National legislatures, and endeavor to enlist the pulpit and the press in our behalf" (20). In doing so, women will be entering and engaging in public and political life, thereby expanding their "sphere of action."

Writing Arguments, p. 685

1. Doubtless, women's rights—and the roles of women as American citizens—have come a long way since Stanton's time. Yet, income disparities between men and women still exist, as do sexism and double standards. Students might consider how social and culture standards, or "codes," persist, even though legal restrictions do not.
2. In saying that "all experience hath shown that mankind are more disposed to suffer, while evils are sufferable, than to right themselves by abolishing the forms to which they were accustomed," Stanton and Jefferson suggest that people are generally resistant to change and perhaps even timid. Students may want to reflect on situations and circumstances nowadays that call for change or action but cannot be resolved because of inaction or complacency. In contrast, students might also provide examples where people have "abolished the forms to which they are accustomed."

Summary of "The Cause of War" by Margaret Sanger, p. 686

Sanger surveys the events, political maneuvers, and justifications leading up to World War I and concludes: "beneath all this superficial turmoil lay the deep-seated impulse given by unlimited multiplication" (para. 16). She also draws on the work of Malthus, Darwin, and others to show the relationship between population growth and war. According to Sanger, "birth control" is the "real cure for war" (18). But since countries and international organizations are reluctant to impose birth restrictions, she suggests that women will ultimately take initiative on their own and "refuse longer to produce the human food upon which [war] feeds" (23).

Reading Arguments, p. 690

1. To support her opening assertions, Sanger focuses on the last hundred years of European history, generally, and the events leading up to World War I, specifically. For Sanger, the Great War is a definitive example, one "sufficient to drive home this truth" (4). She cites the "War Map of Europe," which shows a correlation between the birth rates of countries and international conflicts. Among the most belligerent countries, the rate was high (excepting France, which was "in the way" of Germany); among the consistently neutral countries, the rates are low (6). She also draws on thinkers such as Charles Malthus, Charles Darwin, and John Stuart Mill to substantiate her assertions about the nature and consequences of population growth.
2. Sanger makes an argument by definition when she points out that the justifications for war—the need for "a place in the sun," "a path to the sea," a "route to India"—are just "other names for expansion" (3). The "need of expansion," according to Sanger, is "only another name for overpopulation" (4). She argues by analogy when she compares the attitude of civilized humans toward weaker members of society to the natural checks in the animal world (12–14). She makes a proposal when she argues that "birth control, the real cure for war" be instituted and that nations agree to restrict their birthrates (18). But Sanger acknowledges that such legalistic, international action has proven futile. So her ultimate proposal in this essay is for women to resist imperialism, "pretended patriotism," and the obligation to reproduce. By doing so, women "will kill war by the simple process of starving it to death" (23).
3. According to Sanger, German leaders pointed out that expansion would mean more jobs, more economic prosperity, and more opportunities for Germans abroad; lack of expansion would mean "hard times, heavy burdens, lack of opportunity for Germans, and what not" (9). The German people were given "a startling and true picture of what would happen from overcrowding" (9).
4. Sanger uses deduction in paragraphs 12 and 13 when she establishes general premises about population growth. From these premises, her conclusion is inescapable: "In other words, let countries become overpopulated and war is inevitable. It follows as daylight follows sunrise" (13).

Writing Arguments, p. 691

1. Students might want to research and compare population growth and the causes of war in Sanger's time and in our own. They might also think about this question in the context of current treaties and international agreements on issues such as climate change. For example, is placing restrictions on carbon emissions fundamentally different from restricting birthrates?
2. On the role of women, Sanger cites Napoleon, "the archetype of the militarists of all nations, calling for 'fodder for cannon'" (20). Since the "burden and the horrors of war are heaviest" on women (23), she essentially argues that they should seize power in this public sphere.

Summary of "The Obligation to Endure" by Rachel Carson, p. 692

This essay is taken from Carson's book *Silent Spring*. First published in 1962, the book is often credited with helping to start the environmental movement. But it was also instrumental in raising awareness about the effects of chemicals and pesticides—and even shaped public policy.

Reading Arguments, p. 697

1. Carson supports her assertions about "irrevocable" and "universal" contamination by citing both specific examples of contaminants (Strontium 90) and the "staggering" number of them, which place unnatural demands on humans, animals, and the environment: "500 new chemicals to which the bodies of men and animals are required somehow to adapt each year, chemicals totally outside the limits of biologic experience" (para. 5).
2. Carson claims that "the contamination of man's total environment with such substances of incredible potential for harm" is the "central problem of our age" (9).
3. In different parts of the essay, Carson evaluates modern science and modern approaches to insect control, agricultural production, and policies; but she also makes broader judgments of human beings and civilization itself.
4. Carson's characterization of humans paints them as ingenious, nearsighted, vain, oblivious, and overreaching. She refers to "man's war against nature" (6). She claims that we have a "distorted sense of proportion" (11), that humans have "fallen into a mesmerized state" (22), and that scientists have a "frantic zeal" to "create a chemically sterile, insect-free world" (23). She also notes that humans have much of the "necessary knowledge" to solve many environmental problems, but "we do not use it" (21).
5. Carson acknowledges and anticipates those who argue that chemical insecticides must be used at times: "All this is not to say there is no insect problem and no need of control. I am saying, rather, that control must be geared to realities, not to mythical situations, and that the methods employed must be such that they do not destroy us along with the insects" (12).

Writing Arguments, p. 697

1. Carson's book *Silent Spring,* from which this essay comes, was first published in 1962. For this assignment to take a stand in support of or against Carson's views, students might want to consider how human beings—and views of the environment—have changed (or have remained the same) since then.
2. This is a large question that will involve research by students. You may want to have them narrow the focus of their essays to a specific disease and country. You may also want to allow students to support Carson's position and argue that DDT should continue to be banned.

Summary of "Letter from Birmingham Jail" by Martin Luther King Jr., p. 698

King wrote this letter after he was arrested for participating in the 1963 Birmingham campaign, a nonviolent protest against the racial segregation practiced by the city's government and local retail stores. He was responding to a written statement by eight white Alabama clergymen, who argued that racial injustices must be fought in courts, not through direct action or public protests. King's letter—by turns scholarly, allusive, passionate, ironic, provocative, and conciliatory—contains some of King's most memorable passages, including "injustice anywhere is a threat to justice everywhere."

Reading Arguments, p. 711

1. King's argument is often Rogerian but not naively so: his main point is that the conciliatory, conflict-averse attitudes of sympathetic moderates are a problem. He explains that he shares the same short-term political goal as those who—like the recipients of his letter—want negotiations rather than "direct action": "The purpose of our direct-action program is to create a situation so crisis-packed that it will inevitably open the door to negotiation. I therefore concur with you in your call for negotiation" (para. 11). His argument is Rogerian in a much larger sense, however. King sees the fates (and, implicitly, the interests) of all persons as intertwined: "We are caught in an inescapable network of mutuality, tied in a single garment of destiny. Whatever affects one directly affects all indirectly" (4). He calls on the highest ideals of the United States ("the goal of America is freedom") as well as on shared Judeo-Christian values. These are, King implies, principles and goals that all people of good will share. His argument is confrontational, but it calls upon the proposed ideals of those whom he disagrees with.
2. King deploys various analogies in his letter, drawing primarily from biblical stories. For example, he uses analogies to explain himself and answer his critics who claim he is an "outsider" in Birmingham: "I am in Birmingham because injustice is here. Just as the prophets of the eighth century B.C. left their little villages and carried their 'thus saith the Lord' far beyond . . . their home towns; and just as the Apostle Paul left his village" (3). He compares the

actions of those who defy unjust laws in the Jim Crow South with those who gave "illegal" aid and comfort to Jews in Hitler's Germany (22). He invokes parallels to Jesus, Luther, Lincoln, and Jefferson (31). All these comparisons serve to place the civil rights movement in a long tradition and clearly demarcate right and wrong.

3. Historically, direct action has included everything from boycotts and sit-ins to more aggressive ways of forcing confrontation on an issue or problem. For King, nonviolent direct action "seeks to create such a crisis and foster such a tension that a community which has constantly refused to negotiate is forced to confront the issue. It seeks so to dramatize the issue that it can no longer be ignored" (10).
4. "Letter from Birmingham Jail" is scholarly, allusive, and often stylish, drawing on a broad range of cultural references. But King does more than bring thoughtful, intellectual arguments to bear—after all, he is writing from a jail cell, not from a theology or philosophy department of a university. His language often becomes emotional and deeply person, particularly in paragraph 13, where he addresses those who council him to "wait." King catalogs a long list of injustices, from lynch mobs, murders, and "twenty million Negro brothers smothering in an airtight cage of poverty," to the pain of trying to explain to his crying six-year-old daughter why she cannot go to a segregated amusement park (14). You might want to point out to students how King moves from the general phenomenon of racism and injustice to his own experiences of it.
5. King first confesses his disappointment with white moderates, who, while sympathetic to King's cause, seem "more devoted to 'order' than to justice" (23). He then confesses his disappointment with the white church and white Christian leaders, too many of whom have been "more cautious than courageous" (35). Students should notice how he frames his observations and criticisms here as "confessions" of "disappointment": that is, he had hoped that these figures would have lived up to their higher ideals. How else might he have pronounced this judgment? Why confess disappointment rather than, say, accuse his readers of hypocrisy or bad judgment?

Writing Arguments, p. 711

1. This assignment asks a challenging question: Is there a current law you would consider breaking for the reasons King describes? King's standard is rooted in natural law and moral law; he draws on St. Augustine, Martin Buber, and Paul Tillich, as well as on many historical examples. But he is also depending on conscience, which is personal and subjective. Students should explore King's assertion that breaking unjust laws must be done "openly, lovingly," with the intention of willfully accepting the penalty. According to King, this action expresses "the highest respect for law" (20). How, exactly, does breaking a law express respect for law?
2. Students might want to consider examples from history and literature that support or challenge Niebuhr's statement that "groups tend to be more

immoral than individuals." They might also want to view racism and the civil rights struggle through this lens. For example, was integration achieved by changing the laws and forcing large groups of people (communities, cities, states, etc.) to behave in nondiscriminatory ways, regardless of the personal morality of individuals within these groups? Or was the progress of the civil rights movement more a matter of changing the attitudes of individual people, so that they became more moral in their attitude toward the equality of others?